Teaching, Learning and Assessing Science 5–12

Fourth Edition

Wynne Harlen

SAGE Publications
Los Angeles • London • New Delhi • Singapore

Fourth edition first published 2006
Reprinted 2007 (twice)

SAGE Publications Ltd
1 Oliver's Yard
55 City Road
London EC1Y 1SP

SAGE Publications Inc
2455 Teller Road
Thousand Oaks, California 91320

SAGE Publications India Pvt Ltd
B1/I 1 Mohan Cooperative Industrial Area
Mathura Road, New Delhi 110 044
India

SAGE Publications Asia-Pacific Pte Ltd
33 Pekin Street #02-01
Far East Square
Singapore 048763

Library of Congress Control Number: 2005924504

A catalogue record for this book is available from the British Library

ISBN: 978-1-4129-0871-9 (hbk)
ISBN: 978-1-4129-0872-6 (pbk)

Typeset by Pantek Arts Ltd, Maidstone, Kent
Printed on paper from sustainable resources
Printed and bound in Great Britain by Athenaeum Press Ltd., Gateshead, Tyne & Wear

Contents

Acknowledgements

I wish to thank the many friends, colleagues, teachers and children who have, consciously or unconsciously, contributed to the ideas in this book. One of the themes of the book is that we develop our understanding through testing ideas against evidence and by responding to how others see things. Inevitably I have been influenced by those I have worked with and acknowledge this help with gratitude.

I am also grateful to the University of Liverpool Press for permission to reproduce figures from the SPACE Research Reports: *Evaporation and Condensation* (1990), and *Rocks, Soil and Weather* (1993).

Introduction

Education is an area of human activity that, as with most others, is ever changing. In writing the fourth edition of this book I have attempted to reflect some of the gradual, but perceptible, changes of the past six or so years in our understanding of learning and teaching. In terms of learning, three of the main themes are recognition of the importance of social interaction as well as interaction with objects and phenomena in the environment, the need to motivate learning so that it may continue throughout life, and the need to engage all children in their learning, identified in the concept of 'personalised' learning.

The first of these has brought about a greater emphasis on the value to learning of talk, or dialogue and reflection. The second means that we need to provide learners with the thinking skills and the enjoyment of learning that will provide the ability and desire for lifelong learning. The third requires more attention to involving all learners in making decisions about their learning, about their goals, about their progress and how to continue it. It particularly requires the use of assessment by teachers and learners to help learning.

None of these points is new, but the greater emphasis they are currently being given is in response to evidence that they improve levels of achievement. They apply to all subjects and to all ages of learners. What I have tried to do in the new edition of this book is to reflect what implementation of this change in emphasis means in particular for primary and middle school teachers teaching science. At the same time, many priorities remain the same as before and teachers continue to request more professional development, more time, space and resources for science and a less crowded curriculum. These matters receive due attention as we discuss the various aspects of provision for science at the class and school levels.

The book is organised in four parts. The first is about learning in science, comprising three chapters that provide a model of children's learning and a rationale for selecting particular goals for learning in science. Chapter 1 makes a case for spending time on considering the nature of learning with understanding, based on evidence that how teachers understand children's learning and what they understand the goals of learning to be, frame their decisions about the provision of learning experiences. In turn, how teachers view appropriate learning experiences determines the roles they take, the roles of the children, and the parts that materials and assessment play in the learning experiences. Chapter 2 provides an extended example of children's interaction with materials and each other during an investigation. The evidence here provides the basis for a model of how children learn, from which the importance of encouraging children's development of process skills is drawn. The process (or enquiry or investigative) skills are important in their own right, particularly with a view to a foundation for continued learning, but they are also key to the development of conceptual understanding. The model provides a way of looking at learning as the construction of understanding, in which children start from their existing ideas and use evidence and ideas from others in developing these ideas to become 'bigger' and more useful in explaining things around them. Chapter 3 considers the role of science education in developing 'scientific literacy' and the implications for the teaching of children aged 5 to 12. Through this discussion I identify the goals that are followed through in the later accounts of progression, assessment and classroom activities and interactions. These goals are consistent with but not identical to those identified in particular national curricula or standards. They include the development of scientific attitudes, which are constantly noted in research as important in learning.

The second part of the book comprises three chapters concerning practical matters that are always of immediate concern to teachers. Chapter 4 is about provision of appropriate activities that enable children to develop ideas and process skills. A progression in these aspects of learning is implied, but explicit discussion of the nature of the progression comes later. At this point we are concerned with the overall provision at different stages of primary education. Chapter 5 takes up one aspect of the emphasis on talk, the use of questioning by teachers and how they can respond to children's questions. It brings together a number of points about questioning and listening that experience shows are central to improving classroom interactions between teacher and children. Chapter 6 comprises entirely new material about motivation for learning. This is in recognition of the importance of developing children's willingness and desire to learn, mentioned earlier, and of the growing amount of evidence about the actions that promote, and of others that inhibit, motivation for learning rather than motivation to achieve rewards or to pass tests.

The whole of the third part of the book is concerned with the use of assessment for learning in the context of primary science. Chapter 7 sets out a framework for looking at what this involves. It describes a cyclic process of collecting, interpreting and using information about children's current ideas and skills relating to the goals of a particular section of work to enable children to take the next steps in the progress towards the goals. Chapters 8 and 9 discuss and exemplify what this means and how it can be done in relation to development of process skills. This includes discussion of ways of helping children to develop thinking and enquiry skills and scientific attitudes. Chapters 10 and 11 do the same for children's ideas in science, emphasising again the importance of children talking as a means of developing their understanding. Chapters 8–11 make explicit the progression in learning so that finding where children are enables identification of what children may need if they are to operate at a more advanced level.

However, it is not the teacher alone who considers where the children are in working towards specific goals. Chapter 12 is concerned with the role that the children can take in using assessment for learning. This role depends on children understanding what are the goals of their activities and the quality of work they should be aiming for. They are more likely to understand what this means if they take part in identifying the criteria by which they should be judging their work. Examples of how to do this are described. Children are then in a position to recognise their next steps and, with the help of feedback from their teacher and their peers, how to take them. Self- and peer-assessment are key features of using assessment for learning.

The fourth part of the book is concerned with matters that require decisions at the school level including: how records of children's achievement are kept and communicated to parents and others; decisions about resources for learning science including visits out of school and links with other schools or individuals; and the role of the science subject leader in school-level planning and provision for science. Chapter 13 is concerned with summarising children's learning, that is, with summative assessment as distinct from the formative assessment considered in Part III. The chapter on resources for learning (Chapter 14) inevitably includes references to developments in the use of information and communication technology (ICT) but emphasises that the important role of the technology is to assist in collection and interpretation of evidence from the real world. Relevance of their activities is something that children value and which engages them in learning; the choice of resources and links with events and people beyond the school are key aspects of ensuring this engagement. Much of the work in organising the school programme so that children have a broad, balanced and progressive experience of science activities falls to the science subject leader. Chapter 15 is concerned with this role, which has become even more important as schools are given the responsibility for evaluating their provision for children's learning. Aspects of this leadership role that are discussed include curriculum planning, the evaluation of the programme and opportunities for professional development within and out of school.

To sum up, the aim of this book is, as before, to provide not only accounts of learning and teaching in science, but a rationale for the classroom practices that are suggested. I think that we should be able to justify what we do in classrooms in terms of what is known about how children learn and about how their learning and motivation to learn can be enhanced. The changes made in this edition reflect development in my own and others' understanding of how to bring this about. But there are no easy answers and no prescriptions for success. It is essential for readers to review critically the ideas in this book as they reflect upon and refine their own practice.

Wynne Harlen
Duns

Part I

ABOUT LEARNING IN SCIENCE

Chapter 1

Learning in science

INTRODUCTION

The case of teaching science from the very start of children's education is now universally accepted. But while we no longer need to justify teaching science at the primary level, it is still necessary to examine reasons for teaching it in certain ways rather than others. Within the constraints of school policies and national guidelines, teachers teach in ways that they believe lead to learning. Thus their view of what it means to learn is a key factor in their classroom decisions. For this reason, this opening chapter discusses different views of learning and how they influence these decisions. It provides a rationale for taking the view that effective learning results from active involvement of learners in constructing their understanding of the world around them.

Learning theorists distinguish individual constructivism from socio-cultural constructivism. Here we take the view that both ideas generated in social interaction with others and individual sense-making of investigations of the environment are important in learning science.

The chapter ends with a brief outline of some implications of taking a constructivist view of learning, with reference to where these matters are taken up in more detail later. Thus it acts as an introduction to other parts of the book.

DIFFERENT VIEWS OF LEARNING

What do we mean when we talk of children 'learning'? This is an important question because the answer has a strong impact on how we go about helping children to learn. Without going into details of theories of learning or neuroscience, it is worth reflecting on what we understand to be happening in learning. There are three dominant views of what it means:

- Adding more knowledge and skills as a result of being taught.
- Making sense of new experience by the learners themselves.
- Making sense of new experience by learners in collaboration with others.

The first of these views embodies a rather passive role for the learner, who is considered to take in information from others including, but not only, the teacher. The second gives the learner a more active role in using existing knowledge to build new knowledge. The teacher's role is to create a learning environment that nurtures this gradual extension of ideas and skills and to help the learner to link new experiences to previous ones. The third view gives weight to the social aspect of learning; understanding is created not by individual learners alone but through expressing ideas to others and receiving ideas from others. Of course, one can hold a view of learning that is a mixture of these, depending on what we hope is being learned. However, a general disposition towards embracing one or other of these does affect decisions about the roles of the teachers, the learning materials and how assessment is used. The relationship is illustrated by the two teachers reported in Box 1.1.

Box 1.1: A tale of two teachers

These two teachers, both in their early 30s, taught 10- and 11-year-olds in very similar conditions. Teacher A had the children sitting in rows, all facing the blackboard, working in silence, mainly from books. In discussion she explained why:

> Well, you see, the main thing is – I can't stand any noise. I don't allow them to talk in the classroom . . . I mean they go out at playtime, they go out at dinnertime and so on. But actually in the classroom I like them sitting in their places where I can see them. And I teach from lesson to lesson. There's no children all doing different things. You know, it's formal . . . and of course I like it that way, I believe in it that way.

Asked about the use of materials other than books Teacher A confirmed that all the learning was from books, the blackboard or from her because *'that's the way they learn'*.

By contrast, Teacher B, who taught the same age group (10- to 11-year-olds), and had a similar number of children in the class (32) had the desks in the classroom arranged in rather irregular groups. She spent most of her time moving round the groups and allowed the children to talk while they worked on a variety of activities. She explained:

> I hate to see children in rows and I hate to see them regimented. At the same time, you know, I often get annoyed when people think that absolute chaos reigns, because it doesn't. Every child knows exactly what they have to do . . . it's much more – you could say informal – but it's a much more friendly, less pressing way of working and you find the children do . . . it's nice for them to be able to chat with a friend about what they are doing . . . I mean, adults do when they work. As long I get the end result that's suited to that particular child I don't mind, you know. Obviously if a child's not achieving then I do go mad because at nine, ten and eleven, they should know they've got a certain amount of work to do and the standard one expects of them.

Both of these teachers could have arranged and managed their classes differently. However, what they chose to do was influenced by their understanding that 'this is the way children learn'. Decisions about matters such as whether the children work in groups, whether these are friendship groups or based on ability, whether low-level noise is permitted in the class, whether children can move round the class without asking permission, whether they have materials to explore or learn from books – these decisions are justified in terms of supporting learning of the kind that the teacher values. Where this is not the case, and teachers have to adopt procedures decided by someone else, they may be dissatisfied that they are not able to achieve the learning that they value. Also, teachers may perceive that externally imposed conditions, such as pressure to get children to pass tests, requires them to teach in certain ways. This is a matter we take up later in the book (Chapter 13).

SOME FEATURES OF EFFECTIVE LEARNING

Since the understanding we have of learning is so influential, it is important to consider what is known about learning that would suggest which view is to be embraced. There is a good deal of research on this matter, too, which we will refer to throughout this book. Included in this are studies reviewed by Black and Wiliam (1998a) and by Harlen and Deakin Crick (2003) to show that when children are helped, for instance:

- to see how to improve their work, by feedback that is non-judgemental,
- to try to explain things rather than just describe them,
- to take some responsibility for assessing their own work, finding the errors in their own or a partner's work,
- to talk about and explain their reasoning,
- to understand the goals and the quality of work they should be aiming for,

then their attainment exceeds that of children not given these opportunities. In other words, children learn better under conditions reflecting a view of learning in which the learner takes an active rather than a passive part. SF2

Reflecting on experience

Research evidence based in unfamiliar contexts might not be as convincing as reflecting on one's own experience. Consider for a moment an occasion when you could say that effective learning was taking place. Reflect on the features that made you think that really good learning was happening. Box 1.2 provides two examples of what teachers have recalled.

Some features of the vignettes in Box 1.2 are likely to be found in many 'learning events'. The judgement that learning was taking place was indicated by the links that the children made between what they were doing and previous experience: Benny, in recognising that heating and cooling were part of the same kind of change; Mary and Jon, in realising that the light from the bulb was the result of heating the filament. Both these ideas, though obvious to an adult, are not so to children, who often, as we will see in Chapter 10, have different explanations for different manifestations of the same process. The children were also actively developing their own understanding, without prompting by the teacher, but with the spur of communication with others. Teachers' reflections of learning events often include the way in which children help each other's thinking by expressing their own ideas, leading to children questioning each other, asking for justification and monitoring the meaning that is being made.

Box 1.2: Learning events

Benny
When Benny, aged 10, wanted to show to a younger child that air expands when heated, his first idea was to take a glass jar with a screw-on lid and heat it to a high temperature and then screw on the lid. When it cooled he expected to hear hissing as air was sucked in. The other child said this might be dangerous, so Benny then suggested working 'in reverse', by putting the jar in a fridge and when the air inside cooled, screwing on the lid and bringing it out into a warm room. When it had warmed up he expected to hear hissing when the lid was unscrewed due to air under pressure escaping.

Mary and Jon
When Mary and Jon made a bulb light up in a simple circuit they used a hand lens to look at the filament in the bulb. Mary said it was 'like a little furnace in there'. Jon joined in: 'it's like an electric bar fire. So what makes the fire hot is the same as what makes the light in the bulb'. In their drawings of the circuit they were careful to show the connections to the bulb indicating that current passed through the filament. But they had also made connections in their minds between this and their earlier experience that would help them understand energy transfer.

Learning with and without understanding

Recalled instances of effective learning rarely include recitation of facts or straight recall of information, such as the names of the planets or how long ago dinosaurs lived on the Earth, or which particular objects sink and which float. This is regarded as memorisation rather than understanding. This does not mean that knowledge of facts is unimportant, but that it is far from sufficient. Information needs to be organised if it is to be useful, so the understanding of principles and development of concepts is a key aim. In relation to floating, the important thing is to understand not just what floats but why some things float. These mental structures cannot be 'taught' as such; they have to be created by the active participation of the learner. The reason why some things float could only be memorised as a form of words unless there is understanding of the concepts involved. The role of the teacher is to provide opportunities for new experience that children can link to their existing ideas, to help them make connections and take notice of the conditions that make certain ideas applicable in particular circumstances.

Learners need to develop understanding of what it means to learn. If *they* have a view of learning as the addition of more facts, they will inevitably direct their effort to this end: 'children can learn practically anything by sheer will and effort' (Bransford *et al.*, 1999, p. xv). So a feature of effective learning is a developing awareness of learning as a process of developing understanding and of what is necessary for this. The extent to which young children can think about their own learning may not be as limited as is often assumed. The work on developing process skills, discussed later (Chapter 9), and on self-assessment (Chapter 12) demonstrates how this can be done.

What kind of learning is needed?

What does this tell us about the sort of learning we should be trying to encourage? Clearly if we want children to develop conceptual understanding that helps them make sense of new experiences, to help them become aware of what learning is and to develop the capacity for continuing learning, then the view of learning as just adding information and skills is inadequate. Indeed, Watkins (2003) states bluntly that 'teaching knowledge is an anachronism'. In common with the view of many others writing about the goals of education, he goes on: 'the goals of learning need to focus less on "acquiring knowledge" and more on "generating knowledge"' (p. 27).

The many good reasons for favouring such learning goals include the need to prepare young people for life and work in a rapidly changing society in which they will have to make more choices than did those living in past decades (Claxton, 1999). The ability to continue learning throughout life is acknowledged as essential for future generations and thus it has to be a feature in the education of every student. Developing this ability involves learning how to learn, the achievement of various cognitive, affective and conative outcomes needed to provide the skill, the will, the flexibility in thinking and the energy needed to make effective decisions. This is recognised as being needed by students in all countries, as underlined by the Organisation for Economic Co-operation and Development (OECD):

> Students cannot learn in school everything they will need to know in adult life. What they must acquire is the prerequisites for successful learning in future life. These prerequisites are of both a cognitive and a motivational nature. Students must become able to organise and regulate their own learning, to learn independently and in groups, and to overcome difficulties in the learning process. This requires them to be aware of their own thinking processes and learning strategies and methods.

> (OECD, 1999, p. 9)

IMPLICATIONS FOR TEACHING SCIENCE 5–12

The view of learning developed in this book is described as constructivist (or generative). The key point is that learners are constructing their understanding, sometimes through their own thinking and sometimes in collaboration with others. The label 'constructivist' includes both the second and the third of the three meanings of learning proposed at the start of this chapter. Some learning psychologists (e.g. Vygotsky, 1962; Lave and Wenger, 1991) see the difference between learners 'making sense of new experience by themselves' and 'making sense of new experience in collaboration with others' as being of great significance. This is especially so if 'with others' is interpreted broadly as including reading what others have written in books or on the Internet, as well as directly in face-to-face communication.

In the socio-cultural constructivist view of learning, discussed further in Chapter 11, understanding is seen as being generated by, and residing in, the interaction among members of a group. However, we may still think of the individual as taking from this shared understanding what helps them make sense of their own experience. Thus we consider learning being developed through interaction with objects as well as people. Consequently, in the discussion here, when we refer to experience we mean both experience of the physical environment and also experience of social interaction and dialogue.

As we consider in more detail in Chapter 2, in constructing meaning a learner uses the ideas or concepts already formed from previous experience and attempts to make sense of new experience in terms of these existing conceptions. These tentative ideas about explaining new experience have to be tested out, sometimes mentally and sometimes through a combination of mental and physical activity in the form of an investigation or experiment. The way in which this testing of possible explanations is carried out involves mental processes, which therefore play an essential part in developing understanding in this view of learning. Understanding learning in this way has important implications for experiences needed for children to further their learning and for the role of the teacher, the children and for the learning resources. It also has consequences for how the effectiveness of the provision for children's learning in science is evaluated.

Implications for learning experiences

In the context of five- to 12-year-olds learning science, building understanding has to begin with the objects and events familiar to them. From the ideas used in understanding specific aspects of their environment ('small' ideas), more widely applicable ones ('big' ideas) are created by making links between ideas that explain related but different events. The bigger ideas have greater power (because they help to explain more events); these bigger ideas are themselves linked with others in forming broad theories or principles.

The process cannot proceed in the opposite direction, since the broad theories are necessarily highly abstract and, indeed, meaningless if they do not evoke the many real situations which they link together. Thus, for example, if children develop, through investigation and observation, an understanding that there is interdependence among plants and animals in their own environment – their back garden, the park, the stream or the hedgerow – they may eventually understand the reasons for protecting the rain forests. But if the big issues relating to conservation are the starting points, they may be understood at no greater depth than slogans and the relationships never more than superficially grasped. Moreover, it helps understanding if learners can reflect on what they have learned and the way in which they have learned. From these arguments it follows that experiences that will lead to learning are those that:

- are within the reach of the children's current ideas and ways of processing
- can be linked to their previous experiences
- stimulate children to explore and interact with living and non-living things in their environment
- enable children to test their ideas for explaining phenomena or events that are new to them
- give children access to alternative ideas to test out as well as their own
- help children to develop the skills needed to test ideas scientifically
- give children control of making sense of new experience
- encourage children to reflect on how their ideas and skills have changed.

There is discussion of specific experiences to help the development of process or thinking skills and scientific ideas in Chapters 9 and 11.

Implications for the teacher's role

In the most general terms, the teacher's role is to enable children to build effective ways of investigating and understanding the scientific aspects of their surroundings. In order to do this, teachers need to have a clear idea of the goals of learning and of the path of progression towards those goals. They also have to have the skills to find out where the children start from and knowledge of ways to help them make progress, including sharing with the children the goals of learning and helping them to assess their own work and progress. This knowledge and skill supports the teacher's role, which is to:

- find out the children's ideas and use these as a starting point for building towards more effective, scientific ideas
- promote interaction of the children with the materials and resources through which they can develop understanding
- help children to develop the skills needed to test out ideas scientifically
- provide children with access to alternative ideas to their own, including the scientific one
- promote dialogue and the development of shared understanding
- help children reflect on their ideas and on their ways of thinking
- monitor progress and reflect on the effectiveness of the learning experience provided.

The whole of Part III of this book is concerned with developing these points. Here the teacher's role is conceived as being within the framework of formative assessment, or using assessment for learning (ARG, 1999, 2002a). Assessment of this kind is integral to teaching and is concerned with helping learning, not with assessing outcomes or with labelling children's achievement. It involves children, so that they can judge their work and be helped to recognise the next steps they need to take. There is also a role for summative assessment, to summarise, record and report on what individual children have achieved at different points. This is discussed in Chapter 13.

While there is an important formative role for assessment in all learning and teaching, it is particularly relevant when learning is seen as helping children to construct their ideas. Teachers need to know the starting points in terms of the children's existing ideas and skills so that they can decide on the appropriate next steps and act on this information to help the children to take these steps. The involvement of the children in these decisions (see Chapter 12) has a central part if they are to construct their understanding. Thus, the teacher's role also includes making sure that the children know the purpose of their activities and develop skills of self-assessment.

Implications for the children's role

The active involvement of the children in their learning is an essential feature of a constructivist approach to teaching and learning. This means that they have to be both mentally and physically active and also that they engage in reflection about what they are learning. As noted earlier, there is evidence that even very young children can take part in discussing *how* they are exploring and reasoning as well as what they are finding. Thus their role in learning is to:

- engage in investigations and enquiry into events presented in the classroom and in the world around them
- become involved in developing ideas and skills that help them make sense of their environment
- reflect on how their ideas and skills have changed as a result of their activities
- begin to identify what they have learned from particular activities
- assess their work and take part in deciding how to improve it.

Implications for the role of resources

Resources include physical materials for investigation, equipment used in investigation, books and other sources of information including visits and visitors, which have an essential part to play in learning science. Their role can be summarised as:

- providing opportunities for children to investigate and manipulate things in their environment
- stimulating interest and provoking questions that children can attempt to answer by enquiry

- providing the means and the evidence for children to test ideas

- providing information to help children construct useful ideas.

Matters relating to resources are discussed in Chapter 14.

Implications for evaluation of learning opportunities

Evaluation involves making judgements about the effectiveness or quality of what is being evaluated. Feedback of these judgements to those able to change the situation gives evaluation a formative role in learning. Thus it is important always to be asking the questions: 'Do the children have the opportunities that are intended?', 'Are they learning in a way consistent with the view of how learning takes place?', 'Is the teacher taking the role intended and using resources and assessment to support the learning experiences?' and so on.

However, the judgements depend on the criteria being used. For example, someone observing Teacher A's class (p. 4) using the criterion that an effective classroom organisation is a formal one where children work individually and silently, would judge that class to be effectively organised, while judging Teacher B's class to be ineffectively organised. The judgements would be reversed if the criteria were that an effective classroom organisation enabled children to work collaboratively and share ideas. The criteria to be applied in the context of a constructivist view of teaching and learning would be, for example, that:

- children are engaged in enquiry in new situations, raising questions and attempting to answer them

- children are questioning ideas (their own and others') and testing them against previous experience and against new information

- children are basing their conclusions on evidence and are prepared to change their ideas in the light of evidence

- children are reflecting on how they have tested ideas and how their testing can be improved

- teachers are aware of the children's ideas and are providing opportunities for them to consider and test alternative ideas including the scientific view

- there are sufficient resources available and children are using these effectively

- teachers are using assessment formatively and involving children in assessing their work and deciding how to improve it.

Further discussion of criteria for evaluating children's learning opportunities are included in Chapter 15.

SUMMARY

This introductory chapter has sought to provide:

- a brief account of different views of learning and of the implications for teaching of holding a particular view

- a rationale for endorsing a view of learning that sees learners as constructing their understanding in science through social interaction and through interaction with the physical environment

- some implications for the role of the teacher, children and resources of embracing a constructivist view of learning

- some signposts to later parts of the book where the discussion of these aspects is taken up in more detail.

FURTHER READING

A straightforward account of different views of learning is given in:

Watkins, C. (2003) *Learning: A Sense-Maker's Guide*. London: Association of Teachers and Lecturers (ATL) and Institute of Education, University of London.

A more comprehensive discussion of learning can be found in:

Bransford, J. D., Brown, A. L. and Cocking, R. R. (eds) (1999) *How People Learn: Brain, Mind, Experience and School*. Washington, DC: National Academy Press.

Chapter 2

Children learning

INTRODUCTION

In this chapter we look at how children approach the task of making sense of the events and phenomena that they encounter in the classroom and beyond. We begin with evidence in the form of extracts from a verbatim transcript of a video recording of groups of 11-year-olds working on a problem of why blocks of different kinds of wood floated at different levels in water. Commentary on the actions of the children in the first two groups leads to hypotheses about how they try to make sense of their observations. Evidence from other groups is used to test these hypotheses, and some general themes about children's approach to understanding through active investigation are suggested.

Analysis of these and similar classroom events is used to propose a model of the development of understanding. This shows how the use of science process skills has a key role in the development of scientific ideas.

CHILDREN OBSERVED

The children were working in groups of four or five. Each group was given four blocks of varnished wood of similar size and shape but different density and labelled A, B, C and D, a bowl of water, spring balance, ruler, and an activity sheet as shown below:

1. Float your blocks on the water. Look carefully at the way they are floating.
   What do you notice that is *the same* about the way all the blocks float?
   What do you notice that is *different* between one block and another about the way they float?
   Get one person to write down what you notice, or make a drawing to show how the blocks are floating.
   Check that you all agree that the record shows what you see.
   Put the blocks in order from best floater to worst floater.
2. What other things are the same about the blocks?
   What other things are different? Think about their size, their mass, colour and anything else. Weigh and measure them.
   Make sure you keep a record of what you find.

3. Now discuss all the things that are the same about the blocks. Get one person to put down a list of things that are *the same*. Now discuss all the things that *are different* and make a list of them. For each thing that is *different* about the blocks you should put down what you found about each block. Discuss with your group the best way to do this.

4. Now look at your results of things that are different. Do you see any patterns in the differences? Write down any pattern you find.

● Group 1: 'It's the varnish'

The first group of five will be called Group 1. They are all girls and the extract starts when they have just begun to digest the task:

Jenny	Yes, one person to write down
Anya	I know why – it's the varnish
Cheryl	Just a minute! How do you know it's the varnish when we haven't even looked at it?
Anya	Yes, but look, they . . .
Felicia	That one
	(putting block A into the water) Does it float?
	(all bend down to have a good look at the floating blocks)
Manjinder	Yes, half and half
Others	Half and half
Jenny	(Beginning to write this down) Right!
	(Felicia, Manjinder and Anya each pick up one of the remaining blocks)
Felicia	Shall I put B in?
Manjinder	I'll put C in
Anya	I'll put D in
Cheryl	Leave this A in there
Jenny	Now put B in there

● Group 2: 'A sinks half-way and floats half-way'

Meanwhile a second group, of four boys (Ahmed, Richard, Pete and Femi) and one girl (Rachel), have started in a similar way, putting one block in at a time, and so far A, B and C are floating in the water. Five heads are crowded round the bowl and before D is put in one of the boys says:

Ahmed	C's nearly all gone, so D must sink
Richard	D must sink
	(block D is then put in and floats very high in the water)
Pete	Ah, D's floating on the top
Femi	D's the best floater
Pete	Now why is D the best floater?
Ahmed	Got more air in it
Richard	Got more air
Femi	. . . air bubbles
	(Ahmed takes block D out of the water to look more closely at it)
Ahmed	It's lighter
Richard	It's the lightest
Rachel	It's balsa wood
Pete	(taking the block from Ahmed) Yes, that *is* balsa wood
Rachel	Balsa (taking block and putting it back in the water) (meanwhile Ahmed picks up the spring balance as if to suggest weighing but puts it down again as the attention of the group turns again to the other blocks in the water)
Pete	Now which is floating the worst?
Richard	This one – C
	(he picks C out of the water and hands it to Femi)
	Now feel that one
Femi	That's . . .
Richard	That's terribly heavy
Pete	That's why it's still floating – all wood floats – but, if – the heavier it is the lower it floats
Femi	Yes
Richard	Yes, but it still floats
Femi	(taking B out of the water) B's pretty heavy
Pete	(picking up pencil to begin making a record) So A . . .
Rachel	– A is sort of –
Femi	A is half-way down, and B's . . .
Richard	B sort of flops. It's half-way –
Rachel	– down at one side
Pete	(concerned to have an agreed record) So how shall we describe the way A floats?
Rachel	A equals about half
Ahmed	A sinks half-way and floats half-way
Femi	I think . . .
Pete	(writing) A is medium weight. Block A
Rachel	No, A block –
Ahmed	(to Pete) Yes, block A
Pete	(speaking as he writes) Block A
	(Ahmed turns to Richard while Pete writes and points to blocks B and C)
Ahmed	(to Richard) They're both the same
Richard	(to Ahmed) They're not, that one's lopsided

Pete	(speaking as he writes) . . . is medium . . .
Femi	(joining in with Richard and Ahmed) It's probably because of the varnish it's got on it
Rachel	(also joining in) Right
Pete	(summarising what he has written) So, block A is medium weight and so . . .
Femi	B
Richard	B's lopsided
Pete	(still writing) . . . and so it . . .
Femi	Yes, B's the worst one
Richard	No, C's the worst one
Pete	(reading what he has written and regaining the attention of the others) . . . so it floats with half the wood under the water
Femi	Yes – about that
	(there is a pause, they all look again, putting their heads as low as possible to place their eye level near the water surface)
Femi	Use a ruler – are you sure?
	(he goes to fetch a ruler)
Femi	Here's a ruler

Commentary

Before going any further there is enough here in these children's activity to raise several points about the children's own ideas, mental skills and attitudes as they explore the material given to them. Right at the start Anya throws in what appears to be a wild hypothesis: 'It's the varnish'. There is no evidence for this, as Cheryl immediately points out to her, but it does show a desire to explain. In this case the 'explanation' is a low-level one, stated in terms of an observed feature (the varnish) without any attempt to propose a link between the supposed cause and its effect, although this may have been tacitly assumed. Cheryl's intervention indicates an attitude of willingness to use evidence. They then proceed to gather that evidence by putting the blocks in the water systematically. Their first 'result' is a rough one, 'half and half', but it is recorded at the time.

The second group is also making interpretations ahead of observation at the start of the quoted extract. They have already put three blocks in the water and noticed a pattern (quite accidental) that each one floated lower in the water than the last. Block C has been observed to be 'nearly all gone' and they predict 'so D must sink'. They accept the evidence when they see it, however, and find that D floats higher than any other block. So they are quite willing to change their ideas in the light of evidence. Immediately there is some further hypothesising as to why block D floats best. The initial hypothesis, about air inside it, is overtaken by one finding support within the group, that D is lighter. (Perhaps to the children these are not alternative hypotheses but different ways of saying the same thing: things with more air in them are lighter than things with less air.) They also use their previous knowledge to identify block D as balsa wood.

At the point where the floating of block D seems to have been explained by its being 'the lightest' there is in fact no evidence of this at all. The children have not yet even 'weighed' the blocks in their hands in any way which would have allowed comparisons to be made (although they do this soon after). The process of interpreting observations is clearly way ahead of actually making the observations in this case. But a realisation of the lack of evidence for their statement may be what makes Ahmed pick up the spring balance. He does not persist at this point, sensing that the group interest has passed on to other things, but much later (in the continuation, to come) he is the one who does introduce the balance and initiates the weighing of the blocks.

The hypothesis about the weight of the blocks of wood being related to the way they float seems to direct the next section of their work. Notice how Richard, when he identifies block C as the worst floater, hands it to Femi and says 'Now feel that one'. He is referring to 'feeling' the weight and the observations he is making about the wood are clearly focused and narrowed down by the idea he has in mind. Pete puts the suggested relation clearly, 'the heavier it is the lower it floats', after reminding himself, from previous knowledge, that 'all wood floats'.

Pete then directs his attention to writing down what they have found (he is the recorder). But is it what they have found? What he writes is 'Block A is medium weight and so it floats with half the wood under the water'. Their observation was about the floating not about the weight; in fact they have no evidence about how the weight of A compares with that of other blocks. The statement recorded seems to have given an assumption the status of an observation and made their observation (of the floating) into an explanation for it. The ideas they have, based apparently on no more than jumping to conclusions, have influenced the process of gathering information. But they are still exploring the blocks, the water and the equipment, and as long as the real things are in front of them there is the opportunity for them to reconsider and test out the relationships they have suggested.

● Group 2 continued

While Femi was explaining to Rachel why a ruler was needed, Richard was looking closely at block B floating in the water:

Richard	I can't understand why this is lopsided
Rachel	Well, look, see, it goes down that side
Richard	Yes, that's what I mean, I can't understand it
Pete	(who has not noticed this lopsided debate, having been busy writing the record, finishes writing about A) Now how is B?
Richard	Lopsided
Ahmed	Lopsided
Pete	(taking B out of the water) Now B is . . .
Rachel	Hang on a minute
	(she takes block B from Pete)
Pete	Now is B heavier than A, or lighter?

Rachel	Let's see if it's . . .
	(she uses the ruler to measure the thickness of the block at all four corners; all the others close round to see what she is doing)
Richard	(answering Pete's earlier question) Sort of lopsided, Pete
Femi	Lopsided
Rachel	(after finishing the measuring of B) Yes, it's the same length all the way down, but it's lopsided
Pete	(picks up blocks A and B, weighing them in his hands) Now which one is heavier, do you reckon?
Ahmed	(reaches for the spring balance again) Try this
Pete	(picks up the pan to use with the spring balance)
	If we try this, we can use this – who knows how to set up something like this?
Femi	Well, you put it on the hook
	(he hooks the pan on to the spring balance)
	. . . now you can weigh something on it
Richard	(who has put blocks A and B back in the water and is looking at block B) Lopsided, in'it?
Pete	(picking block A out of the water) Now shake all the water off. Try A first
	(Rachel holds the spring balance while Pete puts block A on the pan)
Rachel	Just put it on
Pete	Now what's it come up to?
	(he ducks under Rachel's arm so that he can put his eye right in front of the scale)
Femi	(also closing one eye and peering at the scale) . . . about sixty
Richard	(also trying to look) . . . about sixty-three
Pete	Is there something we can hang it on, 'cos if you hang it on your hand you're likely to bounce it about

They then seek and find a way of steadying the spring balance. In the course of this they notice the zero adjustment, take the block off and use the zero adjustment and then discuss the reading of the divisions of the scale. From this point their investigation takes on a much more businesslike air. They are not content with the rough 'feel' of the weight nor with describing the floating as 'half-way' for they begin to measure the parts of the block below the water. Pete finds a neat way of recording this by drawing the blocks upside down like this:

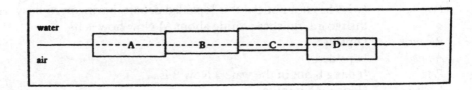

Figure 2.1 Pete's drawing of the floating blocks

so that it is easy to see the direct relation between the length of the submerged part and the weight of the block.

Commentary

The group showed what seemed to be a considerable progression in the way they approached the task. Starting from rather gross qualitative observations, of both the weight and the floating, they proceeded to use measurement to refine their observations. It appeared that this early period of rough observation was one of working out for themselves what the problem was. Once they defined the problem in their own minds they tackled it in a more systematic and precise manner. This took some time (about 30 minutes) in this particular case, probably because the task had been presented to them on a sheet; it was not of their finding. It took time for them to become interested in it and make it 'their own'. When children work on problems they have found for themselves there is no need for this period of 'coming to terms' with it. When they take on problems given to them, and they are generally very willing to do this as evidently happened here, time may be needed for rough exploration before they begin to grasp what is needed and to apply mental skills and ideas at the more advanced level of their capabilities. This is not unlike the scientist who takes rough measurements to 'get a feel' for the problem before setting up conditions for more precise measurement.

The observations, and later measurements, of this group were very strongly focused by their idea that the floating was related to the weight of the blocks. This idea was introduced early on, it was not something they 'discovered' by induction from their observations. It was, in fact, stated before enough evidence had been collected to support it, and became the framework for the observations and measurements they then made. It seemed that there was an immediate attempt to find a relationship that might explain initial observations and that later observations were focused by the desire to test this relationship. In the process another relationship might be suggested which was then tested. Thus all the observations were made for a purpose and not just to gather a range of different kinds of information that later would be put together to find patterns and relationships. It is entirely reasonable that this should be so, for without a purpose it would not be possible to decide what information to gather. The idea was in the children's minds and their investigation was carried out to test it.

So far, from this analysis of the observations, we might hypothesise that the children's approach was to find evidence to test the ideas that they already had about why the blocks were floating differently. They had the idea first and *then* gathered evidence including measurements. The ideas did not *come from* the evidence but preceded it and indeed determined what they looked for and measured. They were using deductive reasoning related to their hypothesis, not an inductive approach, starting from their observations. To see if this applies to others than just this one group, here is another group working on the blocks activity and apparently making much more open-ended observations.

Group 3: 'They're magnetic when they're wet'

There are five girls, Kay, Lisa, Mena, Nicola and Ann (who is the recorder). We join them after about 20 minutes of exploratory activity with the blocks, when Ann has just summarised what they have so far done and is rereading the activity sheet to make sure nothing has been omitted:

Ann	(reading) What do you notice about the way they float? (answering herself) Well, we've found out that they all . . .
Nicola	. . . don't sink (brief laughter at this jokey statement of the obvious)
Mena	I know what it is, none of them float lopsided
Nicola	(who has taken two blocks out of the water and is holding them touching each other) They're magnetic!
Kay and Mena	(repeating what Nicola has done) Yes, they're magnetic
Mena	And if you put them in like that, they go flat, look (she puts the blocks into the water with the largest face vertical and they settle with this face horizontal)
Kay	And D goes flat
Mena	Test with D and B
Lisa	They're getting water-logged now, aren't they?
Mena	This one goes flat last I think
Nicola	Hang on, let's put them all in and see which goes flat last (they do this)
Mena	C
Lisa	C
Kay	No, it may have been B
Mena	I think it shouldn't be that, it should be D
Lisa	That one's the heaviest, so it should go over first because it's heaviest (Four pairs of hands go into the bowl, placing the blocks in vertically)
Mena	I think B should go over first and D should go over last
Nicola	Why?
Lisa	(to Ann) And they're magnetic
Mena	Yes, they're magnetic when they're wet (to Ann, who has been writing all this down) Write that down. They're really magnetic
Lisa	(reading from the worksheet) What other things are different?
Mena	Yes, look, the colour. The lightest in colour is the lightest in weight (Mena and Nicola take up the blocks and 'weigh' them in their hands)
Nicola	. . . and the darkest in colour is the heaviest in weight
Kay	Yes, the darkest in colour is the heaviest
Nicola	Yes, you know it's like white is very cool and dark is very hot
Mena	Yes, you see this is the lightest and it floats the best and this is the darkest so it doesn't float so well
Nicola	The lightest is . . .

Ann	(leaving the report-writing) Let's put it against the side (she picks up the two blocks in question, the heaviest and the lightest and directly compares their dimensions)
	You see, they're all the same size
Lisa	(pointing to the heavier one) It hasn't got so much light in it
Nicola	They're magnetic as well
Mena	That's probably only chance
Lisa	If you get them really wet and then put the sides together
Mena	(puts two blocks side by side)
	No, hang on – no, they are – even though they're shorter, this one's wider
Nicola	They're all the same size, then
Ann	The darkest is the heaviest and the lightest is the lightest
Lisa	Look, get them all wet
	(dips two blocks in the water and holds them with the largest surfaces together)
Nicola	(does the same as Lisa, holding up one block with another clinging beneath it) Yes, they do, look. They're definitely magnetic
Mena	You've got to get them really wet
Kay	Try C and D
Nicola	Try the heaviest and the lightest
	(they try various combinations and find that the heavier block falls off when hanging beneath a lighter one)
Mena	The heaviest ones don't work very well
Kay	A heavy and a light work, but not two heavies (a moment or two later they start weighing and measuring each block; Kay holds the spring balance)
Nicola	Put D on first
Ann	We can see that they're the same length
Nicola	Put D on, then we'll measure them all with the ruler (Kay puts D on the pan)
Nicola	That is . . .
Lisa	(interrupting) But we should dry them all off first because the water may affect them
Mena	But they're water-logged already
Kay	Here you are, here's some dry towels
Lisa	The water may affect them. The water will affect to – er – thing
Kay	(pointing to the wet balance pan) This is wet – better dry that
Lisa	But that's going to be the same in all of them – so it won't matter
Ann	(still measuring with the ruler) They're about 12 cm

(Some time is spent taking measurements of the blocks. They decide to find the average dimensions, for some reason, and Lisa sits aside from the rest of the group doing this. The others stand round the bowl apparently doing nothing in particular, but they are in fact watching the movement of blocks 'stuck' to the side of the bowl. The movement is very slow . . .)

Mena	They'll never come off
Kay	I know, I'll give it a little jog and see which comes down first
	(both bang the sides of the bowl)
	They're not going to come down
Ann	This one should come down first
Kay	Yes, that one came down when I pushed (on the sides) but that one was harder to push down
Ann	So D came down, then A
	(goes to record this. Nicola takes her place and continues to experiment in the same way, with Kay)
Nicola	We got to find patterns, what patterns have we got?
Kay	Well, we've got two dark ones and two light ones
Nicola	That's not a pattern
Kay	I know but . . .
Mena	We've got to find out what sort of pattern the weight goes in – there may be a pattern in the weight
Nicola	Start with D, then A, then C, then B (weight order)
Ann	Press them all down to the bottom and see which comes up to the surface . . . I should say D should come up first
Ann	One, two, three, let go!
Nicola	D, A, C, B, so that went in the heaviest order, because we found that B was the heaviest and D is the lightest
Kay	. . . and D came up first
Ann	. . . so it came out right, so we know our facts are right

Commentary

There are more widely ranging observations made by this group than by Group 2 and some attempt to explain each observation. Not all the ideas are tested, sometimes because other observations divert their attention, and the validity of many of the tests could be questioned. At the start of the extract the girls are following up their observation that if the blocks are placed in the water with the largest face vertical they do not float that way but turn over and 'go flat'. They have noticed a difference in the time taken for the blocks to 'go flat' and, at least in Mena's view, this is connected with the weight of the blocks. They decide to test all the blocks together rather than in pairs. The result does not satisfy Mena who says 'I think B should go over first and D should go over last', even though she saw that C was last. Nicola begins to question the assumption Mena is making and this might have led Mena to reconsider it, either by the force of argument or evidence or both.

They are interrupted, however, by the excitement over the discovery of the 'magnetism' of the blocks. It is interesting that none of the group members questions the use of the term 'magnetic' in relation to the blocks. They may indeed consider the effect to be exactly the same as found with a magnet or they may be using the word metaphorically. In either case the influence of previous knowledge in this interpretation of their observations is clear. The magnetic power of the blocks is tested by seeing if one block will support another hanging beneath it. They find the blocks differ in their ability to do this. Neither the test nor the conclusion from it are very soundly based but there is no challenge, from the teacher or the group, to make them reconsider it. Thus the idea that the blocks were 'magnetic' remained with them and was later reported as a finding from their group work, although not recorded here.

The magnetism sequence is briefly interrupted when Lisa reminds the others that they are to look for other things that were different about the blocks. The colour of the wood is an obvious difference and Mena leaps immediately from the observation of difference to a relationship which is more of an inspired guess than a pattern based on evidence ('the lightest in colour is the lightest in weight'). Indeed it is *after* this statement that the weights of the blocks are estimated by 'feel'. Nicola goes a stage further to try to explain the relationship, 'you know it's like white is very cool and dark is very hot', again using previous knowledge, in this case of differences relating to colour.

In the final part of the extract the Group 3 girls repeat in a more systematic way something that they had already done earlier (not covered by the transcript). They had held the blocks at the bottom of the bowl and noticed a difference in the rate at which they came up when released. They had a clear hypothesis about which block would reach the surface first and tested it by looking, not just for differences, but for whether these differences fitted their prediction. The pattern based on their ideas was indeed confirmed.

COMMON THEMES

The girls in the last group did indeed show the same kinds of approach to their enquiries as the other groups. Classroom observations in other contexts, too, suggest that such exchanges go on among children whenever they are truly co-operating and collaborating on a shared problem. Some of the recurring themes illustrated here are:

- since the problem had been assigned to children and was not one that they had found for themselves, some time was needed for them to 'make it their own'

- there was an initial period of activity in which many predictions and explanations were aired during what seems superficial and non-quantitative exploration, followed by more focused, quantitative investigation

- the children were constantly importing knowledge from previous experience, some relevant and some not

- their explanations, so readily offered, which sometimes seemed like guesses, preceded the evidence of whether or not they fitted the observations

- they used many of the process skills (observation, prediction, measurement), but these were used erratically, rather than being combined in a systematic approach

- although they challenged some of each other's ideas, provoking them to look for evidence to support their ideas, there were still many ideas left unchallenged even though there was no evidence to support them.

⬤ TOWARDS A MODEL OF THE DEVELOPMENT OF UNDERSTANDING

A model is a mental framework for describing and helping to understand a process and should be useful for taking action. A model of change in ideas should not only represent reality as far as possible; it should be able to account for failure to develop understanding in certain circumstances as well as for the incidences of change that lead to greater learning. But any model is no more than a hypothesis. There is no certain knowledge of how children's ideas are formed or how change in them can be brought about. All that anyone can do is to study the evidence in children's behaviour, put forward a possible explanation for it and then see how well this is supported by further evidence.

This is what Piaget (1929) and Bruner *et al.* (1966), and others who have produced theories about children's ideas, have done. They looked in detail at children sorting pebbles, swinging pendulums, solving problems involving physical principles, and so on, and hypothesised about what might be going on in children's minds to explain the outward behaviour they observed. Evidence of this kind is always open to various interpretations and sometimes the evidence itself is disputed. What children do with pebbles or with a pendulum depends on so many other things than their concepts and skills. It depends, for example, on:

⬤ whether they have seen the same or similar things before

⬤ their interest in them or in other things competing for their attention

⬤ how the things are presented to them and by whom

⬤ whether they are in company or alone

⬤ what they did immediately before

⬤ how tired or alert they feel.

Any generalisation about changes in children's ideas must be interpreted as being an account of what is likely to be happening but not one that necessarily will hold in all situations and for all children.

When children encounter something new to them – as in the case of the floating blocks of wood – they call upon previous experience in the attempt to find an explanation for their observations. There may be several ideas that could be used to try to explain the observations in a particular situation. The children refer to ideas that heavy things sink and light ones float; that all wood floats; that things that stick together are magnetic. In all such cases they are trying to use an existing idea to explain the new experience.

Whether the idea is useful in explaining the new experience is then tested. First the reasoning that 'if it is this, then it follows that . . . ' results in a prediction. Then available evidence is used, or more is sought through investigation, to see if the prediction fits and the explanation can be said to work. The evidence is then interpreted in terms of the idea being tested.

The possible outcomes of the testing are that:

- The linked idea is found to 'work' and emerges strengthened by the extension of its range, or it can be made to 'work' by some modification. In either case it undergoes some change as a result of being applied to the new problem and tested.

- It does not 'work' and cannot be made to work, in which case the only way to try to make sense of the new experience is to start again and link another existing idea to it.

So what seems to be happening is that the proceess begins by an existing idea being applied to a new experience or problem, as in Figure 2.2.

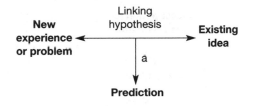

Figure 2.2 An existing idea linked in trying to explain the experience

The double-headed arrow represents the process of linking an idea as a possible explanation (hypothesis) of what is observed or as a possible solution to the problem. From the hypothesis (e.g. 'the lightest floats best') comes the prediction (if we weigh them we'll find the best floater is the lightest in weight). The process of predicting is represented by arrow 'a'. In order to test the prediction, an investigation is planned (arrow 'b' in Figure 2.3) which may mean making changes in the original situation or setting up a new one where some action is taken to see if there is evidence to support the prediction. Further steps follow as in Figure 2.3.

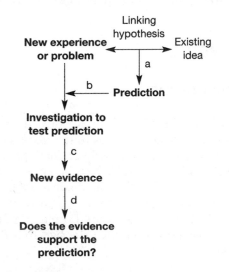

Figure 2.3 The prediction is tested

The test of the prediction may be as simple as weighing the blocks, or in other cases it may involve setting up a controlled experiment. As a result new evidence is gathered (arrow 'c'). The evidence is then interpreted in terms of the prediction (arrow 'd'). This leads to one of the two possible outcomes, as in Figure 2.4.

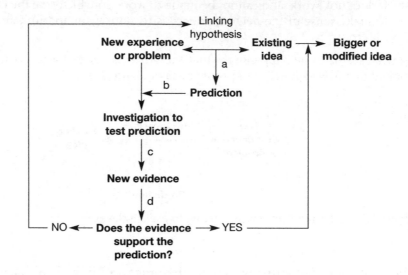

Figure 2.4 The outcome is used to decide whether or not the idea is useful

If the prediction is supported by the evidence and so the idea on which it was based has helped to explain the original observation, this initial idea becomes strengthened or 'bigger' because it now explains the new experience as well as previous experience. If on the other hand the answer is NO, then the idea that was linked has not predicted what was found and another hypothesis needs to be tried, another idea tried.

TESTING THE MODEL

Ideas about floating

Before taking the model further let us see how it accounts for the events in some examples. There were several occasions in the discussions of the groups investigating the wooden blocks when children made predictions about what might or might not happen. After the girls tested to see which block 'went flat' last, Mena said, 'I think it shouldn't be that, it should be D'. Mena made a prediction, tested it and found it did not fit. Later, they pressed the wet blocks against the side of the bowl, above the water level and waited to see which would slip down first. Ann said, 'This one should come down first' based on some idea she had that the force holding them varied among the blocks.

There was also the prediction by Richard's group of the connection between the weight of the blocks and the level at which they floated. This was eventually tested by predicting the relative weights from the way the blocks floated and then weighing them to see if the order was the same. Quite separately, Mena's group, having put the blocks in order of weight, predicted the order in which they would rise to the surface if all the blocks were held down at the bottom and released together. They predicted correctly and concluded 'so it came out right, we know our facts are right'.

The hypothesis that the blocks which stuck together were magnetic was not used to make a prediction and was not tested. It remained an untested assumption, along with several others, for example, about the colour of the blocks being significant. However, we can easily imagine a test of the magnetic hypothesis. They might have predicted that a magnet would pick up a wet block ('a'), tried using a magnet to do this ('b'), observed that the block was not attracted ('c') and interpreted this ('d') as meaning that the idea of magnetism did not explain the fact that the wet blocks stuck to each other. As it was, their investigations just led them to believe that 'they're only magnetic when they're wet'.

Ideas about keeping warm

Another example illustrates how different existing ideas and experiences determine the outcome of children's attempts to understand phenomena. A group of children of a wide age range were discussing the common experience that expanded polystyrene feels warm to the touch. They had a big block of the plastic that was going to form part of the props for a school play. There was general agreement at first that 'there is something hot inside'. The younger children apparently found this quite a reasonable explanation. Their experience, after all, of large warm objects such as hot-water bottles and radiators was that there was something inside that was hot and stayed hot for a considerable time. So their prediction was that the polystyrene block would stay warm, and it did.

The older children, however, brought to this problem the more complex idea that hot things generally cooled down if there was nothing to keep them hot. They knew that there was nothing but polystyrene right through the block and so predicted that if it was warm at one time then it should get cooler as time went on, and it did not. They even tried to make a piece cool down by putting it in a fridge and it obstinately refused to feel cold. It was quite a puzzle to them and they had to think of some altogether other way of explaining the warmth they felt. In the event they came to it through playing with some other pieces of polystyrene in the form of very small pellets. They ran their hands through the pellets and one said, 'It's like putting on warm gloves'. 'But gloves aren't warm, they just keep you warm', said another. 'That's what's happening with the blocks, it just keeps your hand warm, it isn't warm itself.' Here was a possible explanation (though expressed with a great deal of certainty, it was still a hypothesis) and an associated prediction. If the idea was right then the block would not be any warmer than anything else around. This could be checked with a thermometer, and it was.

Note that the 'new' idea was not new in the sense of being discovered from the observations; it was only new in that it had not been brought to bear on the problem before. In itself it was well known to the children that gloves and clothes keep them warm without having any heat source to do this. What they had to do to use this existing idea was, first, to recognise the possible connection, second, create a possible explanation (hypothesis) based on it, third, to use it in making a prediction and, fourth, to test the prediction. And they all learned together from the ideas sparked off by a few of them and picked up by the others.

A role for the teacher?

In reality the thinking often happens in a flash and it is in no way being suggested that children consciously think through from one step to another. After all, it is not possible to account in a rational way for how scientists arrive at new ideas (see Chapter 3). The steps of the model are a convenient way of looking at what happens. In the polystyrene example the same processes led to different emerging ideas for the younger and older children: the younger finding their ideas confirmed and therefore not needing to change them and the older finding a conflict because the ideas they brought to it were different and did not fit the evidence.

In these instances there was no teacher intervention and we don't know how this may have assisted or inhibited the children's investigations. We consider in a later chapter what kind of intervention might be appropriate, but it is worth noting here that, without it, the children with the floating blocks did not use the results of their enquiries as much as they could have done to reflect on their initial ideas or to develop their understanding of floating. Nor was their approach to testing ideas as systematic as it might have been. Nonetheless these observations enable us to see some significant features of how children go about solving problems and making sense of events and phenomena. They also provide a clue to how teachers can intervene so that children's thinking is developed as a result of their activities.

THE ROLE OF SCIENCE PROCESS SKILLS

The model suggests the development of ideas through application and testing in new situations. When ideas are shown to explain further experience, they become 'bigger', more encompassing and more useful. But the model also indicates the role of process/enquiry/investigative skills in the development of ideas. For if the processes indicated by the arrows 'a' to 'd' in Figure 2.4 are not properly carried out, then ideas may be accepted as explanations when they should be rejected and sometimes vice versa. Children sometimes make 'predictions' that they already know to be true and so are not a test of an idea. In setting up a test they may not control variables that should be kept constant. When observing the outcome they may focus on certain observations that confirm their ideas, leaving out of account those that might challenge them. In other words, the way in which the processes are carried out crucially influences the ideas that emerge. It follows that children's process skills have a key role in developing understanding. This is why we pay attention throughout this book to the nature and development of science process skills.

SUMMARY

In this chapter we have looked in detail at the talk and actions of some groups of children investigating the differences in how some blocks of wood floated in water. The close study of their talk showed how they pursued ideas from previous experience to try to make sense of what they observed and used various process skills in their investigations. It was also noted that, although their investigation became more systematic and quantitative as time went on, in the absence of teacher intervention, some ideas went unchallenged and untested.

A model of how ideas are developed through investigation was built up to reflect the way children use and test their existing ideas in trying to explain observations or solve problems. Other evidence from children's activities was used to test the model. An important implication drawn from it is that process skills have a key role in the development of understanding.

FURTHER READING

Transcripts of children's talk are included in:

Qualter, A. (1996) *Differentiated Primary Science*. Buckingham: Open University Press.

Ollerenshaw, C. and Ritchie, R. (1988) *Primary Science: Making it Work*. London: David Fulton Publishers.

The role of talk in developing ideas is discussed further in Chapter 11, where reference is made to:

Barnes, D. (1976) *From Communication to Curriculum*. Harmondsworth: Penguin.

Chapter 3

The goals of science education

INTRODUCTION

The model in Chapter 2 described development of ideas through the use of process skills, leaving open the question of which ideas and skills we should be aiming to develop in children. This is the question taken up in this chapter. We begin with an overview of some recent thinking about the aims of science education in general. The second section looks at views of the nature of scientific activity, since how we view this influences how we represent science in our teaching. The third section then looks at the implications of this discussion for the science education of 5- to 12-year olds, leading to the identification of the process skills, attitudes and ideas that are the focus of discussion in the rest of this book.

WHAT LEARNING DO WE WANT TO ACHIEVE THROUGH SCIENCE EDUCATION?

This is a big question but a fundamental one, given that the answer will help determine, in large measure, how we teach as well as what we teach and when we teach it. The answer at any one time depends on priorities, for there is never enough time or enough resources to teach all that it's possible or desirable to teach. But change in what is taught is gradual rather than revolutionary. Although national curricula and guidelines are revised from time to time, most changes are in finding different ways of expressing the same thing. In practice there is considerable consensus across the world and over the years in national curriculum statements or guidelines both about the breadth of different outcomes that should be embraced and in the particular concepts, skills and attitudes that are felt to be important. Indeed, some would say, as we will see later, that there is too much continuity over time and not enough rethinking of what is relevant to the world today, rather than yesterday.

WHAT LEARNING IN SCIENCE IS IMPORTANT FOR FUTURE CITIZENS?

A modern industrial and democratic society needs citizens who have:

- widely applicable skills
- informed views on matters such as pollution, biotechnology, species conservation and so on
- flexibility in thinking and respect for evidence
- the willingness and ability to continue learning.

The contribution of science education is to:

- sustain and develop curiosity and a sense of wonder about the world around
- provide information that can lead to understanding that helps decision-making about matters relating to health, diet, lifestyle, etc.
- enable informed participation in debates about major issues such as environmental preservation, genetic engineering, the use of energy
- give access to ways of investigation and enquiry that are based on evidence and careful reasoning
- provide satisfaction in finding answers to questions through one's own mental and physical activity.

In the twenty-first century, few will be able to lead a useful and satisfying life without being able to adapt to the accelerating changes in types of occupation, ways of living and in the requirements of any particular job or profession. Clear evidence of this is seen in the emphasis given in upper secondary school courses to the development of key, or core, skills. These are generally taken to be problem-solving, communication, numeracy, using information technology and working with others. Requirement to develop these skills is gradually moving down to earlier stages of education, in response to recognition that they can be developed more satisfactorily the sooner the process begins. So we should be looking to ensure that education at all levels makes a contribution to these vital skills.

SCIENCE EDUCATION FOR ALL

Science education in school has to serve the purpose both of preparing future scientists and technologists and of providing all citizens with sufficient knowledge and understanding of the world around so that they can operate effectively and make sensible decisions about science-related issues that affect all our lives. Although in the curriculum for 5- to 12-year-olds there is no distinction between these two, nevertheless there is a tendency for the requirements of later stages of education to bear down on the earlier stages. The need to educate future scientists still tends to dominate the secondary science curriculum, despite efforts to equalise the weight given to vocational and academic careers. This situation has been widely criticised and curriculum developers are now being urged to consider as a priority the contribution that science education should be making to the education of everyone, irrespective of whether they continue study of science beyond the end of compulsory schooling.

The findings of two groups, who have considered what the contribution of science to the education of all in the twenty-first century should be, give some ideas of how this perspective might change the goals of science education.

'Beyond 2000'

One of these groups was of UK science educators who considered 'the form of science education required to prepare young people for life in our society in the next century' and published their findings under the title *Beyond 2000* (Millar and Osborne, 1998, p. 1). They expressed the outcome of their deliberations in terms of the need for a science curriculum that is 'seen primarily as a course to enhance general "scientific literacy" '. The meaning and implications of this were exemplified rather than being worked out in detail by the members of this group. They emphasised the need to build gradually, throughout education from the age of 5 to 16, 'general understanding of the important ideas and explanatory frameworks of science'.

They also proposed that the development of an understanding *of* science should be an aim of science education. This should come from:

- evaluating, interpreting and analysing both evidence which has been collected at firsthand and evidence which has been obtained from secondary sources

- hearing and reading stories about how important ideas were first developed and became established and accepted

- learning how to construct sound and persuasive arguments based upon evidence

- considering a range of current issues involving the application of science and scientific ideas.

The PISA framework for scientific literacy

The second group that has considered what science education should aim to provide echoed many of the points made in *Beyond 2000*. This was an international group set up by the Organisation for Economic Co-operation and Development (OECD) to advise on the development of tests for the Programme for International Student Assessment (PISA). The PISA project was set up to conduct surveys every three years, beginning in 2000, to assess 'how well students at age 15, and therefore approaching the end of compulsory schooling, are prepared to meet the challenges of today's societies' (OECD, 2003, p. 9). The interest is in the outcomes rather than the curriculum processes, although some information is collected by questionnaire about students' exposure to learning experiences relevant to what is tested. Surveys look at achievement in reading, mathematics and science. In each case what is assessed is described in terms of 'literacy'.

The group deciding the framework for 'scientific literacy' defined it as: 'the capacity to use science knowledge, to identify questions and to draw evidence-based conclusions in order to understand and help make decisions about the natural world and the changes made to it through human activity' (OECD, 2003, p. 133). To take this to a more detailed level meant answering the question: what are the outcomes of science education up to the age of 15 that every citizen needs? The group identified science processes, science concepts and situations (or contexts) in which the processes and concepts are used. The processes identified were formulated in 2003 as:

1. Describing, explaining and predicting scientific phenomena.

2. Understanding scientific investigation.

3. Interpreting scientific evidence and conclusions.

It was recognised that science knowledge is needed for all three processes, although only in the first is the knowledge intended to be the main 'hurdle'. Consistent with the definition above, the group considered that scientific literacy would be indicated by using these processes and applying science concepts in relation to issues that citizens of today and tomorrow need to understand and make decisions about. Ten such 'areas of application' were identified:

Science in life and health:

Health, disease and nutrition

Maintenance of and sustainable use of species

Interdependence of physical/biological systems

Science in Earth and environment:

Pollution

Production and loss of soil

Weather and climate

Science in technology:

Biotechnology

Use of materials and waste disposal

Use of energy

Transportation

(OECD, 2003, p. 139)

Thus the science concepts that are assessed, and considered to be useful outcomes of science education, are determined by the relevance to these real-world issues. The situations, or contexts, in which they are encountered – both in life and in the test items – can affect us as individuals (food, use of energy), as members of a local community (water supply, air pollution) or as world citizens (global warming, loss of biodiversity). It was also thought important to include a 'historical context' reflecting the way scientific knowledge evolves and affects social decisions.

Implications

The focus of both the *Beyond 2000* and the OECD/PISA groups was the whole science education of 5- to 16-year-olds, but what they have to say is relevant not only to the secondary school curriculum but to the age range 5–12 where, after all, the largest part of science education takes place. We take up the implications of this later in this chapter after first completing the discussion of relevant factors, by looking at the view of science that reflects current thinking.

THE NATURE OF SCIENTIFIC ACTIVITY

In *Beyond 2000*, leading science educators in the UK reviewed the science curriculum in the UK and concluded that:

> The current curriculum retains its past, mid-twentieth-century emphasis, presenting science as a body of knowledge which is value-free, objective and detached – a succession of 'facts' to be learnt, with insufficient indication of any overarching coherence and a lack of contextual relevance to the future needs of young people. The result is a growing tension between school science and contemporary science as portrayed in the media, between the needs of future specialists and the needs of young people in the workplace and as informed citizens.

> (Millar and Osborne, 1998, p. 4)

The modern view is quite different from the one that sees science as yielding ultimate truths and providing proofs of objective theorems. It sees science as characterised in this way:

- Science is about *understanding*, that is, arriving at possible explanations of and relationships between observed events, which enable predictions to be made.

- Science is a *human endeavour*, depending on creativity and imagination, and on skills of gathering and interpreting evidence: it has changed in the past and will change in the future as human experience and understanding change.

- Scientific theories at any particular time are subject to change in the light of new evidence and so must be regarded as *tentative* at all times.

- The physical world around is the *ultimate authority* by which the validity of scientific theories and principles is to be judged. Whatever logic there seems to be in hypothetical explanations or relationships, they are only useful in so far as they agree with reality.

Each of these points is now briefly elaborated. In this discussion we take the opportunity to distinguish science from its closest neighbours – mathematics and technology. There are many reasons to combine teaching and learning in science and technology and in some aspects of mathematics. But it is still important for a teacher to know how the learning contributes to knowledge and understanding in each of these subjects.

● Science as understanding

In both learning science and doing science the aim is to understand. In this it differs from technology (see Box 3.1). In practice this means that we have to have an *explanation* for what is known and that predictions made on the basis of this explanation fit the available evidence. In arriving at an explanation – a theory – a scientist uses existing ideas, makes predictions based on them and then makes observations to see whether the predictions fit the facts. For a theory to be worthy of the name, as Stephen Hawking points out, it must satisfy two requirements: 'It must accurately describe a large class of observations on the basis of a model that contains only a few arbitrary elements, and it must make definite predictions about the results of future observations' (Hawking, 1988, p. 9).

If the observations do not fit, the theory has to be changed, assuming that the 'facts' are not disputed. When Copernicus' model (theory) of the universe put the sun at the centre of planets moving in circular orbits, this was a great improvement on the Ptolemaic model. However, the predictions it gave about the movement of the planets did not coincide with how the planets were observed to move. Johannes Kepler then modified the theory, proposing that the planets' orbits were elliptical, not circular. Newton elaborated the model, providing an explanation for the elliptical orbits in terms of the 'law of gravitation', which gave predictions fitting the observations well – that is, until the technology existed that revealed previously undetected phenomena. Then it was Einstein's theory that fitted the events better.

These changes exemplify the gradual development of understanding, where each step is taken from the position reached by a previous one. A scientist does not come to a new phenomenon, or revisit a familiar one, without ideas derived from what is already known. In the same way, a pupil learning science has ideas derived from previous experience which are brought to bear in making his or her personal meaning of events and phenomena. These ideas are tested out against the evidence and modified so that they fit better that which has been observed.

While there are, of course, many differences between the ways of working of the scientist and of the child learning science they are both aiming for understanding and there are broad similarities in the way that understanding is developed. These similarities are certainly enough to support the claim that learning science and doing science are basically the same activities.

● Science as a human endeavour

It is implicit in what has just been said that scientific ideas originate in the way human beings make sense of their experience. So it is perhaps surprising that science is so often depicted as being some kind of objective picture of the world 'as it is', as if facts and theories exist in the objects or phenomena themselves to be teased out by those clever enough to do so. An unfortunate consequence of the term 'discovery learning' is that it gives this impression. We can agree that the answers to how things work do reside within them in that they are to be found by investigation and experimentation, but there is an important difference between regarding the process as 'finding *the* explanation of what is happening' and 'finding the best way for me to explain what is happening'. The difference is not trivial, for the latter formulation admits that there may be other ways of explaining things.

Box 3.1: The relationship between science and technology

The concern with understanding, which is characteristic of science, enables it to be clearly distinguished from *technology*. Technological activity is closely connected in practice with scientific activity. Both are relevant in the education of young children but one should not be mistaken for the other. Technology is about solving problems by designing and making some artefact, whereas science is about understanding. They are, however, more closely related than this simple statement seems to suggest. In the pursuit of scientific activity, problems are often encountered which require technology, as, for example, in devising ways of observing (a microscope results from the application of technology to such a problem) or in handling data (a computer). At the same time the solution of problems by technology involves the application of concepts arrived at through science (the understanding of reflection and refraction of light in the case of the microscope, for instance).

Technology is also involved in the solving of problems in other areas of the curriculum outside science. There is more to science than solving practical problems and more to technology than applying science concepts. Moreover, as Layton (1990) argues cogently, scientific knowledge has to be 'reworked' before the technologist can use it. Scientific knowledge is expressed in terms of theories, which are general and widely applicable, while technology requires knowledge that is particular, specific and tailored to the particular situation.

There is an intriguing question here about just how major changes in ideas come about. How did Kepler come to hit upon elliptical orbits as providing a better model than circular ones? How did Newton arrive at the universal theory of gravitation? In Newton's case we have the apocryphal story of the falling apple, but it still leaves a big question as to how any thinking about an apple was connected with the solar system. Biographies sometimes help to provide an explanation of an event, but inevitably they present it with hindsight, from the position of knowing that the new idea was in fact a useful one. From this perspective the new idea always appears so obvious that it seems surprising that it was not thought of before. At the time, however, it probably emerged from creative reflection, even day-dreaming, rather than rational thinking. Creativity and imagination have played a part in the successive changes that have led to our current state of understanding. The ideas, which appear sometimes to 'come out of the blue', have been seized upon and selected from others by a mechanism that Einstein described as 'the way of intuition, which is helped by a feeling for the order lying behind the appearance' (Einstein, 1933).

Science includes much more than controlled experiment, objective measurement and the careful checking of predictions. It depends on these but just as much on creative thinking and imagination; a truly human endeavour. Learning science through experiencing it this way is more likely to appeal to, and excite, children (and future citizens) than learning it as a set of mechanical procedures and 'right answers'. In particular it is more likely to appeal to the female half of the population who often feel excluded from science because of its masculine image.

The tentative nature of scientific theories

Reference above to the successive models of the solar system and theories of the universe provide an example of how certain ideas have changed. We can confidently add 'and will change', for there is no reason to suppose that this process will not continue. Einstein would have been the last to claim that he had arrived at some kind of final word on the subject. Many examples of changes in ideas in other branches of science could be cited. Without labouring the point, what these changes mean is that, at any particular time in the past – or indeed in the present – the only certainty is that the current theories, although believed to be the most perfect insights, are only passing stages in human understanding.

The consequence of recognising this is that any theory must be regarded as subject to change and therefore as only tentative knowledge, for the chance of finding evidence that disagrees with it is always present. Even though a theory may provide predictions which accord with all existing evidence for centuries (as Newton's did) there is always the possibility of further observations that do not fit (as indeed eventually happened in Newton's case). Hawking expresses this with clarity and authority when he notes that any theory is always provisional, regardless of how much supporting evidence there is for it, since 'you can disprove a theory by finding even a single observation that disagrees with the predictions of the theory' (Hawking, 1988, p. 10).

If this applies to the theories of scientists, how much more seriously must it be taken in relation to the individual theories of learners? At any particular time learners' ideas are those that best fit the evidence available, but soon there are likely to have to be changes in the light of further information or observations. However, if we see for ourselves the evidence which brings the need to change, there will be no confusion but greater clarity. If children are taught science in a way that reflects the tentative nature of all theories, it will seem natural for them to adapt their own ideas as new evidence is presented. It is only when others tell them to adopt different ideas for which they as yet see no reason, that confusion is likely.

Reality as the ultimate test of scientific theories

It may seem obvious that, if science is about understanding the world around, then its theories must be judged by how well it does this. In practice, however, testing how well a theory fits is not always easy. Evidence may not be available, or may be contested, or may depend on such complicated mathematics that few people understand it.

In the history of science there are many examples of factors other than the fit with evidence being used to assess a scientific theory. It took a hundred years for the ideas of Copernicus, that the Earth and planets moved round the Sun, to be accepted even though this model fitted the observations far better than Ptolemy's model of the universe, mainly because the latter's Earth-centred model had been adopted by the Christian Church. There are contemporary examples of theories based on cultural mores which are preferred to scientific theories in certain societies. The extent to which science is culturally neutral is the subject of ongoing, and complex, debate.

So the statement that reality is the ultimate test of a scientific theory is not as uncontentious as it may at first seem. It raises the question of 'whose reality' for one thing. But, while not assuming a single view of science, the statement does help to distinguish the broad area of science from other disciplines. For example, in *mathematics* the ultimate test is the internal logic of numbers and relationships. There is no need for the predictions from mathematical theories to relate to reality (non-rational numbers are an example), in sharp distinction to the theories of science.

WHAT ARE THE IMPLICATIONS FOR 5- TO 12-YEAR-OLDS?

Now that we have looked at contemporary views of science and at what it is considered that science education should aim to provide by the age of 16, we turn to the question of what this means for the goals of science education for 5- to 12-year-olds.

Science education at all stages should help children to understand the world around them. As that 'world' expands, as children grow older, so the ideas they develop become bigger (in the sense of explaining more phenomena, as discussed in Chapter 2) as they encounter more of it. So there should be no incompatibility between the role of early science education in helping children to understand things around them and its role as a foundation for later science education. At all stages they need to develop the process skills, attitudes and motivation that drive the creation of bigger ideas.

Process skills

Our discussion of the nature and outcomes of scientific activity leads to the view that in order to build understanding at any level it is important for learners to be able to:

- raise questions that can be answered by investigation
- develop hypotheses about how events and relationships can be explained
- make predictions based on the hypotheses
- use observation to gather information
- plan and use investigation to search for patterns and test ideas
- interpret evidence and draw valid conclusions
- communicate, report and reflect on procedures and conclusions.

These things involve processing ideas and information and so they are described as 'process skills'. As noted in relation to the PISA processes (which can be mapped to these as in Figure 3.1), they all involve some scientific knowledge. For instance, when we observe, what we look for is framed by using existing knowledge. If we have no knowledge of a situation, we 'see' (or hear or taste) much less than someone with knowledge. (Think of a wine taster, or someone who is very familiar with cloud formations, and how what these experts observe depends on their knowledge of what is significant.) Similarly, interpreting information in science draws upon knowledge of how things behave rather than on fantasy or magic.

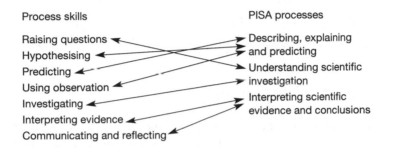

Figure 3.1 Mapping the process skills to the PISA framework

In various curriculum statements, the process skills are expressed in different ways, sometimes in more detail and sometimes less, but their meaning and range is the same. For instance, in the National Curriculum for England they are encompassed in three overarching enquiry skills: planning; obtaining and presenting evidence; and considering evidence and evaluating. It is clear that:

- 'planning' covers raising questions, hypothesising, predicting and investigating

- 'obtaining and presenting evidence' includes using observation and communicating and reporting

- 'considering evidence and evaluating' encompasses interpreting information and reflecting.

The Scottish 5–14 guidelines use three different categories: preparing for tasks; carrying out tasks; and reviewing and reporting tasks. Again it is easy to see how these can be mapped to the seven process skills we have identified.

We are using the longer, more detailed set of labels for two reasons. First, they are clearly related to the model that we used in Chapter 2 to describe learning. This shows that each is different in nature and function, even though several will generally be occurring in a scientific activity. Second, by being more specific about goals we can also be more specific about how to help children achieve these goals. There is no problem about grouping them together for the purposes of reporting children's achievement, but for trying to ascertain what help may be needed it is likely that considering raising questions, hypothesising and predicting separately is more informative than a more general 'planning'.

Scientific attitudes

Closely related to the *ability* to use these skills is the *willingness* to use them. This means willingness to question preconceived ideas in order to test them, to regard ideas as tentative, to change them in the light of evidence. It is important also to add a moral value of sensitivity for the environment, both natural and made, in the course of investigating it. So the goals of science education should include fostering these attitudes and values:

- curiosity
- respect for evidence
- flexibility in ways of thinking
- sensitivity in investigating the environment.

Motivation for learning

An important goal of education in all subjects and at all ages and stages is to motivate further learning. This becomes more important as the pace of technical development quickens and there is no longer any chance of schooling preparing pupils with the skills and knowledge they will need in the rest of their life. Within a decade there will be the requirement for skills that we do not even recognise today (just as most of us would not have known what 'surfing the Net' meant a little over a decade ago). Thus school must prepare students for continued learning throughout life and this means willingness to learn, enjoyment of learning, the development of high-level skills and of understanding how to learn.

We discuss later, in Chapter 6, actions that can be taken to encourage motivation for learning. At this point we note that these actions have to take into account the complex nature of motivation. It is a concept encompassing a number of personal factors that influence whether someone will exert the effort required for learning. These factors include interest, goal-orientation, locus of control, self-esteem, self-efficacy and self-regulation. These are interconnected components of motivation for learning and there is a good deal of evidence that what happens in classrooms, and particularly how assessment is used, has a key role in promoting or inhibiting them and hence in the nature of the learning achieved in particular circumstances.

Scientific ideas

It is relatively easy to identify aspects of the world around children which their science activities should help to develop. These are ideas about:

- living things and the processes of life (characteristics of living things, how they are made up and the functions of their parts, human health, etc.)
- the interaction of living things and their environment (competition, adaptation, effects of pollution and other human activities, etc.)

- materials (their variety, properties, sources, uses, interactions, conservation, disposal of waste, etc.)

- air, atmosphere and weather (presence of air round the Earth, features of the weather, causes of clouds, rain, frost and snow and freak conditions, etc.)

- rocks, soil and materials from the Earth (nature and origin of soil, maintenance of fertility, fossil fuels, minerals and ores as limited resources)

- the Earth in space (Sun, Moon, stars and planets, causes of day and night and seasonal variations)

- forces and movement (starting and stopping movement, speed and acceleration, simple machines, transportation, etc.)

- energy sources and uses (sources of heat, light, sound, electricity, etc.).

Of course such a list could equally apply to secondary school science, even tertiary. What would make it more useful as a guide to practice would be to identify *what* ideas about, say, sources of materials are appropriate at the primary level. But rather than spell them out in detail (for it is not the purpose of this book to develop a curriculum) it is more relevant here to consider the principles that should guide the identification of conceptual goals at the appropriate level.

There is wide agreement that process skills and attitudes have a particularly important role in science for 5- to 12-year-olds, since exploration, seeing for themselves and active learning are essential to learning at this stage. Thus, when we come to consider the content of science activities it is necessary to ensure that the ideas involved are ones that are investigable and accessible to children by using process skills.

This does not mean that we are only concerned with ideas about things children can physically touch and manipulate. Many ideas will be, and should be, of this kind, but it is not necessary to exclude ideas about events in children's experience which cannot be manipulated, such as ideas about the Sun, Moon and stars and about the weather. Children can develop these ideas by collecting information through careful observation and recording, seeking ideas from books and other resources to explain the patterns they observe and checking predictions against further observations. It is also important to keep in mind, as mentioned earlier, that the development of 'big' ideas has to begin with 'small' ones. Therefore we will not be teaching young children directly about, for example, the global impact of deforestation, but this will start if they investigate soil and observe what happens when streams of water flow through it.

Bringing these points together, we can identify principles for deciding ideas that should be given priority in science 5–12. These should be ideas that:

- help children's understanding of everyday events and their experience of the world around them

- are within the grasp of children in the age range 5–12, taking into account their limited experience and mental maturity

- are accessible and testable through the use by the children of science process skills

- provide a foundation for further science education that will develop their scientific literacy.

Applying these principles should enable us to set goals of understanding at appropriate levels for children aged 5–12.

SUMMARY

In this chapter we have discussed the role that science education has to play in enabling young people to become informed and thoughtful citizens of the twenty-first century. We have presented some current thinking about the goals of science education, reflecting new emphasis on education for scientific literacy of all, regardless of whether they will study science beyond the end of secondary school, and about the nature of scientific activity. We have considered some implications for the goals of science education for 5- to 12-year-olds and set out the first steps in identifying the process skills, attitudes, values and ideas that science 5–12 should aim to promote. In Chapter 4 we look at the kinds of experiences that provide opportunities for learning with these aims in mind. More detailed discussion of progression and ways of promoting it are given in Part III.

FURTHER READING

There is interesting discussion of scientific literacy and of views of science in:

Hodson, D. (1998) *Teaching and Learning Science: Towards a Personalized Approach.* Buckingham: Open University Press.

Part II

OPPORTUNITIES FOR LEARNING

Chapter 4

Providing for development 5–12

INTRODUCTION

In this part of the book we look at some overall features of providing opportunities for children's learning in science. This paints a background against which, in Part III, we propose ways of tailoring activities more specifically to the progress of individual and groups of children. It may be helpful, then, to begin with a résumé of where we have reached so far.

In Chapter 1 we considered some implications of holding different views of what the process of learning entails. We argued that both current understanding and motivation for continued learning in the future follow from a view of learning as the construction of knowledge by learners. Chapter 2 developed a model of this constructivist view of learning, illustrated and tested by examples of children engaged in science activities. The model formalised the process of learning as one of changing ideas in the course of trying to explain newly encountered events. An important result of looking at learning in this way was to draw attention to the key role of process skills in the development of conceptual understanding. Then, in Chapter 3, we identified the goals of science education, starting with the broader picture, leading to identifying goals for primary science in terms of the development of conceptual understanding, process skills, attitudes and values, and motivation.

This chapter now considers the consequences of this thinking for decisions about children's activities. While children encounter activities as a whole, it is important for teachers to consider separately two aspects of activities: their content (or subject matter) and the way in which the children encounter or interact with the content. So in the first two sections of this chapter we consider decisions about these two aspects of activities separately, even though they are one as far as the children are concerned. In the third section, we consider the experiences suitable for the early, middle and later stages of education 5–12.

OPPORTUNITIES FOR DEVELOPING IDEAS

Content is closely related to development of ideas, for clearly activities with snails lead to ideas about living things, not about magnets. The relationship between the development of skills and the content is different; activities with both snails and magnets can develop skills of gathering evidence and interpreting it. The content must provide the interest and motivation for children to become involved in an activity that is going to challenge and develop ideas. It must be chosen so that, across the years, children aged 5–12 have opportunities to develop ideas in the eight areas identified as goals of science education in Chapter 3 (p. 40–1).

In order for their activities to be genuine learning opportunities, however, children must be able to engage with the content. There must be incentive for 'minds on' and, where possible, for 'hands on'. Three things about the content will help this engagement:

- the potential to lead to a satisfying degree of understanding
- that it is of interest to the children
- that it is of relevance to understanding things around them.

These kinds of statement can become mere slogan unless we consider what they may mean in practice.

The potential for understanding

Bruner famously said that 'any subject can be taught effectively in some intellectually honest form to any child at any stage of development' (Bruner, 1960, p. 33). In stating this hypothesis he was drawing attention to the importance of taking into account 'the child's way of viewing things'. This is why we need to have in mind the strengths and limitations of children's ways of thinking when we consider what kinds of activities are really learning experiences, as we do later in this chapter. The ideas that satisfy young children are those that answer their questions about their immediate environment. These are conveniently called 'small' ideas because they explain small parts of experience rather than applying across a whole range of experiences. For example, they answer questions about 'what these seeds need to grow' rather than about the needs of living things in general. As time goes on, steps have to be taken to link the small ideas into bigger ones but these will not be effective unless the small ideas have been put in place through earlier experiences. As we have said before, conceptual understanding cannot begin with the broad generalisations. The content has to be such that it can be understood in terms of appropriately small ideas.

Interesting to children

Interest is important for children to engage with and make an effort to understand what is happening in their activities and experience. However, interest is not intrinsic to these happenings; it depends on how they are encountered. The result of 'following children's interests' has often been to narrow children's range of experiences by seizing too early on things in which they have already shown interest instead of attempting to expand their interests. The readiness of children to be intrigued by new things, or new ways of looking at familiar things, shows that interest can be created. It is perfectly possible for children to become completely absorbed in activities that they did not themselves suggest, but this does not mean that their interest can be captured by any activity. The criterion of interest should be applied after there has been chance for children to encounter new phenomena. This makes the question of starting points for topics particularly important.

What makes an activity interesting? It is generally because there is something *puzzling* about it, something that we have an urge to settle in our own minds. If I have always wondered how they make plastic bottles without a seam showing, then I am interested to visit the factory where such bottles are made. If someone shows me a new material that I have never seen before ('Potty putty', for instance) then I am interested to touch it, play with it and perhaps investigate its properties in a more ordered way. Each person's puzzles are slightly different, of course, and so what interests me will not necessarily interest another. It will depend on their previous experience and whether the links between this and new experiences raise questions to be answered.

It is not just the new and unexpected that can puzzle children. The familiar has puzzles in it and these are often the most intriguing to them. Who would have thought that four blocks of wood floating in a tank of water would keep children busily investigating literally for hours? This is what happened to the children quoted in Chapter 2, and not just those children; the same activity invariably creates similar intense interest. There was nothing apparently new except that the materials were selected to make them puzzle about floating in a way that they may not have done before and offered the chance of working on this puzzle. So in seeking to create interest we should have in mind links with previous experience when presenting either novel phenomena or familiar ones in a new light.

Relevance to things around

The difficulty here is the sheer complexity of real things and events. While experience of things around can develop children's ideas of the range and diversity of materials, living and non-living, the degree to which children can understand something as familiar as why the wind blows in a certain direction is limited. So, on the one hand, relevance means using the environment to develop, for example, the idea of the variety of different living things on the shore, at the zoo, in the park, in the wood, according to the location of the school. On the other hand, some ideas are not so directly related to real life, for reality is not simple.

If children tackled real questions raised about their environment the complexity could be so confusing that the underlying basic ideas may not be apparent. A way of avoiding this would be to simplify the real situation and take it apart to study its component ideas separately. But there are dangers in doing this if it means the link with the real phenomenon is lost (Box 4.1).

Box 4.1: Separating the investigation from the real situation

Suppose the question being investigated is why the wind blows in a certain direction at a certain speed. Activities which, to the teacher, are relevant might be to look at how air moves upwards over a source of heat, and then at how it moves towards places where the pressure is reduced and so on. The danger here is of creating activities which the children may not be able to relate to what is happening in the world around and which they cannot combine in puzzling over the real problem. Science activities then become things that the children do in science lessons rather than a means of increasing their understanding of things around them. Fine, if the study of a swinging pendulum really does have some function in helping children to understand things in the world around, but not if the link is theoretical and obvious only to the scientist.

There is no easy solution to this dilemma of how to reduce complexity while preserving relevance. In some cases the better course of action may be to accept the complexity of the problem and in others to break it down into simpler component problems.

It may help in deciding which is better in a particular case to recall two points: first, that the children's ideas at any time need not be the ones that remain with them for ever; second, that they will form some ideas about the things around them even if we, as educators, consider them too complex. If we want children eventually to understand that wind is moving air and how its movement is created, we can discuss and investigate the children's ideas about the wind so that they realise their ideas do not fit all the evidence and they will keep puzzling about it. Or we can ignore the children's ideas and attempt to create the 'right' ones about how air is made to move, through activities designed to illustrate relations, such as heat causing air to rise, and which 'work'.

Experience at the secondary level, where the latter approach has been the traditional one (and with children who might be more able to abstract the relevant ideas), suggests that it is not very successful. Many pupils do not see the point of the activities they do and are far from making a connection with the world around. Research into children's views of their work indicates that, as children get older, relevance is more important to them than enjoyment (Harland *et al.*, 2002).

In practice there is often a compromise to be reached between the two courses of action. Once the children are investigating a relevant problem it may well be possible to separate out one aspect for study, to test out an idea or hypothesis. This does no harm, as the connection with the real problem is already established. Box 4.2 provides an example.

> ### Box 4.2: Using the link to the real situation
>
> The children were working on the problem of how to keep an ice cube from melting (without putting it in the freezer). They wondered whether the same materials they used to surround the ice to stop the 'cold' getting out would or would not keep heat getting out of a warm object. They ended up using food cans filled with hot water and covered by jackets of various materials. This is a fairly common activity, suggested in books at both primary and secondary levels, and can mean little to those undertaking it if it comes 'out of the blue'. For the children who came to it via the ice-cube problem, however, it had a great deal of meaning and marked a considerable advance in their ideas about heat and changes of temperature.

OPPORTUNITIES FOR DEVELOPING SCIENTIFIC PROCESS SKILLS

The most important opportunities for children to develop process skills occur when children are using these skills. This means that children themselves must be raising questions for investigation, suggesting explanations (hypothesising), predicting, planning and conducting investigations, and so on. Obvious though this point may seem, it needs to be made and justified.

First, it means that children must be engaged in situations where these process skills are required and where they are able to use them. The interaction of content and process comes in here. As just discussed, the content has to be interesting and relevant so that children engage with it. It must also be capable of being understood at some level by the children, for only then will they be able to apply their skills to it. For instance, children who can plan a 'fair test' of how well balls bounce on different surfaces may not be able to plan a fair test of something much less familiar to them, such as how the concentration of a liquid affects its osmotic pressure.

Second, the justification. No one learns a skill, mental or physical, only by watching others, talking about what it means or just following step-by-step instructions; everyone needs to try things for themselves. This applies more forcefully to young children who tend to 'think through their fingers'. There is a need for them to experience what it is to make certain decisions as much as to do or observe certain things. Too often children are led through actions in a way that prevents them from manipulating things both mentally and physically. For example, take the activity presented on the work card in Box 4.3.

The activity in Box 4.3, for 9-year-olds, clearly aims to lead children to the idea that it is the temperature of the place where the ice cube is that decides how quickly it melts. Let us leave aside for the moment the inadequacy of this explanation to account for the children's everyday experience of where ice melts. The activity gives instructions that the children could readily have thought out for themselves if there had been some discussion of possible reasons for ice melting and how they might test these out. Had the children decided where to put the ice cubes and that they needed to use ice cubes that were all the same size to be 'fair', then they would have had some ownership of, and a great deal more interest in, the investigation. It would have tested *their* ideas.

Box 4.3: Work card instructions

What makes ice cubes melt?
To find out where ice cubes melt most quickly:

1 Take three ice cubes that are all the same size as each other.

2 Put one by the window inside the classroom.

3 Put one outside.

4 Put the third in a refrigerator.

5 See how long each one takes to melt.

6 Explain why they take different times to melt in the different places.

The activity has another flaw, however, by focusing on the temperature of the surroundings rather than other possible ideas about how ice might be made to melt or, more challengingly, prevented from melting. Children have ideas from their everyday experience about these things; they have seen ice not melting even in warm places (when surrounded by insulating material, in 'cool boxes' for example). It is much more useful for their understanding of everyday experience, as well as for the development of 'big' ideas about change of state of matter, if they test *their* ideas about what is needed to melt ice or prevent it melting.

In one classroom where this was discussed, one child thought that putting ice in a plastic bag would prevent it melting, while another considered that wrapping it in newspaper would be best. Designing the test to be fair was important to them in order to see which prediction was better. It also made them try to explain their findings and they did this in terms of how quickly heat needed to melt the ice could reach it through the material. In their discussion they went on to speculate that a freezer must take heat away from water when it turns it into ice. The whole activity was a genuine learning experience, in contrast with the limited experience of the activity on the work card.

The point here is not that the activity in Box 4.3 was presented on a card, since a teacher could have set up just the same activity by oral instruction, but that it was prescriptive and did not engage the children in developing their ideas or their investigative skills. In planning, therefore, teachers should screen activities by asking questions such as:

- What opportunities are there for the ideas that the children bring to this activity to be revealed?

- What opportunities are there for the children to decide what to do to test these and other ideas?

Unless there are good answers to these questions, the time spent on the activity may not be well spent.

Opportunities for the development of process skills occur when children are seeking answers to questions through active investigation of phenomena in their environment. But different questions require different types of investigation and vary in the degree to which all the process skills are involved.

Different types of investigation

The way in which an investigation is set up and carried out depends on the kind of question to be answered. Different questions require different approaches. For example, the notion of the 'fair test' has been widely used, but it is not helpful to think of all investigations as being of this kind. Fair testing is appropriate where it is possible to separate the things that can vary and to change one variable independently of the others so that the effect of changing it can be judged in an 'all things being equal' way. These kinds of investigation are important because they encourage children to develop understanding of the need to make fair comparisons.

However, not all scientific problems are of the kind where the variables can be separated. Often changing one condition inevitably affects another. For example, if you deprive a potted plant of water you inevitably also deprive it of the minerals dissolved in the water and may well raise its temperature since it will not be cooled by the evaporation of water from the soil. There are also questions that cannot be investigated experimentally because the variables are not susceptible to experimental control in classroom activities. Questions such as: 'Does the Moon's phase affect the weather?' 'Are the trees whose leaves open early in the spring the first ones to drop their leaves in the autumn?' In these cases there is no control over the independent variable (the Moon or the opening of leaves on the trees) and the investigation has to be devised so that the information is gathered from situations which arise naturally rather than those which are created experimentally.

Different types of investigation have been identified during the course of the AKSIS (Association for Science Education and King's College Investigations in Schools) project (Goldsworthy *et al.*, 2000). The project's work with teachers of children across the age range 8–14 produced the six types (with examples of questions provided by the project) given in Box 4.4.

Box 4.4: Types of investigation

1 Fair testing
  – What affects the rate at which sugar dissolves?
  – What makes a difference to the time it takes for a paper spinner to fall?
  – Which is the strongest paper bag?

2 Classifying and identifying
  – What is this chemical?
  – How can we group these invertebrates?

Box 4.4 Continued

3 Pattern-seeking

- Do dandelions in the shade have longer leaves than those in the light?
- Where do we find most snails?
- Do people with longer legs jump higher?

4 Exploring

- How does frog-spawn develop over time?
- What happens when different liquids are added together?

5 Investigating models

- How does cooling take place through insulating materials?
- Does the mass of a substance increase, or decrease, during combustion?

6 Making things or developing systems

- Can you find a way to design a pressure pad switch for a burglar alarm?
- How could you make a weighing machine out of elastic bands?

The sixth type in Box 4.4 is technological in nature and the fifth more appropriate in the secondary school than the primary. The first four are most relevant for 5- to 12-year-olds and illustrate how different types of investigation are needed to answer different questions. Within this age range, however, there are considerable differences in children's capacity for the various kinds of investigation.

We now look at some characteristics of children in the lower, middle and upper parts of this age range which have relevance for the kinds of activities that are likely to provide real opportunities for learning. These are, of course, broad generalisations and provide only a rough guide; there will always be individual children whose development varies from this pattern. For fine tuning, the progress of individual children needs to be taken into account, as we discuss in Part III.

ACTIVITIES AT DIFFERENT STAGES

We consider here the characteristics relevant to learning of children at three stages: early, middle and later stages within the 5–12 age range. These are characteristics, or 'ways of viewing things', which have been described by researchers and confirmed by teachers' experience. The implications for activities that provide genuine opportunities for learning are discussed for each stage.

Learning opportunities in the early years (5–7)

The relevant characteristics of children's ways of thinking at this stage are:

- The need to carry out actions to see their result rather than 'think through' actions. Whereas, for instance, older children could work out that if they increase their size of stride they will take fewer strides to cross the room, the 5- or 6-year-old will have to get up and do it, with small strides and then with longer ones.

- Looking at things from only one point of view, their own. They may not realise that a different point of view makes things look different unless they physically move to the other position. Even then they may not realise that it is a different view of the same thing.

- Focusing on one aspect of an object or situation at a time. For example, the youngest children may identify either Sun or water or air as needed to keep plants alive, but not a combination of these, as do older children (see Chapter 10, p. 137).

- The idea that the cause of a particular effect rests in the presence of some feature or object. So the drum makes a sound 'because it is very loud', the candle burns 'because someone lit it', the washing dries 'because of the Sun'. So-called explanations are often tautologous and merely express an observation in a different way: 'the car went because of the wheels'.

- Identifying only parts of a sequence of events. They are likely to remember the first and last stages in the sequence, but not the ones in between. For example, a 6-year-old, after watching sand run through a timer, was reported as being able to draw the timer and its contents at the beginning and end, but not in between. Given five drawings of the timer as the sand was running out he could not arrange them in sequence (Match and Mismatch, 1977).

These points have clear consequences for the sorts of activities the children will be able to learn from. The children's limitations are obvious. It will be no use expecting them to see patterns in events until they have begun to connect events in a sequence. The notion of a cause being related to an effect is still developing, so the idea of separating two or more variables to test the effect of each separately is still a long way off. Their limited experience will mean that their ideas tend to be based on a few very specific instances, selectively observed, having little explanatory power as far as new experience is concerned.

Equally clear are the indications for the kinds of experience that are appropriate at this age. Action and thinking are closely related to each other, reflecting their even closer identification at an earlier, pre-school, stage. Thus children in the early years need to be able to act on things, to explore, manipulate, describe, sort and group them. Firsthand experience and exploration of objects in their immediate environment is the chief aim of teaching science to infants. The content of the activities is therefore found in what is around the children and suitable topics start from everyday events. Common topics, encompassing activities across the curriculum involving science, include cooking, shopping, travelling, pets, holidays, Christmas and other religious festivals, toys, the park/shore/street, etc.

We shall deal with the teacher's role in planning and implementing activities in Chapter 11. Our concern here is with the overall nature of activities and their goals. Starting from the familiar the content should gradually introduce new experiences to the children (making a periscope with mirrors, for example). Though the main emphasis in terms of process skills used will be on observation, raising questions and discussion, there should be a gradually increasing demand in the use of these and development of other skills. When the children have had plenty of experience of acting on things and using the skills they already have with success, they will become able to replace some action by thought. They are then on the way to rational thinking and the development of higher levels of process skills.

Box 4.5: Appropriate activities for early years children

The children's activities should include plenty of:

- looking, handling, using other senses on material collected and displayed in the classroom

- watching, standing and staring at things in their natural state in the immediate neighbourhood

- collecting things and sorting them

- trying things out

- making things, particularly models, that in some way 'work'

- taking things apart and reconstructing them

- talking about what they have observed and sometimes recording it in pictures and models and in words when they can

- discussing their ideas and trying to think of explanations for things they have noticed.

The most relevant types of investigation are 'classifying and identifying' and 'exploring'.

Learning opportunities in the middle primary years (8–10)

On the assumption that children have had the kinds of experience indicated in the early years, they will reach the middle primary stage having already made some advances in their thinking. A major advance is the ability to use thought instead of action, to think things through, in certain circumstances. The ability to do this develops gradually from the age of 8 or 9. It is limited at first, restricted to those actions with which children are very familiar and which necessarily involve the real concrete objects they have been exploring. The main characteristics of children's thinking at these ages follow from the limited ability to carry out actions in thought. The advances over the previous thinking are that:

- they begin to see a simple process as a whole, relating the individual parts to each other so that a process of change can be grasped and events put in sequence

- they can think through a simple process in reverse, e.g. they can imagine a ball of plasticine that has been squashed out flat being rolled up into a ball again, which brings awareness of the conservation of some physical quantities during changes in which there appears to be an increase or decrease

- they may realise that two factors may need to be taken into account in deciding the result of an action, not just one (for instance, that heat *and* moving air help wet things to dry more quickly); there is some progress towards being able to envisage things from another's point of view, as long as this point of view is one that they have experienced for themselves at some time

- they can relate a physical cause to its effect and are less likely than before to say that, for instance, the leaves fall to the ground because the tree wants to get rid off them.

The limitations are that:

- these kinds of thinking are carried out only on the familiar; they are no substitute for action and firsthand experience when new things are encountered

- thought about whether changes have really happened or are only apparent depends on how strong the visual impression is; thus apparent changes in volume of the same amount of liquid in different containers (which can confuse adults, after all) are less easily challenged by thought alone than changes where reasoning can more easily contradict perception

- the quantities that can be manipulated in the mind are those that can be seen and easily represented mentally, such as length and area; mass, weight and temperature are less easily grasped

- as might be expected, the complexity of a problem or situation influences the ability of children to approach it using rational thinking; they may be able to investigate the effect of one variable but if there are two operating together it is unlikely that their effects can be separated.

The implications for children's activities are that these should be extended in two main ways. The range of content should be increased beyond the immediately familiar. The way in which the children interact with this new content might well be similar to their activity in the earlier phase, mainly finding out by observing, discussing, questioning and recording. Their experience of the variety of living things, for example, may be increased, through visits, books and films. Their knowledge of different materials may be extended by making and handling collections of plastics, rocks, various kinds of wood, metal, fabric and building materials. Their awareness of the way different things work may be expanded by investigating simple machines and mechanisms.

The second type of expansion in activities is a change in the way of finding out more about the already familiar things around them. The children can be helped to realise that some of the questions they ask can be answered by doing more than just observing things closely. They can see what happens when they do something to make a change and do this in such a way that they are sure that the effect they find is the effect of their action and not of something else. The idea of 'fairness' that is involved here is an important step towards investigation in a controlled manner. They also begin to make fair comparisons between things: to find out which toy car goes furthest, which paper towel soaks up water best, which paper dart is the best flyer, etc.

Box 4.6: Appropriate activities for middle primary children

Again, the provision of activities should be such that opportunity is given for children to use the skills and ideas they have already developed and to extend them. Giving them more of the kinds of activities they learned from as infants is not sufficient; there has to be more challenge in the form of:

- a wider range of objects and events to observe and to relate to their existing experience

- tasks that require close observation of detail and sequence of events

- investigations of the effect on some object or system of changing a variable systematically, keeping other things the same

- tasks that require a search for patterns or relations in observations

- problems that demand fair comparisons between objects or materials

- encouragement to try to explain how things work; expectation that they find answers to their own questions by systematic and controlled investigation rather than just 'do something and see what happens'.

'Fair testing' joins 'exploring' and 'classifying and identifying' as the appropriate types of investigation.

Learning opportunities in the later primary years (10–12)

The progression in children's thinking in these years is towards both more widely applicable ideas and more structured and rigorous thinking. The children become able to deal with more complex phenomena and can entertain the idea that more than one variable may be influencing a particular outcome. This has a significant impact on the activities that the children can tackle at this time. Investigations can be carried out in a more controlled manner than before. Children respond to the need for measurement in their investigations, the need for accuracy in observation and precision in the use of words and in recording.

So the strengths of the thinking of children at this stage are that:

- they can begin to handle problems which involve more than one variable

- they can use a wider range of logical relations and so mentally manipulate more things

- they show less tendency to jump to conclusions and a greater appreciation that ideas should be checked against evidence

- they can use measurement and recording as part of a more systematic and accurate approach to problems

- they can think through possible steps in an investigation and produce a plan of necessary actions.

However, there are still considerable limitations to their thinking:

- The ability to separate and manipulate variables is confined to simple cases where the variables are obvious and can be physically separated.

- The things that can be manipulated mentally are restricted to those that have a concrete reality for the child. The reality can be conveyed through books, pictures, television as well as firsthand perception of distant things such as the Sun, the Moon and stars.

As long as these limitations are kept in mind there is a great deal that children of these ages are capable of doing to help their growing understanding of the world around them. They will not generally be able to think in terms of abstractions and theories. Their focus will be on how things behave rather than on why they behave as they do. Their conclusions will be limited and they should not be encouraged to generalise prematurely. 'All the kinds of wood I have tried float' is a more suitable, and accurate, conclusion than 'all wood floats'.

Box 4.7: Appropriate activities for the later primary years

A wide range of activities is now available for these children and the main challenge in providing learning opportunities is to make sure that the full range of kinds of learning is covered. Investigations must extend beyond the 'fair-testing' type and should include all the types identified in Box 4.4. In more detail, the range of activities should include:

- problems that can be tackled by detailed observation carried out for a recognised purpose and involving the use of instruments to extend the senses, such as magnifiers and a microscope, where appropriate and available

- discussions in which children raise questions about phenomena or objects in their surroundings, suggest how the answers to various types of question could be found and so begin to realise that science can answer only certain types of question

- production of plans for investigations before they are carried out

- discussion of their learning, of how problems have been tackled in practice, how to tackle new ones, how observations and results of investigations might be interpreted, how to report work to others

- the creation and testing of possible explanations of phenomena

- extension of knowledge through use of books or other sources of information

- extended investigations that involve using all process skills and a range of different resources.

The emphasis that there was in the earlier stages on *doing* gradually gives way in the later years to a more equal emphasis on doing, planning, discussing and recording. Measurement plays an increasingly important part in investigations. As demands are made for more accurate observation and careful distinctions, measurement has to be refined and the use of new techniques and instruments introduced and practised. Repetition of measurements and regard to accuracy should become part of a more careful quantitative approach by the end of the primary years.

Progress in the skills and attitudes may well depend on children being allowed to try their skills in gradually more demanding and complex problems. So it is understood that the list of activities above indicates what the children should be doing for themselves, through their own thinking, rather than by following instructions for actions devised by others. It is through trying, and sometimes failing, that, at this point as before, development takes place. A child who tackles a problem requiring the separation of variables, but who fails to keep other variables constant while varying one, will get results that do not make much sense. In the discussion of what he or she did he or she may realise the mistake and take a step towards a new way of thinking about such problems. Without being allowed to make the mistake the child may well not have learned so much. However, while a certain amount of learning by mistakes is a good thing it is important that children do not keep repeating mistakes that could be avoided by review, reflection and planning.

SUMMARY

This chapter has discussed aspects of classroom activities that have to be taken into account if they are to be genuine *learning experiences*. In relation to the selection of content, the main points that have been made are that:

- it has to engage the children, be interesting and seem to them to be relevant and to provide a satisfying degree of understanding

- finding activities with these characteristics is not unproblematic since the interest created by real-life situations has to be set against the complexity of real life and the advantages of providing simple experiences that enable basic ideas to be developed.

In relation to the process skills needed for learning with understanding, the chapter has emphasised that:

- opportunities have to be provided for firsthand experience of using these process skills

- there are different types of investigations that provide opportunities for children to develop understanding through using process skills.

In order to identify appropriate activities for children at different stages, we have considered the strengths and limitations of children's thinking at the early stage (5–7 years), the middle stage (8–10 years) and the later stage (10–12 years).

FURTHER READING

De Boo, M. (ed.) (2000) *Science 3–6: Laying the Foundations in the Early Years.* Hatfield: Association for Science Education.

Chapter 5

Teachers' and children's questions

INTRODUCTION

This chapter is about questions that teachers can ask, and about ways in which they can respond to children's questions, to increase opportunities for learning. We generally think of questioning by teachers in the context of finding out what children have remembered or what their ideas are or what they already know as a starting point for a new topic. These are important uses of questions, but there are several other ways in which questions can help learning. We will consider here also questions for focusing attention on gathering relevant evidence, questions for promoting collaborative group activity and questions at the end of an activity for provoking reflection on what has been learned. So the first section of the chapter concerns questioning by teachers for different purposes. The second section discusses questions by children: why they are important, how to encourage questions and how to respond to them in ways that support curiosity and further learning.

TEACHERS' QUESTIONS

Observations in classrooms typically find that a high proportion of talk by teachers takes the form of questions. These include a number of questions such as:

> Are you listening to me, Thomas?
>
> Have you put the date on your work?
>
> Why have you not got your notebook ready?

These are points made for control or to give instructions that are put in the form of questions; answers are not really expected. Other questions have quite a different purpose, for example:

> How did you arrive at that idea?
>
> What do you think will happen if we . . .?
>
> How will you find out if your idea works?

These are intended to provoke thinking about the process of investigating and making sense of what they find. The concern here is with these kinds of questions, which are designed to help understanding.

Form, timing and content of questions

Three aspects of questions that contribute to their effectiveness in helping learning are form, timing and content. They are interconnected but all need to be considered in framing questions. When considering the content of questions, which relates to different purposes, some points about form and timing need to be kept in mind, so we look at these first.

Form

This refers to the ways in which a question is expressed. Two of the important ways in which teachers' questions can vary in form are: 'open' or 'closed' and 'subject-centred' or 'person-centred'.

Open questions invite an extended response, as opposed to closed ones, to which there is a short or one-word answer; they leave more options for answering. For example:

> Open: What you do notice when the water is put into the jar with the soil in it?
>
> Closed: Do you see the bubbles coming up from the soil when the water is added?

It is easy to see that the open version is more likely to provoke a range of responses, while the closed one focuses on one particular feature. Which is preferable depends on the purpose of the question. The open form is useful if the interest is in all the observations children might make, whilst the closed form has a place when the purpose is to focus on a significant feature that is not to be missed.

Person-centred questions are phrased to ask directly for the children's ideas, with no implication that one idea is more 'correct' than others. Subject-centred questions, by contrast, ask about the content in a way that suggests that there is a right answer. For example:

> Person-centred: What do you think the bubbles might be?
>
> Subject-centred: What's inside the bubbles?

It is much less easy to give a tentative or speculative answer to the second of these than to the first. If a teacher is interested in children's ideas then the person-centred and open form is the way to express the questions. Closed and subject-centred questions are less useful for this purpose, but may have value for other purposes, such as probing what children have found in their practical activities, when information is being sought from the children, or focusing attention to develop ideas or skills. However, in practice the balance of different forms of question is already too much on the closed side, judging from the research that shows that only a small proportion of teachers' questions are open.

Timing

The timing of asking questions, however, also has to be kept in mind. Jos Elstgeest (2001) drew attention to this aspect by pointing out that even a well-framed question can be ineffective if it comes at an inappropriate point in children's activity. Teachers often ask a question at the wrong time because of their eagerness to press ahead too quickly, he suggests. As an example, he cites a teacher asking children who were listening carefully to the range of sounds around them, 'how do you think these sounds are produced?' The question strangled the very enquiry that the teacher hoped to encourage. This question could have been the right one to ask at a much later stage, but what was needed at the time were questions to encourage more exploratory activity, such as 'how can you make a sound like . . . the rustling leaves . . . or a car horn . . . or a church bell?' There is also the matter of timing in allowing children time to answer, which we discuss later.

Content

Obvious though it may be, it is worth saying that questions have to be worded so that the answer requires the behaviour that is the purpose of asking the question. So if we want to know the ideas children have about something, we ask them for their ideas either directly, as in:

What idea do you have about what is going on here?

or, more usually, indirectly:

What do you think is the reason for . . .?

Why do you think this happens?

but not for an answer that can be given without expressing an idea, such as:

What do you see happening here?

What do you think will happen if . . .?

These questions ask for process skills to be used. Of course both kinds will very often be used in one activity, but they should not be confused. We should not ask questions without a reason and without interest in the answer. If the answer is to be useful then it has to give the kind of information required.

Table 5.1 suggests some questions for different purposes, using as a context some activities where children are investigating shadows.

Table 5.1 Teachers' questions for different purposes

Purpose	Comment	Examples
For finding out children's ideas	For this purpose the more open and person-centred the better. These examples might be used if children are making shadows of various opaque and translucent objects, using a torch beam directed onto a wall.	• What do you think makes the shadow? • Why do you think these things make darker shadows than these? • How do you explain the shape of the shadow?
For developing children's ideas	Questions for developing ideas are likely to follow up the ideas the children have expressed. They would be designed to encourage children to link different observations and see if their ideas work in all cases. They would also encourage children to consider different ideas, by 'scaffolding' the use of other ideas. They are likely, therefore, to be rather less open than questions for finding out ideas.	• How would your idea explain why the colour of the shadow is the same for all the objects? • What other idea could explain the shape of the shadow? • If the object cuts off the light from the wall, how would this explain why the shadow is bigger if the object is closer to the torch?
For finding out children's process skills	Questions here ask for process skills to be used in response. The answers may be actions as well as words, giving the teachers opportunity to see what skills the children already have. Again, the questions are open and phrased to encourage the children to answer without seeking a 'right' answer.	• What would you like to find out about shadows? (raising questions) • What do you think will happen if we move the object this way? (prediction) • What could you do to find out what makes a difference to the size of the shadow? (investigation) • What have you found out about whether there is a connection between the position of the torch and the size of the shadow? (interpretation)
For developing children's process skills	The questions suggested for finding out about use of process skills also provide opportunity for development. Similar questions, but more focused, are thus appropriate for this purpose. Some will involve some scaffolding, providing support for thinking along certain lines, such as about variables or relating what they found to their initial question.	• What do you find if you measure the size of the shadow before and after moving the torch? (observation) • If the shadow gets bigger when you move the torch this way, what do you think will happen if you move it the other way? (prediction)

▶

Table 5.1 Continued

Purpose	Comment	Examples
For developing children's process skills		• How will you make sure that it is the position of the torch and not something else that makes the difference? (investigation) • What have you found out about how you can change the size? (interpretation)
For encouraging collaboration and sharing ideas	These questions encourage children, when working in groups or pairs, to work in genuine co-operation, not as isolated individuals or in competition with each other. They require a group response that reflects combined thinking, which might be about how to explain some observations or how to plan an investigation, etc. In practice they would be posed within a structure where a group report is prepared after a set time for discussion.	• How many different ideas can you suggest in your group to explain what you found? • After each of you have explained your idea, is there one that seems best? • Of all the ideas, which ones could you test? • What do you agree is the way to find out which idea works? • What would each person in the group do in this investigation?
For encouraging reflection	These questions aim to ensure that children go over in their minds what they have done and become conscious of how their ideas have changed. Without this reflection their ideas are likely to slip back to their previous way of thinking. These questions require children to talk about what they have learned and how they have learned so that they learn about learning as well as about the things they have investigated.	• What have you found out that you did not know before? • Have you changed your mind about . . .? • What made you change your mind? • What is there that you don't understand about . . .? • Is there something that you still want to find out? • If you did this again, what would you change so that you could learn more?

Allowing time for answering

The questions suggested in Table 5.1 are designed to provoke thinking; they require a thoughtful response. It is no use asking a carefully worded question and not giving time for children to think and give an answer that really reflects their understanding. There is, perhaps, a place for the quick-fire test of memory, or quiz, but that's not what we are concerned with here. Pressure to respond quickly reduces the value of questioning for the purposes we have been discussing. So it is necessary to signal to children that a thoughtful, not a quick, response is required. This can be done in several ways:

- By increasing the 'wait' time. This is the time between asking a question and expecting an answer. Research (Budd Rowe, 1974) found that teachers waited on average less than one second after asking a question, if no response was offered, before rephrasing or giving a hint or asking an easier question. It is as if they could not endure silence. When the teachers were asked to increase the wait time to eight or nine seconds, the quality of children's responses increased dramatically.

- Avoiding rephrasing a question if it is not readily answered. Putting the question a different way inevitably makes it more closed and less useful. When this happens regularly children realise that, if they wait, the teacher will ask a simpler question, often indicating the answer expected.

- Some teachers find it best not to allow children to raise their hands to answer these kinds of thoughtful question. They expect everyone to be able to answer, given time to think. So the teacher allows thinking time and then calls on certain children to contribute. This signals that thought, not speed, is valued.

- Another strategy, suitable for some questions and situations, is to suggest that children discuss their answers with a partner or group for two or three minutes before the teacher asks for contributions (Black *et al.*, 2003).

CHILDREN'S QUESTIONS

The importance of children's questions

Given that many questions that children ask are difficult to answer and interrupt the teacher's flow, we might well ask, 'why encourage questioning?' Indeed many teachers unconsciously discourage questioning in the way that they respond to the ones that are asked. So it's important to bring together a few answers to this question:

- We all, adults and children alike, ask questions when we don't know or don't understand something; it enables others to know how to help us.

- Children's questions show the 'cutting edge' of their understanding and so enable teachers to identify the next steps.

- Their questions often indicate children's ideas and misconceptions that enable teachers to help them construct a more sound understanding.

- In science, particularly, children are able to answer some of their own questions by investigation and through this gain satisfaction and motivation for learning.

The last point is particularly important in relation to helping children to understand that science answers certain kinds of question but not others. Being able to identify different kinds of questions and how, or if, they can be answered is also necessary for continued learning.

Encouraging questioning

So how can questioning be encouraged? What can teachers do when their pupils don't seem to ask questions? We discuss this further in Chapter 9. At this point note that action which teachers can take to make explicit that questions are welcome includes:

- providing interesting and thought-provoking material to explore, time to handle, examine and wonder about them

- encouragement to ask questions and opportunities to discuss ways of finding the answers

- displays with a notice 'what would you like to know about these things?' and perhaps a box for questions

- after exploring objects, giving children time in small groups to think of questions before bringing them together in whole-class discussion.

Types of questions that children ask

When children do ask questions, however, how does the teacher respond to them? It helps to begin by identifying various kinds of questions that children commonly ask. It is also useful to remember that children sometimes ask questions for motives other than curiosity. Sometimes they are seeking attention and sometimes seeking approval or hints about what the teacher expects.

Children's questions can usually be categorised in terms of five common types: questions that are really expressions of wonder or interest; questions that ask for information that cannot be found by investigation; complex questions; philosophical questions; and investigable questions. Most of these types are represented in this list of questions asked by children while handling pieces of rock.

- What are rocks made of?
- Where do rocks come from?
- How do they get their colour?
- Why are they hard?
- How do rocks get their shape?
- Why do rocks have holes in them?
- What is the name of this rock?
- Why are rocks sometimes smooth and flat?
- Is gold a rock?
- Why is diamond the most valuable rock?
- Why are there rocks on the earth?

(Adapted from Osborne et al. 1982)

Questions expressing wonder or interest

Some of these questions are ways of expressing interest rather than asking for information. The researchers who reported this list collected questions from separate classes of children and found 'Why are they different colours?' sometimes and 'How do they get their colours?' in other cases. The exact words used are not carefully chosen and so we should not read too much into them. 'How do rocks get their shape?' could easily be expressed as 'Why are rocks different shapes?' Questions such as these are a way of saying 'Look at all the different shapes' or 'I've just realised that rocks are not all the same colour'. An appropriate response to such questions is therefore to share the children's interest and perhaps take it further: 'Let's see how many different shapes/colours there are.' A teacher will be able to judge from the children's reaction whether there is particular interest in the shapes and colours or whether these were passing comments expressed as questions.

Questioning for information

Children's questions always include some of a second kind, asking for straight information: 'Is gold a rock?' 'What is the name of this rock?' or perhaps one that well might have been in the list, 'Where were these rocks found?' The answers to these can be given directly, if the teacher knows, or the children can be referred to a source of the information. They are facts, some a matter of definition; they add to children's knowledge, which is important to their understanding of the world but is by no means all of it.

Complex questions

Questions of this type are the ones that often give teachers most difficulty because there are scientific answers but they are complex, not factual, ones. Many teachers may not know the answers and those who do will realise that the children's existing concepts are not sufficient to enable them to understand the answer. 'Why are they hard?', 'Why do they have holes in them?', 'Why are rocks sometimes smooth and flat?' are examples of these. They ask for an explanation, but in fact if the children were to be given the explanation they would probably not understand it, and might well be deterred from asking such questions in future. So teachers should not feel inadequate at not answering such questions from their own knowledge; in most cases it would be the worst thing to attempt.

Philosophical questions

These are questions that appear to be of the kind 'What is the meaning of life?' They appear to be this way because they begin with 'Why', which can often be interpreted as requiring an answer in terms of some fundamental cause. Alternatively it could require a more 'down to earth' answer. For instance, 'Why is diamond the most expensive rock?' could be answered in terms of its rarity and attractiveness (factual) or requiring an answer as to why it is found attractive. Similarly 'Why are there rocks on the Earth' could be interpreted as 'Who put them on the Earth?' (philosophical) or 'How did rocks form on the Earth?' (complex).

Investigable questions

These are the questions most readily answered by exploration or investigation by children. If the children had asked 'Which is the hardest?', this could have been directly investigated by the children. Until they have some practice, children don't often express their question in a form that is readily open to investigation. However, as suggested below, many questions can be turned into investigable ones.

Handling children's questions

In the discussion of these types of question we see that the meaning is not always clear. It is often necessary to get some clarification by discussing their questions with children. It is helpful to have these five categories in mind since, once the meaning is clear, there are particular ways of handling each type which takes away some anxiety about how to respond to the question. The word 'handling' is used as opposed to 'answering' since a direct answer is not always possible, nor desirable. This will be some relief to teachers, but it is not an invitation to ignore children's questions, but to see that they can be used to help children's learning in different ways. Since we are concerned with science, the aim of handling the more challenging questions is to turn them into ones that children can investigate. Although this will not give them complete answers, it will provide information of the kind the children can understand, leaving further questions to be pursued at a later stage.

Handling questions expressing wonder or interest

For example: Why is it raining today?

Children do not pause for an answer when they ask questions of this kind. They require only sharing of interest. There may be an opportunity to develop this interest into an investigable question, by asking, for instance: 'How many days this week has it rained?' 'How can we keep a record of the weather?'

Handling questions asking for information

For example: Does it rain more often in England or in Wales?

Here an answer is expected and if it requires only factual information, the teacher may supply it directly, or suggest a source where the child may find it, or undertake to find out at a later time. Factual information is useful in testing ideas and there is no reason to withhold it or to insist that children must find out everything for themselves. Learning to use sources of information helps children to expand the evidence on which their ideas are based.

Handling complex questions

For example: Why are rocks sometimes smooth and flat?

Some complex questions can be turned into investigable ones, the ones that are especially valued in science education. So, instead of presenting a problem to the teacher these questions actually present the opportunity to help children define investigable questions, ones that they can answer from investigations. For example, this question about rocks could be used to lead to an investigable question by asking:

- Where do you find rocks that are smooth and flat?

- What is the same about places where smooth flat rocks are found?

- What is different about places where rocks are not smooth and flat? Could these differences account for the shapes of the rocks?

- Could we make a rough rock into a smooth one?

The end point may be a series of questions such as: 'Does rubbing one rock against another make them smooth?' 'Does putting them in water make any difference?' 'Do you need a harder rock to rub against a softer one to make it smooth?' Once children embark on answering any of these questions, inevitably others will occur. And since the further questions are generated in the context of activity, it is likely that many of them will be framed by the children in terms of things they can do themselves. Thus once begun the process of defining questions is self-generating.

Handling philosophical questions

For example: Why are rocks hard?

As noted earlier, these questions often require some clarification in discussion with the children. They may be philosophical in nature, if, for example, the intention was 'Who made the rocks hard?' These kinds of questions cannot be answered and are best treated as expressions of interest. But if the question is one that can be answered but only with a complex response, it may be necessary to say that 'the reason is too complicated for me to explain, but we can find out more about it'. The question need not be dropped, however, for it would be possible to turn it into an investigable one, for example, by finding out if all rocks are really hard. How can you decide whether one rock is harder than another? Where are hard and soft rocks found? Soon this leads to several investigable questions from which the children may find the answers at the level which satisfies their curiosity for the moment.

Handling questions that are investigable by the children

For example: What happens if we plant the bean seeds the other way up?

Children's questions of this kind are not often expressed in a form that is already investigable, but can readily be made so. There may be a difficult decision for teachers as to whether to supply the simple answer or whether to devote the time needed for children to investigate the question for themselves, in which case they will learn more than the simple answer. The opportunity to find the answer from the things themselves by their own actions gives children valuable experience of scientific activity, not just the information about whether the bean will or will not grow upside down.

Children soon realise from experience what kinds of questions they can and cannot answer from investigation and what kinds require a different approach. Ten-year-old Stephen, looking at a giant African land snail, wanted to know why it grew bigger than other snails he had seen, how long it was and what it could eat. He set about answering the last two questions for himself and, when asked how he thought he could find out the answer to the first, said 'I suppose I'd have to read a lot of books'. Knowing how to answer different kinds of questions is more important to children than knowing the answers, but it comes only through experience of raising questions and discussing the process of answering them.

SUMMARY

In this chapter we have discussed questions in the classroom: questions by teachers and by children. In relation to teachers' questions the main points emphasised have been to match the form and content of questions to the purpose of asking them. We have considered questions for purposes of finding out and developing children's ideas, finding out and developing children's process skills, encouraging collaboration, and encouraging reflection. The importance of allowing time for children to think before answering has also been noted.

In relation to children's questions we have also considered both asking and answering – or rather handling. We have argued for the importance of encouraging children's questions and have suggested that handling them is helped by considering them in terms of five types: questions as expressions of interest, for information, those requiring complex answers, philosophical questions and investigable questions.

FURTHER READING

The following two chapters in the same book provide key ideas about questioning:

Elstgeest, J. (2001) The right question at the right time. In W. Harlen (ed.), *Primary Science: Taking the Plunge* (second edition). Portsmouth, NH: Heinemann.

Jelly, S. J. (2001) Helping children raise questions – and answering them. In W. Harlen (ed.), *Primary Science: Taking the Plunge* (second edition). Portsmouth, NH: Heinemann.

Chapter 6

Motivation for learning

INTRODUCTION

In this chapter we look at another aspect of the teacher's role in providing opportunities for learning, in this case establishing conditions that motivate learning and which hopefully set children on the path of continued learning throughout life. But since motivation is a complex concept, we first consider its different forms and components. We then discuss how different aspects of motivation for learning influence learners' behaviour and how the aspects that promote learning can be fostered. This is followed by reference to work on identifying and measuring the characteristics of lifelong learners, which adds evidence to arguments about the classroom practices that help children to enjoy learning, begin to reflect on it and become better learners. We end with some implications for classroom practice that apply to science and other areas of learning.

THE IMPORTANCE OF MOTIVATION FOR LEARNING

There can be no doubt that preparing children to continue learning beyond school and throughout their lives is a key aim of education today. We have already mentioned some reasons for this in discussing the goals of science education in Chapter 3. Many other reasons can be added, referring to the rapid change in employment and social structures that require us increasingly to be resourceful, reflective and resilient in dealing with complexity and change. It may seem that our primary school children are a long way from facing these challenges, but there is every reason to include preparation for continued learning in the goals of primary education. Habits of learning, or not learning, views of what it is to learn, beliefs about their capacity to learn – all are established early and are difficult to change if early experiences do not foster 'learning power'. Further, primary teachers are in a position to create the links that are known to be important in developing good learners, as we discuss later in the chapter (see Box 6. 2).

So, accepting that it is important, what is motivation for learning and how it is to be fostered? Unfortunately there are no simple answers to these questions. For a start there are different kinds of motivation.

DIFFERENT KINDS OF MOTIVATION

There is a sense in which we can say that all actions are motivated. This is because we always have some reason for doing something. It is difficult to think of an action for which there is no reason, even if it is just to fill an idle hour, or to experience the sense of achievement in meeting a challenge, or to avoid the consequences of taking no action. People read, play games, look after pets, climb mountains or take heroic risks for these reasons. We may undertake unpleasant and apparently unrewarding tasks because we know that by doing so we avoid the even more unpleasant consequences, for ourselves or for others, of inaction.

There are, however, different kinds of motivation. In tasks that we enjoy, the motivation may be in the enjoyment of the process or in the product; we might take a walk because we enjoy the experience or because the destination can only be reached on foot, or because of the knowledge that the exercise will be good for our health. In such cases the goals are clear and the achievement, or non-achievement, of them is made evident in a relatively short time. In the case of learning, however, while these points apply, the value of making an effort to learn is not always apparent to the learner.

Motivation for learning is all about willingness to make an effort, but this can be for different reasons. There are times when effort is made in undertaking a learning task because of the enjoyment in the process and the satisfaction in the knowledge or skills that result. There are also times when the effort is made because either there are penalties for not accomplishing a task according to expectations or there are rewards that have little connection with the learning task (such as a new bicycle for passing an examination). These describe two ways of motivating learning with important differences:

- *intrinsic motivation*, when the learning process is a source of satisfaction itself and the learner finds enjoyment in the skill or knowledge that results

- *extrinsic motivation*, when the potential gains from learning are not related to what is learned and learning is a means to an end, not an end in itself.

Intrinsic motivation is seen as the ideal, since it is more likely to lead to a desire to continue learning than is learning motivated extrinsically by rewards such as gold stars, certificates, prizes or gifts. Motivation to learn may disappear without such external incentives if they are the reason for making the effort.

However, it's not that all extrinsic sources of motivation are 'bad' and all those of intrinsic motivation are 'good'. There are undoubtedly some learning tasks that are not intrinsically enjoyable and some rewards, particularly praise, help to maintain engagement. What matters is *what* is praised. It should be the effort put in, not the achievement of a gold star or being quicker, smarter, etc. than others. Some intriguing research studies (Kohn, 1993), in which some children have received rewards and others have not been rewarded, have shown that the effect of rewards has been to reduce the quality of children's work. The rewarded children are less thoughtful, wanting to reach the answer through short-cuts, and less creative in their work than the non-rewarded children.

Aspects of motivation

Intrinsic and extrinsic are descriptions of overall forms of motivation, but to understand how to promote intrinsic motivation in individual learners it is necessary to consider some underlying factors. Rewards and punishments are only one way of influencing motivation and people vary in their response to them; the reward has to be valued if it is to promote the effort needed to achieve it. The effort required for learning is influenced by a number factors including interest, goal-orientation, locus of control, self-esteem, self-efficacy and self-regulation. A brief description of each of these is given in Box 6.1 and in the next section we look at their role in learning.

Box 6.1 Some components of motivation for learning

Interest: the pleasure from and engagement with learning, which may come from previous personal experience in the content or from the situation, such as novelty.

Goal-orientation: whether the goal is to learn in order to understand or to perform well in the short term (which may not reflect secure learning).

Locus of control: how much learners feel their success or failure is under their own control as opposed to it being controlled by others.

Self-esteem: how a learner values him or herself as a person and as a learner.

Self-efficacy: how capable a learner feels of succeeding in a learning task.

Self-regulation: the capacity of learners to evaluate their own work and to make choices about what to do next.

FOSTERING MOTIVATION FOR LEARNING

Interest

Interest is a response of a person to certain features of an event or task and has a powerful influence on learning. It can reside in the person, as an already existing interest, or it can be a feature of the context in which the event or task occurs. Individual interest is considered to be a relatively stable response to certain experiences, such as a liking for music, football or painting. Situational interest resides in certain aspects of the environment that attract attention and may or may not last.

Not surprisingly those with personal interest in particular activities persist in them for longer, learn from them and enjoy the activities more than those with less personal interest. Thus it is important in the school context to create personal interest in tasks children do not initially find interesting. Where personal interest is absent, situational interest is particularly important for involvement in learning. So features of learning activities – such as novelty, surprise, links to existing experience, providing a meaningful context – can help to engage students' interest. Some potentially boring activities can be made interesting through, for example, making them into games. It has also been found that changing the social environment can encourage interest; for instance, some students show more interest when working with others than when working alone. Interest is also more likely to be created when children see the point of learning something.

Goal-orientation

When someone undertakes a learning task, he or she may see the purpose or goal of doing it in different ways. Different kinds of goal determine the direction in which effort will be made and how a person organises and prioritises time spent on learning. The two main types of goal are described as 'learning goals' and 'performance goals' (Ames, 1992). Research shows that:

- those who see the point of a task in terms of *learning goals* apply effort in acquiring new skills, seek to understand what is involved, rather than just committing information to memory, persist in the face of difficulties and generally try to increase their competence

- those who are oriented towards *performance goals* seek the easiest way to meet requirements and achieve the goals, compare themselves with others and consider ability to be more important than effort.

Learning goals are clearly what are wanted rather than performance goals. So what can teachers do to ensure that learners identify goals in terms of learning? The type of goal embraced by children is open to change by teachers, particularly in the way that tasks are introduced. If told that a task is one in which their performance will be assessed, this orients them to see the goal in terms of performance. Whereas if a task is introduced as one that offers the opportunity of learning something new, the effect is to create a learning goal-orientation.

Researchers (for example, Elliott and Dweck, 1988; Dweck, 1999) have demonstrated how apparently small changes in wording of how tasks are presented produce marked changes in response. Schunk (1996) found that introducing a task as one where 'you'll be trying to learn how to solve these problems' had quite a different impact from 'you'll be trying to solve these problems'. When repeated frequently this slight difference in wording can have an important impact on learning motivation and learning outcomes.

Locus of control

When some learners succeed in a task they attribute their success to something within themselves, either their effort or their ability. Others may think of their performance as being the result of something outside, perhaps a good teacher or just good luck. The first of these is described as an internal locus of control and the second an external locus of control. Since these differences refer to failure as well as success they have implications for learning. Those with an internal locus will be prepared to try harder in the face of difficulties, as they see themselves as in control, while those with an external locus will have less motivation to make an effort because they don't think it will make any difference.

These differences matter particularly when children meet challenges, such as at points of transition from class to class and school to school. Unfamiliar surroundings, a new teacher who takes time to get to know the class, perhaps new subjects – all these present challenges which those who hold the view that with effort they can succeed will seek to overcome far more than those who fear they will fail. Those who have found that success comes easily, without much effort, are particularly vulnerable at such times of change as they do not believe that with effort they can overcome problems.

So it is important for teachers to help all children to recognise that effort is needed to succeed and that with effort they can succeed. Strategies that they can use to do this include:

- making clear that problems and failures are opportunities to find where more effort is needed and so are to be welcomed not hidden or avoided

- helping children to direct their effort more usefully and discuss how to overcome problems

- encouraging children to judge themselves by how much effort they apply rather than how bright they are

- encouraging the view that effort is needed from everyone, even geniuses, by talking about famous and successful people in history.

Self-esteem and self-efficacy

Self-esteem refers to how a person sees him or herself both as a person and as a learner. It shows in the confidence that the person feels in being able to learn. Those who are confident in their ability to learn will approach a learning task with an expectation of success and a determination to overcome problems. By contrast, those who have gained a view of themselves as less able to succeed are likely to be tentative in attempting new tasks and deterred by problems encountered.

Self-esteem is affected by how people perceive themselves to be judged by others and so how they come to judge themselves. Since some children will always be better at something than others if they are compared, such comparisons should be avoided. Rather, as a regular part of work, teachers should encourage children to focus on the progress each of them is making, not on whether they are better than or not as good as others.

Some evidence of the impact of the introduction of national tests for 7-year-olds in England is worth noting in this context. Davies and Brember (1998, 1999) conducted a study beginning two years before the introduction of national tests and extending for several years afterwards, using successive cohorts of Year 2 (7-year-old) and Year 6 (11-year-old) students. They administered measures of self-esteem and some standardised tests of reading and mathematics. For Year 2 children, self-esteem dropped with each year, with the greatest drop coinciding with the introduction of the tests. Of particular importance was the finding that it was the self-esteem of the lower achieving children that declined most.

Self-efficacy is closely related to self-esteem and to locus of control, but is more directed at specific tasks of subjects. It refers to how capable the learner feels of succeeding in a particular task or type of task. Psychologists regard it as a learned response, the learning taking place over time through the learner's various experiences of success and failure. As with self-esteem, assessment can be an important factor in this experience. So the more assessment is used to support learning, to encourage and direct effort, rather than to label children, the better.

Self-regulation

Learners who are able consciously to control their attention and actions so that they are able to solve problems or carry out tasks successfully are described as self-regulating. Those not able to regulate their own learning depend on others to tell them what to do and to judge how well they have done it. Self-regulated learners' consciousness of their learning enables them to talk about what and how they have learned and so become aware of successful learning strategies. This is also described as meta-cognition. Both self-regulation and meta-cognition enable effort to be directed to improve performance.

In order to develop self-regulation, children need opportunities to take responsibility for what they are doing. This can come from having a choice in what to do or how to carry it out. Even a choice from a limited range of options provided by the teachers leads to commitment to the task, whereas being told what to do does not.

MOTIVATION FOR LIFELONG LEARNING

In order to encourage motivation for learning, we have to know where children are in this aspect of their development and to have some means of identifying whether steps taken have had an effect. Recognition that very little attention had been given to measuring orientation to learning (compared with that given to measuring educational achievement) led to the development of the Effective Lifelong Learning Inventory (ELLI) (Deakin Crick *et al.*, 2002).

The inventory comprises a number of statements to which learners respond by indicating their agreement or disagreement on a five-point scale. It provides a profile of a learner's characteristics relating to willingness and enjoyment of learning. It can be used with learners from the age of about eight onwards. The statements have been found to relate to seven dimensions, each of which is an aspect of effective learning, summarised in Box 6.2.

Box 6.2: The dimensions of learning power from the ELLI profile

Growth orientation – referring to the belief that learning is itself 'learnable'. This dimension is similar to the distinction between those who regard their ability as fixed or changeable through effort.

Critical curiosity – the desire to find things out, to come to their own conclusions, contrasting with being passive and accepting what they are told.

Meaning-making – making links between what they are learning and what they already know. This contrasts with 'fragmentation' and learning piecemeal.

Dependence and fragility – relating to the response to challenge and the risk of failure. Those at one end of this dimension are dependent on others for their learning and sense of self-esteem, and show little perseverance. Those at the other end like a challenge and are resilient and robust, and can recover from frustration.

Creativity – referring to the liking for 'playing with ideas', and not always knowing where trains of thought are leading. In contrast are those who tend to be rule-bound and unimaginative.

Interdependence – relating to the balance between being able to work alone and being collaborative and sociable. At one end are those who like to learn with and from others but also recognise that some learning requires individual study. The contrast is with those who either are too dependent on others or unwilling to engage with others.

Strategic awareness – refers to those who have awareness of themselves as learners, are able to talk about learning, evaluate their learning and take responsibility for it. At the other end of the dimension are those who are described as 'robotic' and self-conscious rather than self-aware.

(Based on Deakin Crick *et al.*, 2002, pp. 7–9)

Intervention for lifelong learning

When the inventory was given to a large sample of children of all ages from 8 to 19 there was 'an alarming drop in the mean of all of the effective learning dimensions' from the younger to the older children (Deakin Crick *et al.*, 2002, p. 14). The greatest drop was in creativity, imagination and playfulness, accompanied by an increase in dependence and fragility. This raised the crucial question of how to reverse this trend so that children would become more, not less, oriented to lifelong learning as they progress through school. To answer this question the researchers worked with teachers as they decided how to take action in response to the inventory results from their children. An example is given in Box 6.3.

Box 6.3: Taking action to reduce dependence and fragility and improve awareness of learning

In a class of 8- to 9-year-olds, the inventory results indicated a lack of resilience when faced with uncertainty and a need to develop skills of 'strategic reflection'. The teacher focused her intervention on helping the children to take ownership of the learning and become more reflective. Her own observation was that many children were unsure of how to organise their time independently and had difficulty in using freedom. They were unsystematic unless given adult support to point them in the right direction or were happy to rely on taught procedures without which they were unsure how to proceed. Some would regularly copy others' work in order to guarantee accuracy and nothing was being brought in from home, 'which suggested that students were not making many links between learning at home and learning at school' (Deakin Crick *et al.*, 2002, p. 23).

The teacher's attempt to make learning more 'connected' involved breaking down the sharp divisions between one subject and another and between home and school. Time spent on each subject was made more flexible and opportunities were given for reflecting on the links between subjects. She also set up more 'real-life' situations, encouraged children to bring things from home, and set aside time to talk about them and link them with school work. Time was provided for 'dialogue about learning. This meant verbalising strategies, sharing and learning from mistakes, supporting each other and affirming resilience' (Deakin Crick *et al.*, 2002, p. 24). The teacher would also model meaningful strategies for problem-solving, by 'thinking aloud' about *what do I already know? what am I learning now? where do I go from here?*

As a result the teacher noted these changes in the children:

- The amount of copying decreased noticeably when children were encouraged to point out and share their errors in a positive, relaxed atmosphere.

- Children gradually took over from the teacher ways of modelling learning for each other.

- They were more pro-active in bringing material from home or setting up science experiments at home.

- They began to act more collectively, being prepared to work with different partners and supporting each other.

- There was more collaborative learning and increased perseverance.

Although only a small-scale action research project, the results were a clear demonstration of what can be done by a teacher and school committed to improving motivation for learning. Indeed, the results of re-administering the inventory after five months showed a significant increase in all the targeted dimensions.

IMPLICATIONS

The work of the ELLI project began from the dimensions of motivation discussed earlier and has added to our understanding of how to help children to enjoy and want to continue learning. Putting together some insights from both these sources leads to proposing the conditions set out in Table 6.1 as ones that teachers, working with their pupils, should strive to bring about and others that they should avoid. They are readily applicable to teaching primary science.

Table 6.1 Implications for planning, presenting and discussing classroom activities

More of this:	Less of this:
● Activities linked to real life and across subjects	● Firm demarcation of subjects
● Activities introduced as opportunities to learn	● Activities introduced without reference to learning
● Valuing effort and engagement in learning	● Valuing products; praising outcomes achieved without effort
● Time spent on reflection on how learning has been achieved	● Discussion only of what has been learned
● Self-assessment of what they have learned	● Dependence on others' judgements of what they have learned
● Allowing for mistakes and learning from them	● Frowning on mistakes so that children conceal them
● Collaborative learning with and from each other	● Comparison and competition with others
● Choice in activities or how to tackle them	● Firm directions for activities and how to tackle them
● Discussing children's own ideas and meaning derived from activities	● Discussing whether children have reached the 'right' answers

SUMMARY

This chapter has considered the importance of motivation for learning and the nature and components of this complex concept. In particular we have discussed how learning is affected by learners' interest, goal-orientation, locus of control, self-esteem, self-efficacy and self-regulation and how these aspects of motivation can be fostered. We have also looked at the outcome of work developed from these aspects of motivation, which has led to the identification of the characteristics of lifelong learners. Using the inventory of these characteristics enables teachers to focus on what is needed to help their pupils to become more conscious and reflective learners.

We have seen that among the actions found to promote motivation for learning are several concerned with children's understanding of the goals of their activities, with helping them make choices and take responsibility for them and with establishing practices of self-assessment. While in this chapter these have been discussed in general terms, applicable to any subject area, in Part III we consider them in more detail and specifically in the context of teaching science to 5- to 12-year-olds.

FURTHER READING

A brief account of the research that links summative testing to impact on learners' motivation is given in:

ARG (2002b) *Testing, Motivation and Learning.* Available from the Institute of Education, University of London and as a pdf file from the Assessment Reform Group website: www.assessment-reform-group.org

A readable account of a range of research studies on how views of whether personal qualities can be changed or are fixed is given in:

Dweck, C. S. (1999) *Self-Theories: Their Role in Motivation, Personality and Development.* Philadelphia, PA: Psychology Press.

Part III

USING ASSESSMENT FOR LEARNING

Chapter 7

Helping learning: a framework for decisions

INTRODUCTION

In Part I of this book, we discussed learning in terms of the processes taking place. Chapter 2 provided a model of the steps in thinking that can lead to learning. This model gives some clues in very general terms as to how to facilitate learning by, for example, helping children to develop process skills or helping to forge links between new and previous experience. But it doesn't answer questions about how a teacher can decide what kind of help is needed, when and how best to provide it. These are the questions taken up in Part III, which is concerned with the role of teachers and children in helping learning during regular work. The overarching framework for this part of the book is the notion of formative assessment, beginning in this chapter with what it is, and dealing with how to do it in Chapters 8–12.

This chapter introduces formative assessment as a framework for making classroom decisions. It is a framework in which both teacher and children look at the skills and ideas being developed and use this information to help further learning. We begin by considering what teachers need to do to support learning that leads to understanding. The processes described are then presented in the framework, which is identified as one of using assessment to help learning, or formative assessment. The last part of the chapter justifies using the term 'assessment' in this context, where it is used as part of teaching and learning, rather than in the more familiar context of reporting on learning. We end with reference to evidence that this approach can raise children's achievement.

THE TEACHER'S ROLE IN LEARNING WITH UNDERSTANDING

A key feature of learning with understanding, discussed in Chapters 1 and 2, is that children are active in constructing knowledge through their mental and physical activity, not passive receivers of knowledge from others. This involves a learner linking new experiences to past ones, testing existing ideas and reconstructing them according to what he or she finds. Although the learner is seen as in control of the learning, nevertheless the teacher's role is to ensure that suitable new experiences are provided. What we mean by suitable experiences are such as have been described in Chapter 1 and developed in Chapter 4. They are activities that are within the reach of children's existing ideas and skills but provide enough challenge to extend them so that the children make progress towards the development of the ideas and skills that are the goals of learning.

How will the teacher choose activities of appropriate content and difficulty? Could it be by following a programme of activities that have been worked out by others and usually shown to 'work' for most children? All children are not the same and following a pre-packaged course slavishly will inevitably mean that for some the experiences may be too distant to be understood or too familiar to challenge current ideas. Most teachers will use ideas from programmes or from other teachers, but will adapt them to suit the current understanding and skills of their children. To do this they need to know where the children are in the progress, that is, what are their existing ideas and skills in relation to the goals of learning.

It takes much more than knowing what point the children have reached, however, to ensure that they move forward. So the framework that we present in this chapter – and which is the rationale for the subsequent chapters in this part of the book – begins with identifying where children are in relation to the goals of a particular lesson or section of work and ends with action that provides experiences to help progress towards the goals. The decisions in between involve both the teacher and the children.

INTRODUCING THE FRAMEWORK

Where are the children in relation to the goals?

The first step the teacher needs to take is to gather information about where children are in relation to the goals. Of course this means being clear about just what these goals are. While obvious in theory, in practice this is not always so evident, since teachers are often so concerned about what children will *do* and with making preparations for this that they pay less attention to what they intend the children to learn (see Chapter 12 for more on this).

The information about where the children are may come from previous work, or exploratory activities on the topic, or discussion at the start of a lesson. In Chapters 8 and 10 we discuss a range of methods for collecting relevant evidence. For the present purposes, let's suppose that A in Figure 7.1 represents some activities related to the goals. These activities provide opportunities for the teacher to gather some evidence about where the children are in relation to the development of skills and ideas that the work is intended to promote. The gathering of evidence is followed immediately by interpreting it in terms of the goals. These steps may seem to occur together, but it is quite important to separate them because we have to be sure of the evidence before drawing conclusions about it. It is often tempting to jump to the conclusion that children have grasped an idea when, in fact, careful listening to the words they use, or attention to the detail of their drawings, shows that a misconception exists.

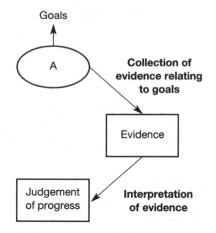

Figure 7.1 Building the framework: collecting and interpreting evidence in relation to the goals of learning

The 'judgement' of progress may seem a rather formal way of describing the interpretation, but it is not a formal judgement that is used to label children. Rather it is a necessary point from which to decide what are the next steps that the children need to take in order to make progress towards the intended goals. It involves comparing the evidence with what is expected at various points of progression towards the goals. Ways of doing this are discussed in Chapters 9 and 11.

The next step might be to address a misconception, or to extend current ideas by applying them more widely. Or it might be to develop a process skill, such as planning an investigation or drawing conclusions from evidence. Having decided the next step in learning for the children, the teacher's next step is to decide how to help them take this. Again, these two – deciding the next steps and deciding how to take them – may often coalesce, particularly if the means to help the next step is readily available (as in scaffolding the development of a process skill). However, it is useful to understand them as separate steps. The decision about how to help the children take the next step leads to Activity B, as in Figure 7.2.

What Figure 7.2 shows is the beginning of a cycle of collecting and using evidence to help learning. There are two more features to add. One is to represent this as a continuing cycle, and one that moves towards the goals. So Activity B is the context for a further collection of evidence about progress, which leads to further decisions and further steps to reach Activity C, and so on. Of course this is a theoretical framework of the process and in reality:

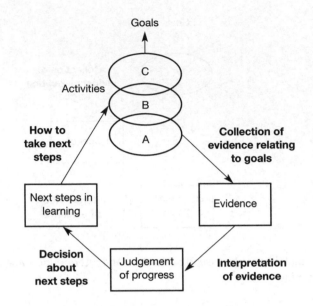

Figure 7.2 Building the framework: using evidence to help learning

- Activities B and C may not necessarily follow immediately; they may take place some time later, when the topic is revisited or when similar types of investigation are encountered some time in the future.

- Although described as a series of steps, in practice the processes within a cycle often run together and are more of a whole. See the example in Box 7.1.

- Because information is gathered frequently as part of teaching it is not necessary to try to cover all aspects at any one time. In one 'cycle' the focus might be on children's reports of their work; in another, their ability to raise questions and to plan ways of answering them, or on linking up experiences to develop ideas relevant to the content of the activities. One group might be a focus for observation for a particular lesson, other groups being the focus at other times.

The second feature to add is the role of the children in the process. A key theme throughout this book is the development in children of awareness of their learning and their central role in it. So they need to know what they are aiming for, the purpose of their activities. They can then take a part in: providing the information about what they understand and can do; seeing where they are in relation to the goals of their activities; identifying their next steps; and deciding what they have to do to take them. So in Figure 7.3 the children are at the centre of the process. The double-headed arrows indicate that they are not just the object of decisions by the teacher but help in the process of their learning.

Some of the features of this framework are illustrated in the example in Box 7.1

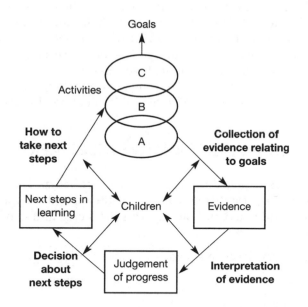

Figure 7.3 The complete framework

Box 7.1: The framework in action

Julie's group (of 8-year-olds) had been collecting seeds of many different kinds. Julie added a sticky bud with the scales removed to the collection. She told the teacher that the things inside were seeds. When the teacher asked her what she thought was surrounding the little 'seeds' she said they were leaves that would grow into horse-chestnut leaves. She was convinced, however, that the things inside were the seeds of the tree. The teacher recalled the 'conkers' that they had collected some months earlier and how some of them had sprouted. But although Julie seemed to appreciate that conkers would grow into trees, they did not seem to fall into her idea of seeds. The teacher asked Julie how she would be able to collect the 'seeds' that she had identified. She said they would show when the sticky buds opened. So more twigs were gathered and Julie and other children observed the buds regularly as they opened. Later they continued observation of the opening of buds on the tree from which the twigs had been taken and noted that the 'seeds' turned into flowers and the new small conkers began to form. These various activities extended Julie's idea of the life cycle of plants as well as her notion of the variety of forms that seeds can take. At the same time all the children learned that trees had flowers, which they had not recognised before.

In the example, evidence was gathered by observing, listening and questioning during the seed collection (Activity A). To interpret the evidence, the teacher clarified whether Julie knew that the twig and conker were related to the same type of tree. It appeared that the problem was not this, but Julie's narrow conception of seeds as small and spherical. The next step was to help Julie to recognise a wider range of things that were seeds. The teacher first tried to make a link with earlier experience, by reminding Julie of the sprouting conkers. However, although the link to earlier experience was made, Julie persisted with her idea. The teacher then helped Julie to test her idea in a way that she found convincing, leading to further activities (Activities B and C) that advanced her understanding of seeds and life cycles.

THE FRAMEWORK AS FORMATIVE ASSESSMENT

The framework depicted in Figure 7.3 is described as 'formative assessment'. Why 'assessment'? Because there is evidence gathered and interpreted systematically and the result is used in a particular way. This fits the definition of assessment as an activity that involves:

- collecting evidence in a planned and systematic way
- interpreting the evidence to produce a judgement
- communicating and using the judgement.

Why 'formative'? Because the assessment is used to help, or to 'form', learning. Indeed the same process is also called 'assessment for learning'. This makes clear the purpose and the distinction from 'summative assessment' or 'assessment of learning', which depicts assessment used to summarise and report achievement at a certain time. Both purposes of assessment are important in education, but since formative assessment has a key role in learning with understanding, as we pointed out at the start of this chapter, in this book we give most attention to it.

Before looking in more detail at the essential distinction between formative and summative assessment it is useful to consider the different ways in which the above three components of an assessment can be carried out.

Collecting evidence

The range of methods of collecting evidence extends from observation by the teacher during the usual interactions between teacher and children, to marking written tests or examination papers. Observation, which includes watching and listening, can be structured so that children are observed responding to particular tasks or questions. Some evidence will be in the form of a permanent record that can be studied after the event in which it was produced, but if there is no permanent record then it is necessary to gather the information by observation at the time. However, even where there are drawings, writing or other products to be assessed, information about when and how these were produced is important in the assessment. This applies particularly to young children, whose products may need to be discussed at the time and annotated by the teacher if they are to convey meaning later.

Making a judgement

In making a judgement the evidence is compared with some standard or criterion. In educational assessment the three ways of doing this are:

- comparing with the standard of others of the same age and/or experience (norm-referenced)

- comparing with criteria for certain levels of performance (criterion-referenced)

- comparing with the individual's previous performance (child-referenced or ipsative).

In the first of these the outcome of a child's assessment will depend on how other children perform as well as on his or her own performance. In formal standardised tests the 'norm' is a certain mark derived from testing a representative sample of children and finding the average. In a less formal way a teacher may apply standards derived from experience of other pupils in deciding what is the expected level of performance.

When criterion-referencing is used, the assessment is in terms of how the child's performance matches criteria describing certain kinds of performance. This judgement does not depend on how other pupils perform, although the choice of criteria is likely to be influenced by what it is reasonable to expect of pupils of comparable age and experience.

Ipsative or child-referenced assessment judges a child's progress against what he or she has done previously and results in the teacher giving different feedback to different children, thus appearing to use different standards. This is appropriate when assessment serves a formative purpose but not for other purposes.

Communicating and using the judgement

There are several points to be considered here: feedback to the child; use by the teacher; and ways of communicating to others. The form of feedback to children about their work has an important impact on their self-esteem and the effort they put into their work. Research has shown that the use of judgemental comments, marks or grades is best avoided (see Chapter 12). The feedback should help the children take the next steps, which may be to move on to new activities or to improve the quality of what they have done.

Evidence used by teachers to help their classroom decisions about the children's next steps will exist as informal records of the evidence of progress in the form of notes or collections of children's written work. These records can be summarised at points in the year when formal summative assessment judgements have to be reported. For communicating with others it is important that information is conveyed in the amount of detail that the recipient can use and that the basis of judgements in terms of levels, grades or standards is made clear (see Chapter 13).

FORMATIVE AND SUMMATIVE ASSESSMENT COMPARED

Formative assessment

Formative assessment (assessment for learning) is essentially carried out by teachers as part of teaching, as described in the framework. This means that it is ongoing and a regular part of the teacher's role. However, the fact of being carried out regularly does not necessarily mean that assessment serves a formative purpose. Regular tests are not necessarily formative in function; it depends on how the results are used and who uses them. The use is the chief difference between assessment for formative and summative purposes. So it seems best to describe the types of assessment in terms of function rather than frequency of occurrence.

Formative assessment includes diagnostic assessment. The term 'formative' is preferred, however, since 'diagnostic' carries the connotation of concern with difficulties and errors, whereas formative assessment is relevant at all times. It helps the teacher to decide the appropriate next steps in learning both for those who succeeded in the earlier steps and for those who encountered difficulty.

Characteristics of formative assessment

Together these points lead us to characterise formative assessment as in Box 7.2.

Box 7.2: Characteristics of formative assessment

Formative assessment:

- *is an integral part of teaching for understanding*

When learning is understood as the construction of understanding by learners, formative assessment is not optional; it cannot be taken away without changing the whole nature of the teaching and learning.

- *is related to progression in learning*

The evidence sought is about 'where the children have reached' rather than 'have they achieved this or that knowledge or skill'. This has implications for the criteria used in assessment, which are best expressed in terms of a progression.

- *leads to action that supports further learning*

Unless the assessment is actually used in helping children to take the next steps in their learning, it is not formative.

● *can be used in all learning contexts*

All actions and interactions of children in educational contexts provide information about what they can do and about what they understand. Thus any situation in which children learn is one in which formative assessment can help their learning.

● *provides information about all learning outcomes*

This follows from the last point and it also means that information is not restricted to what can be measured or tested, since gathering relevant evidence (validity) is more important than accuracy (reliability).

● *involves children in assessing their performance and deciding their next steps*

The extent of this involvement will vary with the children's age and experience of self-assessment, but some form of reflection on their work can begin from the first years of formal education.

It may seem questionable to be saying that it is less important that the assessment is reliable than that it is based on valid evidence. After all, reliability seems to be the hallmark of good assessment and it is argued that in any case assessment that is unreliable cannot be valid (see Chapter 13). But there are two reasons why the reliability in formative assessment can be less stringent than for assessment for other purposes. First, the information is both gathered and used by the teacher, so he or she knows the basis on which it was produced. Second, the cyclical nature of the process means that repeated observations are made that will soon reveal any errors in judgement that may have been made and at the same time provide the opportunity to change the decisions that resulted.

Summative assessment

Assessment that serves a summative purpose indicates individual children's achievement at a certain time. It summarises learning at that time and is used to give this information to others, mainly parents, other teachers, and the children at the primary level. At later points in schooling, information is needed by employers and post-secondary institutions. Summative assessment may take place frequently, as in a regular weekly test (more usual in mathematics or language learning than in science), or more commonly at the end of each term or year.

As just indicated, an important difference between summative and formative assessment lies not so much in the way of gathering evidence as in the use made of it. The process is not cyclical and the information does not have an immediate impact on future learning experiences, although it may do so in the longer term. Further, since the end point is to be a summary, in a readily communicable form, the degree of detail about each aspect of achievement is necessarily limited. These and other differences are evident from comparing Figure 7.3 with Figure 7.4.

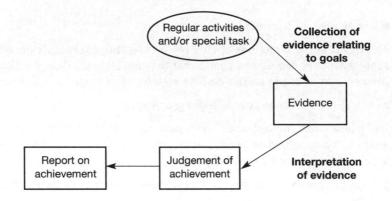

Figure 7.4 Representation of summative assessment

The differences arise from the purposes of these two types of assessment. Formative assessment is used to find out where children are in order to decide their next steps. There is no need to give a label to 'where they are' by using levels or grades. Summative assessment, however, has to be a summary and a convenient way of providing this is to use a level or grade, which represents what has been achieved. The levels or grades must mean the same for all children. Those receiving reports summarising achievement need to be assured that the information is reliable so that, if necessary, children can be fairly compared with each other. This means that the basis for making the judgement of evidence has to be the same, strictly in terms of criteria related to the goals. By contrast, formative assessment can take into account individual circumstances and effort and so is described as ipsative, or child-referenced (see p. 89).

The need for reliable judgement in summative assessment reduces the involvement of children in the process. Although some involvement is beneficial, for the same reasons as given in the case of formative assessment, ultimately the judgement must be reliable and it is the teacher's responsibility to ensure fairness in judgements for all the children. This is particularly important if the assessment is to be used by other teachers or schools for selection or grouping by achievement.

These points lead us to characterise summative assessment as in Box 7.3.

Uses of summative assessment

Other purposes of assessment and some of the uses to which summative assessment information is put, such as for school evaluation, are discussed in Chapter 13. At this point our attention is on formative assessment and so it is appropriate to end this chapter with reference to evidence of the positive effect of formative assessment on learning and hence a strong reason for improving its implementation.

Box 7.3: Characteristics of summative assessment

Summative assessment:

- *takes place at certain intervals when achievement is to be reported*

There should be a clear reason for a summative assessment, which may be for internal school purposes, such as monitoring progress of individual children, or reporting to parents, or for external purposes for certification or selection.

- *relates to progression in learning judged against publicy available criteria*

The information needs to be expressed in a form that the users of the information can understand. So 'levels' and 'grades', which represent developmental criteria, should be explained.

- *gives results for different children that are based on the same criteria and so can be compared and combined if required*

There needs to be some rigour (quality assurance) in the assessment so that the same mark or grade means the same point in progression and is not biased by taking non-relevant information into account.

- *requires methods that are as reliable as possible without endangering validity*

Too much emphasis on accuracy may limit the range of information provided, thus a compromise is necessary and users of the information should understand that no assessment is completely 'accurate'.

- *involves some quality assurance procedures*

Particularly where important decisions are attached to the assessment there should be checks on procedures and moderation of coursework and teachers' judgements.

THE CASE FOR USING ASSESSMENT FORMATIVELY

An extensive review of research on classroom assessment published in 1998 by Black and Wiliam (1998a, 1998b) concluded that 'formative assessment is an essential feature of classroom work and the development of it can raise standards' (Black and Wiliam 1998b, p. 19). This emerged from studies where various steps had been taken to strengthen formative assessment, and which had explored the conditions under which the greatest effects were found. The effects on achievement were indeed large, much greater than changes in other learning conditions, including class size, have been found to produce. The research was clear, too, about the changes to current practice in classroom assessment that need to be made if the potential benefits are to be gained. Black and Wiliam discuss these desired changes under three headings: the self-esteem of children; self-assessment by the children; and the evolution of effective teaching.

Protecting children's self-esteem

The way in which teachers feed back their judgements to children was found to be a key factor in relation to children's self-esteem. Where judgements are in terms of grades or ranking within the class, then children 'look for the ways to obtain the best marks rather than at the needs of their learning which these marks ought to reflect' (Black and Wiliam, 1998b, p. 9). Children focus on seeking clues to the 'right' answer and the easiest way to get the best marks. Meanwhile those who get low marks or ranking feel discouraged and may take these judgements as indicating a limit to their ability and give up trying to improve. To avoid these negative effects, feedback should be given about how the work could be improved, with no judgemental grade, or mark. Even giving praise is less effective than a constructive comment about the work, because when praise is given, children do not attend to any other comments that are made.

Self-assessment

The research evidence gave strong support for children being involved in self-assessment. This should involve children knowing what the desired goals of particular activities are, of being able to recognise where they are in relation to these goals and knowing how to take further steps towards achieving them. There is not a great deal of good practice in these matters but Black and Wiliam (1998b, p. 10) claim that: 'When pupils do acquire such an overview, they then become more committed and more effective as learners: their own assessments become an object of discussion with their teachers and with one another, and this promotes even further that reflection on one's own ideas that is essential to good learning.'

Effective practice

Some aspects of practice that were identified as effective in improving formative assessment were: including formative assessment in planning; teachers' questioning; and dialogue between children and teacher that encourages thoughtful responses, explores understanding and gives all children the chance to express their ideas. Key factors in improving learning through formative assessment are given in Box 7.4.

> **Box 7.4: Key factors in improving learning through formative assessment**
>
> Assessment used to help learning requires:
>
> - the provision of effective feedback to pupils
>
> - the active involvement of pupils in their own learning
>
> - adjusting teaching to take account of the results of assessment
>
> - a recognition of the profound influence assessment has on the motivation and self-esteem of pupils, both of which are crucial influences on learning
>
> - pupils to be able to assess themselves and understand how to improve.
>
> (ARG, 1999, pp. 4–5)

SUMMARY

This chapter has presented a framework for looking at classroom actions that support learning with understanding. These actions are designed to ensure that information about the existing skills and understanding of children is used in decisions about how to help further learning. We have argued that they are essential features of learning viewed as construction of understanding by learners. The description of the framework as formative assessment has been justified by reference to some of the features and purposes of assessment (others are discussed in Chapter 13). In particular a distinction has been made between assessment for summative and formative purposes. Having begun with a theoretical argument for formative assessment, we have ended with reference to empirical evidence of its impact in raising pupils' achievement.

FURTHER READING

Two short pamphlets summarise the findings from the Black and Wiliam review:

ARG (1999) *Assessment for Learning: Beyond the Black Box*. Available from the Institute of Education, Univeristy of London and as a pdf file from the Assessment Reform Group website: www.assessment-reform-group.org

Black, P. and Wiliam, D. (1998b) *Inside the Black Box*. London: NFER-Nelson.

Chapter 8

Gathering and interpreting evidence of children's science process skills and attitudes

---

■■■ INTRODUCTION

In this chapter we look at the collection and interpretation of evidence of children's development of process skills and attitudes. These are the first two stages of the formative assessment framework in Figure 7.3. In Chapter 9 we cover the final two stages of the cycle, concerned with deciding and taking action in relation to children's next steps in this aspect of their science learning.

It is convenient to consider together the collection or gathering of evidence and the interpretation of the evidence, since they are conceptually linked. We do this for the development of concepts in Chapter 10. Gathering evidence implies that we know what information to gather, that is, we have an idea of what is relevant and significant for the purpose of gathering the evidence. This means we need a clear idea of the meaning of the process skills and attitudes we want to help children develop; this is the purpose of the first section of this chapter. The second section is concerned with methods of gathering evidence and the third with interpreting the evidence. Although in separate sections, it's important to remember that gathering evidence and interpreting it are very closely connected. We can't interpret evidence unless it is relevant, so how the evidence is to be interpreted influences what is gathered. The final section considers planning for collecting evidence systematically about the full range of process skills.

■■■ CLARIFYING MEANINGS OF PROCESS SKILLS AND ATTITUDES

The terms used to describe process skills and attitudes vary. One reason for this is that any definition of separate skills and attitudes is a convenience rather than an attempt to describe reality. The skills and attitudes identified in Chapter 3 are components of the complex activity that we call enquiry, or investigation. We look at the component parts so as to help children develop skill in all aspects of enquiry. Different people at different times identify the aspects in different ways, as we saw in Chapter 3. Here the whole has been divided into seven skills and four attitudes. Boxes 8.1 and 8.2 summarise briefly the meaning to be attached to each one.

Box 8.1: Meaning of some process skills

Raising questions
In the context of science activities, our concern is with questions that can be answered through scientific enquiry. Although raising questions of all kinds is important to children's learning, in developing children's understanding in science we are concerned with one particular kind of question, ones that are investigable. In Chapter 5 different kinds of questions that children ask were discussed, with some ideas of how they can be turned into investigable ones. We are not intending to give the impression that these are the only kinds of question worth asking, but for learning science they are the ones that lead children to find out about what there is in the world and how it behaves. Within the range of questions that science attempts to answer we are particularly concerned, in the education of 5- to 12-year-olds, with a small subset of questions. These are the questions to which children can find answers through their own activity. So raising questions in this context means asking questions that lead to enquiry (investigable questions) and recognising the kinds of questions that can be answered in this way.

Developing hypotheses
The process of hypothesising is attempting to explain observations or relationships, in terms of an idea. There were several examples of hypotheses put forward by the children quoted in Chapter 2: 'It's the varnish . . .', 'got more air . . .', 'the heavier it is the lower it floats'. Hypothesising involves the notion of applying: an idea found to explain things in one context is applied in a new situation. If the new situation is almost the same as the previous one, it is a matter of recall rather than application. Hypothesising is a process that acknowledges that there may be more than one possible explanation. This is consistent with the view that scientific theories are tentative.

Predicting
Predicting plays an important part in the model of learning described in Chapter 2 and for that reason alone it is necessary that its meaning is made clear. Predicting often has a close relationship with hypothesising. Although a prediction may not seem to be based on a hypothesis, it invariably is so implicitly if not explicitly. For example, the prediction that 'this cup will be better than that one for keeping coffee hot because it is thicker' includes the hypothesis that thick cups retain heat better than thin ones. The prediction as to which will be best then follows from it, even though it preceded the hypothesis.

It is important to distinguish predicting from guessing. Neither hypotheses nor predictions are the same as guesses. They both have a rational basis in an idea or in observations and a guess does not have this property. Guessing is exemplified in the actions of a teacher with a group of reception children while cutting open fruits of various kinds to see what was inside. Before the grapefruit was cut, the children were asked to 'guess' how many pips there would be in it. Their answers were indeed guesses, for even if they had used existing knowledge of grapefruit to suggest a number of the right order, there was no way of predicting how many would be in that particular fruit.

Box 8.1: Continued

Using observation
Observation means using all the senses to gather information, but it is more than merely 'taking everything in'. Observations are directed by preconceptions and expectations, that is, the tendency to see what we are looking for, while missing other things that may be right under our noses. Observations are quantified through measurement, sometimes by directly comparing one thing with another or, where appropriate, comparing with standard units of measurement.

Planning and conducting investigations
Children use evidence in building their understanding through enquiry and investigation. The evidence may come from direct experience with materials, but also at secondhand by consulting books, the media, experts, discussion with other children and, of course, their teacher. Investigating through direct experience involves making decisions about what, when and how observations or measurements are to be made, and what materials and equipment to use. These decisions are not necessarily made before action takes place. For young children, planning and performing an investigation are interwoven; they may plan no further than the first step and from the result of this think what to do next. Older children can be helped to plan things before setting out on an investigation, but they will often need to make changes in the light of unanticipated events.

Interpreting evidence and drawing conclusions
An investigation usually involves collection of various observations or findings of different kinds. Interpreting these findings means using them to answer the question that the investigation or enquiry was designed to address. According to the type of enquiry, this may mean:

- putting together various pieces of information so that something can be said about the whole that is different from recounting each separate piece of information

- finding a trend or pattern in a set of observations or measurements

- relating the result of testing a prediction to the idea on which the prediction was based.

Communicating, reporting and reflecting
Communicating, reporting and reflecting are put together since it is through attempting to make things understandable to others that we are caused to examine them for ourselves. Communication is two-way. It involves, on the one hand, using speech, writing, drawing or an artefact to share things with others and, on the other hand, listening to or looking at information or argument from others or other sources. Effective communication means being clear and systematic in presenting information and using forms of communication appropriate both to the type of information and to those who are to receive it. It requires knowledge of conventions of communicating information in various forms, such as through graphs, tables and symbols on charts. It also includes communicating with oneself through keeping notes and records.

Box 8.1: Continued

In the context of science activities, reflecting means deliberately looking back over what has been done, to see if procedures could have been improved or ideas better applied. It is related to the attitudes of respect for evidence and flexibility but relates to making a more conscious effort to consider alternatives to what has been done. In practice it may be manifest in self-critical comments, in repeating part of an investigation or even starting again in another way. On the other hand, there may be no critical comment to make; the recognition of having taken a useful course of action is also evidence of having reviewed what has been done.

Box 8.2: Meaning of some scientific attitudes

Curiosity
A child with curiosity wants to know, to try new experience, to explore, to find out about things around him or her. It is obvious that this is an attitude that will help learning of all kinds and especially learning by enquiry. Curiosity often shows in asking questions, but this is not the only sign of curiosity nor the only manifestation to be encouraged. The stimulation that comes from satisfying curiosity will help children reach a more mature stage where interest is sustained for longer and questions are more thoughtful. Then curiosity appears not so much as a flow of questions but as wanting to know. This desire to find out stimulates effort to find out, perhaps by investigation, perhaps by using a library or making a special visit. When children have reached this stage, putting new experiences in their way is more likely to lead to learning through their own effort.

Respect for evidence
Developing understanding in science is essentially a process of gathering and using evidence to test or develop ideas. Although a theory may have its beginning in an imaginative guess, it has no status until it has been shown to fit evidence or make sense of what is known. Thus the use of evidence is central to scientific activity; this is true at school level as much as at the level of the work of scientists, so attitudes towards evidence are of great importance in science education. Children talking among themselves have a keen sense that an unsupported statement is not necessarily to be believed. 'How do you know that's true?' and 'Prove it' feature in their private arguments in one form or another. A desire to obtain and use evidence to decide between ideas is a sign of development of this attitude.

Flexibility
Flexibility of mind bears a similar relation to the product of scientific activity as respect for evidence does to the process. The concepts that we form to help our understanding of the world around change as experience adds more evidence to develop or contradict them. For example, the idea of energy develops from being related to how 'energetic' people are, to being associated with moving things, to being possessed by things that

Box 8.2: Continued

can move other things, to a realisation that energy exists in a variety of forms. The changes are most rapid in children's early years since their limited experience means that their first ideas are often quite different from what they need to understand wider experience later. Unless there is flexibility, each experience that conflicts with existing ideas would cause confusion and create a rival idea instead of modification and growth of an existing one. Flexibility is needed to adapt existing frameworks to fit increased experience.

Sensitivity in investigating the environment
In science education children are encouraged to investigate and explore their environment to understand it and to develop skills for further understanding. Unless investigation and exploration are governed by an attitude of respect for the environment and a willingness to care appropriately for the living things in it, such activities could result in unnecessary interference or even unpleasant harm. So it is important that growth in skills of enquiry and concepts should be accompanied by a development of sensitivity towards living things and responsibility towards the environment. Young children soon pick up the signs that certain living things have to be treated differently from non-living things. To extend this further to the made environment requires commitment, and a degree of understanding, not reached by many children in the primary years. In the meantime it is necessary to ensure that children are willing to obey simple rules designed to prevent thoughtless harm to the environment. At first, rules will have to be imposed by the teacher and discussed with the children so that they appreciate that there are reasons behind them. Later the children can be involved in deciding the rules and procedures as part of the preparation for investigating beyond the classroom.

GATHERING EVIDENCE OF PROCESS SKILLS AND ATTITUDES

Process skills and attitudes show in what children think and do. In some cases the outcomes of this thought and action, expressed in written or oral reports of their work, are useful indicators of the skills that have been used. In other cases, particularly for young children, it is necessary to observe the action as it takes place. But what is observed may not be easy to interpret without asking about, for example, why things were done in certain ways. Thus gathering evidence about process skills and attitudes is likely to require a combination of:

- observing children's actions
- questioning and discussing
- studying written work designed to reveal the use of process skills and attitudes.

Observing children's actions

Observing all the individual children in a whole class is a formidable task and is indeed an impossible one to accomplish at any one time. It becomes possible through planning and focusing. *Planning*, as suggested later, should be used to ensure that evidence is collected about different groups of children at different times. In any single activity one group is the target for detailed observation, while the teacher interacts as normal with all groups. Planning for gathering evidence is taken up later in this chapter. *Focusing* involves having a mental checklist of what to look for. Such a checklist could be derived from the list of process skills and attitudes which are the goals of learning science. It might take the form of questions such as:

- Does the child raise questions?

- Does the child attempt to explain things (develop hypotheses)?

- Does the child make predictions?

- . . . and so on.

This would require a considerable amount of interpretation by the teacher for each question. It would certainly be difficult to give a decided 'yes' or 'no' to these questions. What does 'making predictions' mean in terms of what the children might be doing? Does it mean the same for children at, say, the age of 7 as for children at the age of 11? Further, different meanings given to words such as 'hypotheses' might mean that evidence of different kinds is collected by different teachers.

Having more detailed statements for each item, incorporating some answers to these questions, although making the list very long, can help by:

- making it a little more certain that we all mean the same thing when we say a child is able to do something (although there can never be certainty about this, here or in other contexts)

- giving more specific help about what to look for as evidence of skills being used

- indicating progression in the development of skills.

In the case of attitudes, the notion of a progression in development common to all children is less clear. However, there are indicators that can focus observation, leading to suggestions of how to help children develop scientific attitudes.

The sets of statements given in Boxes 8.4 and 8.5, describing progression in process skills and indicators relating to attitudes, are proposed as a basis for interpreting evidence (from written work as well as oral reports and actions), as we discuss later, but they also have an important role in focusing observation. Having these indicators in mind helps teachers to plan and prepare to collect evidence by observation that is used to decide where children need help in developing certain skills and reflect on progress. Teachers have found them useful in these ways:

- As part of planning, the statements focus observation on significant aspects of children's activities, that are the goals of the particular activities. Not all activities involve all process skills, but even in complete investigations, it is advisable to focus on one or two process skills particularly. The evidence for all process skills has to be accumulated over several different kinds of activity (see the section on planning later in this chapter).

- During the classroom work, having the statements in mind enables teachers to identify opportunities to help children develop the process skills that are the goals of the activities. In some cases, immediate action can be taken, as in helping children to look more carefully at the situation they are investigating. In relation to recording evidence for later reflection, all that a teacher can reasonably do is to make a mental note, and in some cases a note on paper, of relevant evidence.

- After the lesson the statements can be used to decide where there was evidence of the various aspects being shown. This leads to decisions about future learning opportunities, as discussed in Chapter 9.

The lists in Boxes 8.4 and 8.5 at first sight seem over-long. However, the detail is necessary since it enables the teacher to identify the help that children may need in developing their process skills. Becoming familiar with this approach takes time; experience shows that it is helpful to begin by selecting only a couple of process skills as a start and gradually extending the list as the items become internalised.

Questioning and discussing

The observation of children's actions does not always indicate their thinking and it may often be necessary to ask for some explanation. It would be inappropriate constantly to interrupt practical work to ask 'why are you doing it that way?' for the answer often emerges in what children do subsequently. But occasionally it helps to clarify the intention behind an action when going over the activity after it has been completed. For example, when some children were dropping balls onto different surfaces to see if the surface made any difference to the rebound, the teacher noticed that the balls were held at the same height each time. Later he asked the child 'How did you decide where to hold your hand when you dropped the balls?' The answer came back in terms of convenience in relation to the height of the table; there had been no deliberate decision to control this variable, as might well have been assumed.

Questions that provide evidence of how children are using process skills have to be worded so that they require the process skill of interest to be used in answering the question; for instance: 'what do you think will happen if . . .?' for evidence of predicting; 'what do you notice about . . .?' for evidence of observation. The features of these questions have been discussed in some detail in Chapter 5 and summarised in Table 5.1.

Children's written work

The records and reports that children write will add to the evidence obtained by observation. However, rarely do the reports of primary children indicate the detail that is needed to judge the extent to which various skills have been used. The example in Box 8.3 illustrates this point.

Box 8.3: An investigation of materials

In an investigation of materials, as part of an overall topic on clothing, a group of girls took eight pieces of different kinds of material. They grouped them according to whether they were natural or man-made and compared the resistance to wear for each group by rubbing them against the ground. The teacher observed that they chose the same piece of ground to test all the materials and they counted the number of rubs it took to make a hole. They kept to the same procedures and the same person rubbing. This method took a considerable time, however, and Michelle suggested it would be quicker if they put a stone inside the material. So they wrapped each sample round a stone and started again. Their results were entered in a table drawn up for them by the teacher. Figure 8.1 shows the results recorded by Michelle's group.

At first the children used the results in Figure 8.1 to conclude that 'natural material is better than man-made'. The written work alone gives no evidence of the extent to which they attempted to control variables or how they came to their conclusion. The teacher's observations provided evidence in relation to variables, but in order to find out how they came to their first conclusion it was necessary for the teacher to discuss their thinking. This revealed that they had ignored the finding that the two methods they had tried had led to different results. It also caused them to articulate how they were using their findings to reach an overall conclusion. After discussing their results with their teacher, they wrote:

> We don't know what's the best Material because when we done our second test Natural got the most points And man-made got the least points. But man-made material got the most point's with our first test so we think Man-made and Natural have strong points.

Through the discussion the teacher was able to judge their use of evidence in arriving at conclusions, which enabled him to see where these girls needed more experience.

Natural	Rubs	Manmade	Rubs
felt (wool)	20	cotton + polyester	108
rubber	210	Viscose	57
cotton	67	Satin	20
linen	15	nylon	2

rubber was the strogest material it took 210 rubs. Nylon was the weakest material it took two rubs rubber took 208 rubs more than nylon

Figure 8.1 One group's results from the fabric activity

INTERPRETING EVIDENCE OF PROCESS SKILLS AND ATTITUDES

In order to find out where children are in development of ideas, skills and attitudes, and to use this information to identify next steps, we need to know what is the course of development. This assumes that there is a typical and identifiable progression in development of skills. Not everyone agrees that this is the case.

Skills and attitudes are always applied in relation to some content that influences their deployment. It is not difficult to show, by considering extreme cases, that the influence could be quite large. For example, an 11-year-old who is able to find and use patterns in data concerning the girth of trees and their height might not be able to pick out patterns in the chemical properties of elements that explain their arrangement in groups. It would be unreasonable to judge the 11-year-old's pattern-finding ability in the latter context, but quite reasonable to do so for a 17-year-old studying chemistry.

Because of this context dependency, some people argue that skills do not develop, and that children become progressively more able to deploy them in relation to more complex content and a wider range of situations. However, evidence supporting the notion of development of process skills has come from research and from classroom experience where children are using skills with familiar content. For example, the findings of the surveys of science performance carried out between 1980 and 1985 by the Assessment of Performance Unit (APU) gave evidence of how children's competence in using enquiry skills develops. More recently, the PISA results are reported in terms of levels of development of processes. There is undoubtedly a need for more systematic study to determine more reliably the course of progression in skills. Meanwhile, the approach offered here uses the evidence and experience currently available.

The evidence comes from a combination of:

- the experience of classroom teachers and subject specialists

- research into children's learning

- information about achievements of children at different ages and stages obtained by survey and monitoring programmes.

There is never enough firm information from these sources, however, and the course of development that is mapped out is tentative and always subject to refinement in the light of new evidence. The products have been described in various ways; an Australian project calls them 'progress maps' (Masters and Forster, 1996). To some extent the sequence of attainment targets in the National Curriculum and in other similar curriculum guidance, such as the the benchmark for Science Literacy set out by the American Association for the Advancement of Science (AAAS, 1993) provide 'maps' of development. However, these are coarse-grained statements suitable for summarising attainment. For helping learning, finer-grained statements are needed, describing progression in more detail without necessarily relating to levels or grades.

Interpreting evidence of process skills

The lists in Box 8.4 attempt to map the development in the process skills. Under each heading, the items are arranged in a sequence that reflects typical progression. The sequences have been created from currently available information, but it is important to note that:

- the path they describe is not necessarily one that all children will follow (it describes typical progress but no two children learn in exactly the same way)
- they are not a description of a purely 'natural' sequence of development, but one that results from the experiences we conventionally provide as well as general mental development
- they are not a prescription for a learning sequence
- the earlier statements indicate skills that are likely to be developed before those later in the lists, but a child will not generally demonstrate all skills up to a certain point and none beyond; rather there will be a point where there will be most from below and some from above.

Although the range of the statement has been carefully chosen to be appropriate to the ages 5–12, no attempt has been made to identify where children of a certain age or stage within this range ought to have reached. *This is not necessary for formative assessment, where all that is needed is to see where children are in making progress* and where the next steps ought to take them. In Chapter 13 we will consider how evidence collected by the teacher and used for formative assessment might be reviewed and judged against standards or levels for summative purposes.

Using indicators of development

Earlier in this chapter we noted that the list of questions for process skills and attitudes have two roles in formative assessment: helping to focus observation on significant aspects of behaviour and helping to interpret observations after evidence has been collected. Their role in interpreting evidence is in fact wider than helping to interpret evidence gathered by observation, and extends to making judgements about evidence of all kinds: from children's talk, artefacts, writing and drawings. Evidence from these sources can be used to compare with the statements to see where in the progression the children seem to have reached. Finding where the answer is 'yes, there is evidence of this' and where it is 'no, there is no evidence of this' – or, more realistically, where it becomes difficult to say yes or no – locates the child's development within the progression. Furthermore, and crucially, this process indicates the next step, which is to consolidate the skills and ideas around the area where 'yes' turns into 'no'. Finding where progress is to be made is the whole purpose of formative assessment.

Box 8.4: Indicators of progression in process skills

Things children do that are indicators of raising questions

1 Ask a variety of questions.

2 Participate effectively in discussing how their questions can be answered.

3 Recognise a difference between an investigable question and one that cannot be answered by investigation.

4 Suggest how answers to various questions (investigable and non-investigable) can be found.

5 Attempt to turn their own questions into a form that can be investigated.

6 In science, generally ask questions that can be investigated.

7 Recognise that only certain questions can be answered by scientific investigation.

Things children do that are indicators of hypothesising

1 Attempt to give an explanation which is consistent with the presence of certain features or circumstances.

2 Refer to a related experience rather than the idea that links it (e.g. 'sugar' rather than dissolving).

3 Attempt to explain something by naming a relevant idea but going no further to say what this means (for example, 'gravity').

4 Suggest a possible cause, even if it would be difficult to check (for example, about how a current flows in a wire).

5 Show awareness that there may be more than one explanation that fits the evidence.

6 Give explanations that suggest how an observed effect or situation is brought about and which could be checked.

7 Show awareness that explanations are tentative and never proved beyond doubt.

Things children do that are indicators of predicting

1 Attempt to make a prediction relating to a problem or question even if it is based on preconceived ideas.

2 Recognise that a prediction is different from a guess.

3 Make some use of evidence from past experience in making a prediction.

4 Make a reasonable prediction based on an explicit hypothesis (possible explanation of what is going on).

5 Implicitly use patterns in observations to make predictions.

6 Explain the reason for a prediction in terms of patterns in available evidence.

7 Justify a prediction in terms of relevant science concepts.

Box 8.4: Continued

Things children do that are indicators of using observation

1 Identify obvious differences and similarities between objects and materials.

2 Make use of several senses in exploring objects or materials.

3 Identify points of similarity between objects where differences are more obvious than similarities.

4 Take an adequate series of observations to answer the question or test the prediction under investigation.

5 Use their senses appropriately and extending the range of sight using a hand lens or microscope as necessary.

6 Distinguish from many observations those which are relevant to the problem in hand and explaining the reason.

7 Take steps to ensure that the results obtained are as accurate as they can reasonably be and repeating observations where necessary.

Things children do that are indicators of planning and conducting investigations

1 Suggest a useful approach to answering a question or testing a prediction by investigation, even if details are lacking or need further thought.

2 Make suggestions about what might happen when certain changes are made.

3 Identify the variable that has to be changed and the things which should be kept the same for a fair test.

4 Identify what to look for or measure to obtain a result in an investigation.

5 Select and use equipment and measuring devices suited to the task in hand.

6 Succeed in planning a fair test using the support of a framework of questions or planning board.

7 Spontaneously structure a plan so that variables are identified and steps taken to make results as accurate as possible.

Things children do that are indicators of interpreting evidence and drawing conclusions

1 Compare what they find with what they predicted or expected.

2 Identify patterns or trends in their observations or measurements.

3 Draw conclusions which summarise and are consistent with all the evidence that has been collected.

4 Discuss what they find in relation to their initial question or hypothesis.

5 Use patterns to draw conclusions and attempt to explain them in terms of scientific concepts.

Box 8.4: Continued

6 Recognise that there may be more than one explanation that fits the evidence.

7 Recognise that any conclusions are tentative and may have to be changed in the light of new evidence.

Things children do that are indicators of communicating, reporting and reflecting

1 Talk freely about their activities and the ideas they have, with or without making a written record.

2 Listen to others' ideas and look at their results.

3 Make a short written report that indicates what was done, and why, and what was found.

4 Use drawings, tables, graphs and charts when these are suggested to record and organise results.

5 Choose a form for recording or presenting results which is both considered and justified in relation to the type of information and the audience.

6 Use appropriate scientific language in reporting and show understanding of the terms used.

7 Compare their procedures after the event with what was planned in order to make suggestions for improving their way of investigating.

Interpreting evidence of scientific attitudes

The discussion of four attitudes – curiosity, respect for evidence, flexibility and sensitivity in investigating the environment – in Box 8.2 suggested some behaviours that indicate these attitudes. While it is possible to identify these indicators, there is less certainty about progression. This may be because attitudes depend on experiences that foster them more than on age or stage. Thus in the case of the attitudes in Box 8.5 the indicators can simply be used to identify desirable behaviours and thus, when these are not found, where help needs to be given to foster development of these behaviours.

Box 8.5 Indicators of scientific attitudes

Things children do that are indicators of curiosity

● Give some attention to new things.

● Explore things and ask questions about them in response to invitations to do so.

● Examine things carefully and ask questions about 'how' and 'why' as well as 'what'.

● Explore and investigate things around to answer their own questions.

● Spontaneously seek information from books or other sources to satisfy their own curiosity.

Box 8.5 Continued

Things children do that are indicators of respect for evidence
- Attempt to justify conclusions in terms of evidence even if the interpretation is influenced by preconceived ideas.

- Realise when the evidence does not fit a conclusion based on expectations.

- Check parts of the evidence which do not fit an overall pattern or conclusions.

- Accept only interpretations or conclusions for which there is supporting evidence.

- Recognise that no conclusion is so firm that it cannot be challenged by further evidence.

Things children do that are indicators of flexibility in ways of thinking
- Readily admit to a change in their ideas.

- Modify ideas to incorporate new evidence or arguments.

- Show willingness to consider alternative ideas, which may fit the evidence better, or as well as, their own ideas.

- Relinquish or change ideas after considering evidence.

- Spontaneously seek other ideas that may fit the evidence rather than accepting the first that seems to fit.

Things children do that are indicators of sensitivity in investigating the environment
- Take part, with supervision, in caring for living things.

- Look after living things responsibly with minimum supervision.

- On visits outside school recognise and observe a code of behaviour which protects the environment from litter, damage and disturbance.

- Minimise the impact of investigation in the environment, e.g. by replacing disturbed stones, returning animals caught for study in the classroom.

- Take responsibility for ensuring that living things are cared for in the classroom and for protecting the environment outside from damage and pollution caused by their own action.

- Help to ensure that the actions of others as well as their own do not neglect living things or damage the non-living environment.

PLANNING TO ASSESS PROCESS SKILLS AND ATTITUDES

Process skills can be used in relation to any content. Unlike conceptual understanding, their use and development does not depend on the subject being studied. So, at least in theory, there are frequent opportunities to assess children's process skills. Similar points apply to attitudes.

Most science activities should involve children in thinking and doing, and thus provide the teacher with opportunities to assess and help children to develop process skills. If this is not the case then there is a need for serious evaluation of the learning opportunities being provided. But assuming that there are *frequent opportunities*, this means that it is not necessary to assess all children at a particular time. As we have seen, observation is a key to assessing skills, supplemented by discussion and studying written work. It is better to observe a small number of children thoroughly throughout an activity so as to achieve a detailed picture of their skills than to attempt to cover a larger number more superficially.

Does the activity content matter?

It may take two or three months to complete the observation of all children in the class, and it will mean that different children are assessed when carrying out different activities. This is not a problem in the context of formative assessment, for two main reasons. First, since no comparison is being made between children then, providing the activities give opportunity for the skills to be used, the context of one activity is as good as another. If the purpose were to assign a grade or label to the children then the variation in content of the activities would be a source of error in the results, but when observations can be repeated and the purpose is to help the children's learning in a particular context, it is not a problem. Second, the skills we are concerned with are ones that are assumed to be generally applicable and so, again, it is the case that one context is as valid as another, given that they provide similar opportunity for skills to be used. This is not to deny that the context influences the use of skills, however. With this in mind it may be useful to make observations during various activities over a period of time before deciding what help may be needed.

Focusing on a small target group at one time does not mean that other children are neglected. The children will be unaware of when they are targets, for the teacher interacts with all children in the normal way. When interacting with the target children, the teacher will observe, question and probe with the indicators in mind and interpret this evidence to decide whether to take action immediately or later.

Groups or individuals?

In referring to a group of children here there is some ambiguity about whether the evidence is gathered about the group as a whole or about individual children. Teachers generally have no difficulty in identifying the separate contributions of children even when they are combining their ideas and skills in a group enterprise. But, we might question whether, *for the purpose of informing teaching*, it is always necessary to assess individual pupils. If the information is used to make decisions about the activities and help to be given to children as *a group*, then assessment of the group is all that is needed for this purpose. For group work, differences among children are not a disadvantage, since there is convincing evidence that in heterogeneous groups all pupils benefit when they are encouraged to share ideas and skills. Thus a group assessment may be considered to be all that is necessary where the activity is genuinely collaborative and ideas are pooled. Evidence of the achievements of individuals can be found from the products of their work and discussion of these products.

SUMMARY

This chapter began with brief accounts of the meaning being given to the seven process skills and four attitudes identified among the goals of science education. It then looked at how evidence of these skills and attitudes can be gathered in the context of formative assessment, where detailed information is required. Ways of gathering evidence by observation, questioning and looking at children's written work have been discussed. For interpreting the evidence in relation to process skills, statements mapping progression in each skill have been set out. Although these maps cannot be exact, since development is the combined effect of experience, maturation and teaching, they give a basis for identifying the help children need to operate at a more advanced level. For attitudes, it has been noted that the notion of progression is less certain, but indicators can still be used to identify how to help the development.

FURTHER READING

SCRE (1995) *Taking a Closer Look at Science*, Edinburgh: Scottish Council for Research in Education (SCRE), provides examples of children's work with comments on aspects that signify achievements and indicate likely next steps.

The ACER (Australian Council for Educational Research) published an Assessment Resource Kit (ARK) which includes M. Forster and G. Masters (1997) *Assessment Methods*, Camberwell, Victoria: ACER, giving ideas that are useful for assessment in all areas of the curriculum.

Chapter 9

Helping development of process skills and attitudes of science

INTRODUCTION

Here we complete the formative assessment cycle in relation to process skills and attitudes of science by considering the two stages that follow on from gathering and interpreting evidence, discussed in the last chapter. In the first section we take the seven skills one at a time and consider for each how children can be helped to make progress, according to the next steps that have been identified. From this it becomes clear that there are common strategies across the process skills, which it is useful to keep in mind. These are drawn out in the second section. The final section of the chapter deals with what teachers can do to help children develop attitudes that support their learning.

PROMOTING THE USE OF PROCESS SKILLS

We begin by considering action in relation to each of the process skills briefly defined in Chapter 8. The specific action in a particular situation will depend not only on the point of development reached by the children but also on the context and on the children involved – on their recent progress and range of experience, for instance. So it isn't possible to prescribe what to do in particular cases, but we can identify useful strategies from which teachers can choose what to deploy. Here these are discussed and summarised for each of the process skills.

Raising questions

The concern here is to help children identify the kinds of questions that can be answered through scientific enquiry. This is a key factor in developing an understanding of the nature of scientific activity and it is important to lay a foundation for this in the early years. Science addresses questions about what there is in the world and how it behaves. In answer to such questions assertions can be made which can be tested; for instance: 'Does wood float?' and 'Do you find trees on top of mountains?' Answers can be found by investigation or by consulting someone who has found out. These are science-related questions. The situation is very different, though, for questions such as: 'Is happiness the only real aim in life?' or 'What is knowledge?' These are philosophical questions and are not answered from observation or logical argument. Nor can science address questions of value or aesthetic judgement. It can tackle 'Which watch keeps better time?', but not 'Which watch is more attractive?' or 'Which is worth more money?' These different kinds of questions and how to handle them have been discussed in Chapter 5.

Children come to realise the distinction between questions that can or cannot be answered by enquiry by considering their own questions. So an important role for the teacher is to encourage children to raise all kinds of questions and, through discussion of these questions, to help them realise which ones can be answered by information obtained in different ways.

There are two key features of encouraging questioning: plenty of materials and objects to explore and handle; and a classroom climate that encourages questions.

The materials can include both the unusual and the familiar; ones brought in by the children and those selected by the teacher. The unusual stimulate curiosity, particularly if they are striking in shape, colour or movement. The familiar give children chance to find and wonder about differences among things that they may have previously assumed to be all the same. For instance, a collection of different kinds of bolts and screws may raise questions about why there are so many different kinds, what purposes they serve, what is a screw, anyway? In all cases the displays should be accompanied by written questions that children can ponder and in some cases answer by interaction with the materials.

This goes some way to creating the climate conducive to questioning, by giving a sign that questions are useful. Other ways of showing that questions are welcome and indeed expected are devices such as:

- a question box in which children can post written questions, which are discussed at a certain time in the week

- asking children what questions they would like to ask about a topic and what they would still like to know at the end of an investigation

- introducing a 'question of the week' for children to think about (as suggested by Jelly, 2001)

- providing sources of information so that children can answer some questions for themselves.

Making time to discuss questions, as a whole class or in groups, not only gives public recognition of the value of questions, but also provides opportunities for helping children to identify investigable questions. It helps to ask them what information they would need to collect to answer a question. If this is not clear then the question may need to be reworded. Some examples of questions that are useful for this kind of discussion are given in Goldsworthy *et al.* (2000).

Box 9.1: Helping development in raising questions

The teacher's role in the development of raising questions can be summarised as:

- Providing opportunities for children to study objects and materials that can provoke questions and be used to answer some of them through enquiry.

- Responding to children's questions according to the type of question they are, as suggested in Chapter 5.

- Encouraging questions by inviting children in various ways to raise them and ensuring that time is made for discussing them.

- Helping children to consider how questions can be answered, so that they identify ones that are investigable.

- Making sources of information available to enable children to answer some of their own questions.

Hypothesising

As defined in Chapter 8, this process skill includes the application of concepts and knowledge in attempting to explain things. Hypotheses may be based on existing knowledge applied to the new situation or the generation of an explanation from a hunch or imagination. The difference between these is not as great as it may at first seem, for there is generally a reason for a suggestion that seems to 'come out of the blue' even though it may not be articulated. Both ways of attempting to explain should be encouraged for, although it is important to help children to use information or ideas learned previously in making sense of new experience, it could give them a closed 'right answer' view of science if this were the only approach used. The question put to children in asking for an explanation should more often be 'What *could be* the reason?' rather than 'What *is* the reason?' For instance, what could be the reason for:

- some pieces of wood floating higher in the water than others?

- apples turning red when they ripen?

- pigeons sometimes puffing out their feathers?

- snow melting on the footpath before it does on the grass?

- Julie's salt dissolving more quickly than David's?

To all of these questions there could be more than one answer. A worthwhile task for children to undertake in small groups is to think of all the possible answers they can. Their combined ideas will be richer than those of any individual. Furthermore, in groups, the children are less worried about contradicting each other and turning down far-fetched ideas or ones that would not explain the phenomenon. For example, in a group discussing why the snow melted on the path:

John	People walk on the path and not on the grass, so that took it away
Peter	But it was on the path as well at the start and went before anyone walked on it, didn't you see? Can't be that. I reckon the path was wet – wet sort of dissolves the snow . . .
Mary	They put salt on roads . . .
John	Yes, that's it

Peter's idea, too, was later challenged but he stuck to it because there was no convincing evidence against it so it went down on their list of possibilities. It was noteworthy that as this discussion went on the children began to talk in terms of what *might* be happening instead of the more certain earlier claims of what was happening. Another feature of the situation was that what they were trying to explain was a shared experience and one that provided the chance for them to check some of their hypotheses. Other ideas needed information from further observations or tests, depending in this case on the co-operation of the weather. The important thing was that they were not trying to advance grand theories to explain a whole range of phenomena (e.g. energy is needed to cause a change of state), but making sense of particular things in their immediate experience. Success and enjoyment in doing this would help the development of the ability to hypothesise which could serve them well later when they might have to entertain alternative bigger ideas.

As well as the ideas generated within a group, the children should have access to ideas from others outside the group. Listening to what other groups have proposed is one way, but they should also be able to consult books and other information sources (see also Chapter 11). Part of the teacher's role is to make available relevant books, posters, pictures, CD-ROMs, etc., selected so that the children can easily find ideas in them. For younger children it helps to place appropriate books next to the aquarium or the display or have them ready when a particular topic is to be discussed. Older children might be expected to find books for themselves.

Box 9.2 Helping development in hypothesising

The provision for development of hypothesising involves the teacher in:

- selecting or setting up phenomena which children can try to explain from their past experience

- organising groups to discuss possible explanations

- encouraging the checking of possibilities against evidence to reject those suggestions that are inconsistent with it

- providing access to ideas for children to add to their own, from books and other sources (including the teacher and other children).

Predicting

Predictions can be based on hypotheses or on patterns in observations. In either case, the prediction is an important step in testing the hypotheses or patterns. The question 'does this idea really explain what is happening?' is answered in science by first predicting a so far unknown event from the explanation and then seeing whether there is evidence of the predicted event taking place. For children, the explanation may be in terms of associated circumstances rather than mechanisms, but the same applies. For example, the appearance of a misty patch after breathing on a window-pane may be explained 'because my breath is warm and the window is cold'. Although there is much more to the explanation than this, it is still possible to use this idea to make a prediction about what will happen if the window is warm and not cold. Investigation of 'breathing' on surfaces of different temperatures would test predictions based on this hypothesis.

It is not easy to encourage children to make genuine predictions, as opposed to guesses, on the one hand, or a mere statement of what is already known, on the other. At first it is useful to scaffold the process by taking the children through the reasoning that connects the making of a prediction to the testing of an idea: 'according to our idea, what will happen if . . .?' and so 'if that happens, then we'll know our idea is working so far. Let's see.' It is also important to check whether 'we already know what will happen'; only if the answer is not already known is it a real prediction and a genuine test of the hypothesis or pattern.

The prerequisite for this kind of interaction is that the children are engaged in activities where they can generate hypotheses to test or observe patterns. Such activities include those where an explanation can arise from the observations, as in the behaviour of a 'Cartesian diver', or why footsteps echo in some places but not others, or why moisture forms on the outside of cold containers taken from the fridge into a warm room.

Box 9.3: Helping development in predicting

The teacher's role in helping children to make predictions includes:

- providing opportunities where children can investigate their ideas through making and testing predictions

- discussing with them how to make a prediction and test it (scaffolding)

- helping them to recognise the difference between a prediction and a guess by asking them to explain how they arrived at their prediction

- expecting them to make predictions of something that is not already known in order to test their ideas.

Using observation

The main purpose of developing children's skill of observation is so that they will be able to use all their senses (appropriately and safely) to gather relevant information from their investigations of things around them.

Development of observation is fostered by opportunities for children to make wide-ranging observations. Materials that can potentially interest children abound in their surroundings and can be brought into the classroom for closer inspection and for display. The choice of materials and the way in which these are displayed can increase the information children can gather from their observations. For instance:

- Shells and pebbles might be displayed not only dry, but in water, so that their colours show more clearly.

- Snail shells of different sizes but of the same type provide a chance for children to find out through observation how the shell 'grows'.

- Children can also get some idea of mechanisms from observation of objects that can be taken apart, like a bicycle bell, torch or clock (preferably one made for this purpose).

When new material is gathered or provided to start a new topic it is always worth while to allow a period of time for children just to look, touch, smell and perhaps listen, before suggesting a task. Time is also an important element at later stages in an investigation, so that observations can be checked, refined and extended. When watching a group of children with new materials it is interesting to see how they often appear to observe very superficially at first. This may well be just a first quick run through; given time and encouragement they start again, more carefully, sometimes using measurement to decide whether or not differences they think they have seen are real. If the teacher stops the activity after their quick tour of what there is to see, then the only observations they make are the superficial ones and they are prevented from going into depth.

Some children need few 'invitations to observe' but others are more reluctant and may be easily distracted after a superficial glance. There can be many reasons for this; likely ones include the effective discouragement of detailed observation by allowing insufficient time, or the teacher plying them with questions too soon. Reluctant observers can be helped by a teacher making a comment that might encourage observation rather than a question, which can seem threatening. For example, 'Look what happens to the pebbles when you put them in water' is more of an invitation than 'What happens to the colour of the pebbles when you put them in water?'

Discussion plays a major part in encouraging observation at all stages. In the early stages of development, talking about their own observations and hearing about what others have observed helps children to make some sense of what they have found, to fit it into their understanding of the things just observed and of the others like them which they may have encountered previously. They may find that what others report differs from their own view, so they may want to return to observe more carefully, focusing on the particular feature that will decide the issue.

The move towards focusing is a sign of progress in developing observation skill. It is then appropriate to help this development with questions: do the snail shells all have the same number of turns? Is there any connection between the size and the number of turns? These questions encourage the children to focus the observations for themselves. Problems in which objects or events have to be placed in some sequence are useful for this purpose, for they demand that the children find and focus on the feature that determines the sequence.

The narrowing effect of focused questions should be moderated by more open ones: what else is different about the shells of the same type of snail? What things are the same about shells of different types? Answering these questions helps children to realise that their focused selective observation uses only part of the information that is available. It can prevent them becoming blinkered by existing ideas which lead them to observe only what they expect.

Box 9.4: Helping development in using observation

The teacher can help the development of ability to gather evidence through observation by:

- providing interesting materials or objects to observe and appropriate aids to observation (such as magnifiers)
- allowing sufficient time to observe them
- giving 'invitations to observe'
- encouraging children to make wide-ranging *and* focused observations (by comments and questions)
- enabling children to talk informally about their observations, to each other and to the teacher in a whole-class discussion.

Planning and conducting investigations

Planning is a complex skill requiring experience and ability to think through to the possible outcomes of actions. In practice it does not always precede carrying out an investigation. It is characteristic of young children that they think out what to do in the course of doing it; they do not anticipate in thought the results of actions, unless the actions are already familiar to them. So children need to be introduced to planning gradually, starting with simple problems which make no greater demand than just 'tell me what you're going to do'. By about the third year, more can be expected, such as the planning of a fair comparison, supported by a series of questions, orally or on a worksheet:

- What are we trying to find out?
- What are we going to change?

- What are we going to look at or measure?
- How will we make sure it is a fair test?

The teacher can 'scaffold' more detailed planning by identifying steps to be thought through. These will vary for different types of investigation (see Chapter 4). For a 'fair test' investigation, these steps are:

- defining the problem in terms of what is to be investigated
- identifying what is to change in the investigation (the independent variable)
- identifying what should be kept the same so that the effect of the independent variable can be observed (the variables to be controlled)
- identifying what needs to be observed (measured or compared) when the independent variable is changed (the dependent variable)
- considering how the evidence is to be used to solve the original problem.

For pattern-seeking investigations, the steps are:

- defining the problem in terms of what is to be investigated
- identifying and observing the variable of interest
- arranging these observations in sequence
- identifying and observing possible associated variables
- looking for other variables that follow the same sequence as the variable of interest.

In interpreting the results of a pattern-finding investigation, it is important to recognise that any pattern found between variables does not prove a cause–effect relationship. We return to this in relation to interpreting evidence below.

Although they should have the chance to plan an investigation quite frequently, children do not have to plan out every activity for themselves. It is particularly useful to provide guidance in planning in those investigations where they have only one chance to make the observations and mistakes cannot be easily rectified by starting again. This may apply to gathering information during visits or using materials that are strictly limited in availability.

Development of this skill can be aided by reviewing the steps after the investigation has been carried out, whether or not the children planned the investigation for themselves. This is best done during discussion when the equipment is still at hand. Questions that probe how decisions were made, whether fair comparisons were made, how measurements or observations could have been made more accurately, etc. can be asked without implying criticism. The supporting structure the teacher provides can be gradually reduced as children grasp what is involved in investigating. Children will gradually be able to take over responsibility for reviewing their work if the teacher introduces it as a regular part of the discussion that should follow any practical activity.

Box 9.5: Helping development in planning and conducting investigations

The teacher can help the development of skill in planning and carrying out investigations by:

- providing problems but not instructions for solving them, thus giving children the opportunity to do the planning

- supplying a structure (scaffolding) for the planning appropriate to the children's experience (in the case of fair-testing investigations, questions to take them through the steps of thinking about variables to change, to control and to observe)

- sometimes reviewing what is being done during an investigation in relation to what was planned, recognising that not everything can be anticipated beforehand

- always discussing activities at the end to consider how the method of investigation could have been improved with hindsight.

Interpreting evidence and drawing conclusions

Although this process is the key to children learning from their investigations, it is often neglected. Sometimes time runs out and the important discussion after the completion of practical work is not held. Children go on to the next activity without bringing together what they have already found (cf. Douglas Barnes's comment on p. 161). All investigations should begin with a clear idea of the problem or question under investigation; all should end with some statement of how the findings relate to the problem or question. But before such a statement can be made there are often several stages of bringing individual observations together, which is generally helped by looking for patterns.

So an important aspect of interpretation and drawing conclusions is looking for patterns that relate together observations or data that might otherwise remain disconnected from each other. The ability to do this enables children to make sense of a mass of information that would be difficult to grasp as isolated events or observations. But not all patterns are easily detected; they may be obscured by features that vary unsystematically. So, in helping children to search for patterns, it is useful to provide some activities where the patterns can be easily picked out. For example:

- the distance a toy car rolls before it stops when started on a ramp at different heights

- the pitch of a plucked stretched string when its length is changed

- the pitch of different notes made by striking bottles with different amounts of water in them.

Those who have difficulty will be helped by discussion and hearing what others have found, so arranging for children to talk about the patterns they find in their results is important. The way in which they refer to a pattern may indicate whether they are taking account of all the information. For example, children often describe the relation between the length and pitch of a plucked string in these ways:

- The longer the string the lower the note.
- The longest string gives the lowest and the shortest the highest.
- A long string gives a low note.
- If you change the length the note changes.

Each is correct, but the last three give less information than the first. The teacher's task is to find out whether children who give an incomplete account of the pattern have actually grasped it as a whole but cannot express it as a whole, or whether they do not see the pattern that links all the information, as in the first statement. There have to be opportunities therefore for a great deal of talking about patterns and about different ways of describing them. Generally, much too little time is used in this way.

Checking predictions against evidence is an important part of pattern-finding work, as well as contributing to an attitude of respect for evidence. So the organisation of this work has to allow for toing and froing between making observations or finding information and discussing it. Children might also be encouraged to speculate about the patterns they expect to find, before gathering data and checking carefully to see if there is evidence to support their ideas.

As children's ability to detect and express straightforward patterns becomes established their experience can be widened, taking in situations where the relation between two quantities is not an exact pattern. For example, there may well be a general relation between the size of people's feet and their height but there will be people who have larger feet than others who are shorter than they are. Discussion of these cases is useful in encouraging caution in drawing conclusions from patterns. Clearly, with foot size and height there is no cause–effect relation; the pattern shows only that these are features which tend to go together, though not invariably. This is probably because they are both related to other features, ones that determine growth. It often happens that a pattern is found between two things that each relate to a third variable, or a string of other variables, but have themselves no direct cause–effect relation. (Success in school and month of birth is an example, winter-born children tending to be more successful than summer-born children, until about the age of 11 or 12. There is nothing about the time of year that itself makes any difference; it may be related to time in school which in turn is related to success in school.)

This digression has been made to show that there are good reasons for resisting the temptation to draw conclusions about cause and effect from observed relations. Causes have to be established through controlled experimentation. Children cannot be expected to realise this, but when interpreting findings or information they can, and should be expected to, keep to the evidence.

It requires a delicate touch on the part of the teacher to encourage children, on the one hand, to try to relate together different pieces of information but, on the other hand, not to assume a type of relation for which there is no evidence. We also want children to try to explain the patterns and associations they find but to realise that when they do this they are going beyond the interpretation of evidence and making use of previous knowledge, or imagination, in their hypotheses.

Box 9.6: Helping development in interpreting evidence

The role of the teacher in encouraging children to interpret evidence and draw conclusions involves:

- making sure that they use their findings to address their original question or problem that was the reason for the investigation

- providing opportunities in the form of activities where simple patterns or more general trends can be found (practical work)

- enabling children to talk about their findings and how they interpret them (by questioning and listening)

- expecting them to check interpretations carefully and to draw only those conclusions for which they have evidence (discussion and practical work)

- organising for interpretations of findings to be shared and discussed critically.

Communicating, reporting and reflecting

The dual role of communicating, as a means of giving or gaining information and as an aid to thought, makes it a particularly important skill. But the fact that communication may be going on all the time may mean that no special effort is made to promote it. Recent re-emphasis on developing literacy has drawn attention to the fact that communication is going on all the time and that each subject area has a contribution to make. So we have to be concerned with two complementary aspects of communication in science:

- using it to develop general literacy skills

- using literacy skills to develop children's scientific understanding.

The way in which science activities can contribute to general literacy skills is well illustrated by Feasey (1999). She sets out examples of how science activities can be used in language lessons to encourage skills such as oral retelling of experiences, the use of labels and captions, using new vocabulary, using dictionaries, sequencing events, asking and answering questions, making notes and writing for various purposes and audiences. In the case of making notes, for example, the suggested science activity (based on an idea from the Nuffield Primary Science unit on Materials) is as follows:

Give children a sheet of paper divided into 6–8 sections. Ask them to tell, in a set of pictures, the story of an object, such as a spoon or a glass, from the origin of the material or materials of which it is made to the finished product.

Discuss with children their ideas on how a particular object was made, looking for similarities and differences. Ask them to justify what they have put, where possible drawing on evidence they might be able to offer, such as personal experience.

Provide children with access to either non-fiction books of an appropriate level or video or CD-ROM material. Ask them to use the reference material to find out the key stages in making the material under discussion.

(Feasey, 1999, p. 44)

In many such activities learning science and literacy skills are combined, although there may be a greater emphasis on one or the other. In this activity the discussion is particularly valuable to the development of ideas. Equally strong arguments are made for the value of writing to learning. But, as with talking, the fact that some kind of writing goes on all the time does not necessarily mean that children have opportunities for the kind that is most useful for their learning in science.

Few children spontaneously record what they are doing as they go along. As Wright (2004, p. 4) points out, 'not only are they keen to get on with the best bits, many of them have a strong conviction that they will remember it all, even repeated measures, so there is no need to write it down'. The use of a personal notebook and keeping a diary are devices for encouraging children to use writing to aid their memory and to help sort out their thoughts. For this purpose it is best if they are regarded as personal and not 'marked' by the teacher. The teacher, however, can make suggestions about what might go into the notebook – observations and particularly measurements, which may be quickly forgotten. Teachers who wish children to use these things have to arrange to supply not just the materials, but the incentive and the time to use them. Once they have experience of making a record, the children begin to realise the value as part of investigation and not just for reporting. As Wright suggests, a record helps children to become more detailed and accurate in their observation, notice patterns, remember what they have done so that they work more systematically and reflect on their work and learn more from it.

More formal written communication in science often involves use of non-verbal forms: graphs, charts and tabulated numbers. The techniques of using these are usually not difficult to learn; what is more difficult and more important is the selection of the appropriate form to suit particular purposes and types of information. Skill in selecting among possible symbolic representations comes with experience, but experience is more likely to bring development if it is discussed. The critical review of activities could, with advantage, include discussion of the form of presentation of findings. The teacher can also help in this matter by displaying in the classroom good examples of information appropriately and clearly presented.

Box 9.7: Helping development in communicating, reporting and reflecting

The teacher can help the development of communication, reporting and reflection skills by:

- organising the class so that children can work and discuss in groups

- providing a structure in the children's tasks which encourages group discussion and the keeping of informal notes

- allowing time for records to be made and used in reporting and reflecting

- introducing a range of techniques for recording information and communicating results using conventional forms and symbols

- discussing the appropriateness of ways of organising and presenting information to suit particular purposes.

COMMON STRATEGIES FOR PROCESS SKILL DEVELOPMENT

Looking back now over what has been said about the role of the teacher in regard to the development of process skills some repeated themes are apparent. There are certain aspects of the teacher's role that enable children to use and develop all the process skills. These are brought together in Box 9.8.

Box 9.8: Summary of common strategies for helping process skill development

Actions that teachers can take to help children to develop process skills include:

- providing opportunity for children to encounter materials and phenomena to explore at firsthand

- arranging for discussion in small groups and in the whole class about procedures that are planned or have been used, to identify alternatives and ways in which the approach to particular investigations might be improved

- providing access to alternative procedures through discussion, books, etc.

- setting challenging tasks while providing support (scaffolding) so that children can experience operating at a more advanced level

- teaching the techniques needed for advancing skills, including the use of equipment, measuring instruments and conventional symbols

- encouraging children, through comment and questioning, to check that their ideas are consistent with the evidence available

Box 9.8: Continued

- helping children to record in ways that support systematic working and review
- encouraging critical reflection on how they have learned and how this can be applied in future learning
- using questioning to encourage the use of process skills, for example:
  - What would you like to know about . . .?
  - Why do you think x is growing better than y?
  - What do you think will happen if . . .?
  - What differences do you notice . . .?
  - What will you do to find out . . .?
  - Have you found any connection between . . .?
  - What is the best way to show what you found?

The common factors in the approach to teaching for development of all the process skills constitute both an advantage and a disadvantage. The advantage is that if the teacher does put all these things into practice then the conditions exist for the various skills to be developed in step with each other; observation advances at the same time as interpretation and communication, for example. Gradually, the cumulative effect of successive activities builds up the skills.

This creates the case for what some might consider to be the disadvantage, that opportunities for process skill development have to be provided frequently, if not continuously. It is no use allocating one or two sessions to developing 'raising questions' or 'planning investigations' and then forgetting about these process skills. Not only will the skill drop out of use but it will probably be actively discouraged if an approach to teaching is adopted which excludes children raising questions and doing their own planning.

Table 9.1 attempts to bring together the components of the teacher's role in developing process skills and some of the purposes that each serves. It highlights the close interplay of development of ideas and process skills, since these aspects of the teachers' role anticipate those that help children to develop their ideas, as discussed in Chapter 11.

HELPING THE DEVELOPMENT OF SCIENTIFIC ATTITUDES

Attitudes are more generalised aspects of people's behaviour even than process skills. They can be said to exist only when a general pattern of reacting in certain ways to certain types of situation has been established. One observation of a child spontaneously

Table 9.1 Components and purpose of the teacher's role in process skill development

Role	Purposes
Providing the materials, time and physical arrangement for children to study and interact with things from their environment	For children to have the evidence of their own senses, to raise questions, to find answers to them by doing things, to have concrete experience as a basis for their thinking and to be able to check ideas they develop against the behaviour of real things
Designing tasks that encourage discussion among small groups of children	For children to combine their ideas about how they are gathering and interpreting evidence, to listen to others, to argue about differences and to refine their own ideas through explaining them to others
Discussing with children as individuals and in small groups	For children to explain how they arrive at their ideas; for teachers to listen, to find out the evidence children have gathered and how they have interpreted it, to encourage children to check findings and to review their activities and results critically
Organising whole-class discussions	For children to have the opportunity to describe their findings and ideas to others, to hear about others' ideas, to comment on alternative views and to defend their own; for teachers to offer ideas and direct children to sources that will extend the children's ideas and skills
Teaching the techniques of using equipment and conventions of using graphs, tables, charts and symbols	For children to have available the means to increase the accuracy of their observations and to choose appropriate forms of communication as the need arises
Providing books, displays, visits, visitors and access to other sources of information	For children to be able to compare their ideas with those of others, to have access to information that may help them to develop and extend their ideas and skills, to raise questions that may lead to further enquiry

checking a suggested conclusion by seeking more evidence is not a sufficient basis for assuming that the child has developed 'respect for evidence'. But if he or she did spontaneously check so often that one could confidently predict that he or she would do so in further instances, then the child might well be described as having this attitude.

As in the case of process skills, there is a great deal that is common in encouraging the development of different attitudes. They cannot be taught, for they are not things that children know or can do; rather they are 'caught', for they exist in the way people behave. They are transferred to children by a combination of example and selective approval of behaviour that reflects the attitude. Indeed, quite frequent reference has already been made to the encouragement of certain attitudes during the discussion of opportunities for process skill development and it must already be obvious that there is much in common in the approaches required to foster attitudes and skills. This is confirmed by looking briefly at ways of fostering the four attitudes that we have been discussing as goals of science education. These are summarised in Box 9.9.

The general strategies represented are for teachers to

- show an example of the attitudes in their own behaviour
- create a classroom climate that gives approval to the behaviour that signifies the attitude
- provide opportunity for the attitude to be shown
- provide time for children to complete their work to their own satisfaction
- make allowances for individual differences.

Box 9.9: Ways of fostering children's scientific attitudes

Curiosity
- Sharing in the excitement and questioning about things; 'wondering why' with the children.

- Welcoming children's questions and comments that show curiosity, storing these questions if they cannot be dealt with straight away and making sure of returning to them later.

- Providing new stimuli that will encourage curiosity; refreshing displays.

- Encouraging those who show fleeting curiosity as well as those whose interest is more sustained.

- Providing time for curiosity to be satisfied rather than frustrated.

Respect for evidence
- Teachers providing the evidence for the statements they make; not expecting children to accept them without evidence.

- Asking children to say what is behind their claims and statements; encouraging them to question each other and ask for evidence.

- Ensuring plenty of time for interpreting evidence and considering how sure they can be about conclusions drawn.

- Reminding children of evidence that they may have ignored.

- Providing time for discussion when findings are being reviewed so that alternative interpretations can be considered.

▶

Box 9.9: Continued

Flexibility in ways of thinking
- Participating in discussions about ideas that have changed, being prepared to say 'I used to think that . . . but now . . .'

- Avoiding associating ideas with individuals ('Daniel's idea') so that children do not defend ideas in order to protect self-esteem.

- Planning opportunities for children to think of alternative ideas; introducing new ideas to try.

- Providing ways of dealing with conflicting views that support the separation of ideas from their sources and treat all as open to test.

- Providing time for thinking about problems in different ways.

Sensitivity in investigating the environment
- Providing opportunities for children to look after living things, including invertebrates, and become aware of their needs.

- Showing, by checking frequently on any living things in the classroom, the importance of regular and appropriate care.

- Ensuring that living or non-living material (e.g. rocks) taken from the environment for study are returned to where they were found.

- Discussing and agreeing simple rules for protecting the environment, both living and non-living, when they are studying it or using it for recreation.

SUMMARY

This chapter has continued the discussion, begun in Chapter 8, of actions that can be taken to help children take the 'next steps' in learning, once these have been identified by gathering and interpreting evidence of their current achievements. The focus here has been on process skills and attitudes. In relation to process skills, the action appropriate to the various skills has been considered for each one separately. This has revealed a degree of commonality across the skills in relation to what needs to be provided. These common strategies have been summarised in Box 9.8 for process skills and Box 9.9 for scientific attitudes.

FURTHER READING

Discussion of questioning can be found in:

Elstgeest, J. (2001) The right question at the right time. In W. Harlen (ed.) *Primary Science: Taking the Plunge* (second edition). Portsmouth, NH: Heinemann.

Goldsworthy, A., Watson, R. and Wood-Robinson, V. (2000) *Investigations: Developing Understanding*. Hatfield: Association for Science Education.

Jelly, S. J. (2001) Helping children to raise questions – and answering them. In W. Harlen (ed.) *Primary Science: Taking the Plunge* (second edition). Portsmouth, NH: Heinemann.

Ideas for using science in developing children's literacy can be found in:

Feasey, R. (1999) *Primary Science and Literacy*. Hatfield: Association for Science Education.

Primary Science Review, 84, Sept/Oct 2004, which has several articles on the theme of 'Recording and Communicating'.

Chapter 10

Gathering and interpreting evidence of children's ideas

INTRODUCTION

Throughout this book the interdependence of concepts and process skills has been stressed. Children's learning experiences in science inevitably offer opportunities for both to be assessed and developed and both are likely to feature in lesson goals. However, they are different aspects of learning – concepts depending on subject matter and process skills on the way of dealing with the subject matter. Some separate treatment of how to gather and use evidence about these two aspects is thus appropriate. Chapters 8 and 9 considered these matters in relation to process skills. This chapter is the first of two looking at how the formative assessment cycle can be used in helping children's conceptual development. Here we are concerned with gathering and interpreting evidence; in Chapter 11 we complete the cycle by considering how to help children take further steps in their conceptual understanding in science.

We begin by discussing ways of gathering evidence about children's ideas. This is followed, in the second section, by some examples of children's ideas. As discussed in the third section, these examples show that there are general characteristics in the development of ideas across quite different content areas. These characteristics enable us to identify, in section four, a progression in ideas that can be used to identify 'next steps' in learning. Finally we emphasise the importance of planning to collect and use evidence to help development of children's scientific ideas.

WAYS OF GATHERING EVIDENCE OF CHILDREN'S IDEAS

There is some overlap between methods that can be used to gain access to children's ideas on the one hand and their skills and attitudes on the other, discussed in Chapter 8. There are, however, differences in emphasis. Conceptual understanding shows less in what children do than in how they talk about or represent what they think is happening. So the methods that are most useful in relation to accessing ideas are mainly:

- Listening to the words children use.
- Questioning.
- Discussing events.
- Studying non-written products.
- Asking for drawings and writing.
- Using concept maps.

Listening

Paying attention to the words children use when talking while they are working in groups gives evidence of how they are representing things to themselves. For example, words such as 'melt', 'dissolve', 'disappear' might be heard in activities on the solubility of substances and the way in which they are used indicates the meaning they have for the children. In the activity with different fabrics, briefly described in Box 8.3, the teacher heard the fabrics being variously described as 'manufactured', 'natural', 'see-through', 'strong'. The children's meaning for words such as these needs clarifying and the teacher might well do this by questioning later rather than interrupt the flow of activity at the time.

Questioning

As we discussed in Chapter 5, certain types of teachers' question are more effective than others in revealing evidence of children's ideas. The most effective forms of question for this purpose are open and person-centred questions.

Open questions invite an extended response, as opposed to closed ones, to which there is a short or one-word answer. This means that questions to which the only answers are 'yes' or 'no' are unlikely to be useful. A question such as 'What difference do you think it will make to how quickly the salt dissolves if the water is stirred?' is preferable to 'Will the salt dissolve more quickly if the water is stirred?'

Person-centred questions are phrased to ask directly for the children's ideas, not the 'right' answer. So, a question such as 'Why do you think the cress grows better in this soil?' is preferable to 'Why does the cress grow better in this soil?'

So the teacher's questions in the fabrics investigation (Box 8.3) would be:

- What is it about these materials that made you decide that they are manufactured?
- What do you think this was before it was made into this piece of cloth?

These kinds of questions are also very relevant in the discussion after practical work to help children reflect more consciously on the meaning of what they have found. They also help to reveal the extent to which ideas have been changed:

- Why did you think that one would be most wind-proof?
- What do you think it is about materials that make them waterproof?

Discussing events

It is helpful to have particular events to discuss in order to probe children's ideas. These can be suggested by real events or posters or devices such as concept cartoons. Events involving the children can be captured by a digital camera and displayed on a computer screen or even an interactive whiteboard (as in an example described by Lias and Thomas, 2003) as a basis for recalling the event and finding out what the children were thinking at the time.

Posters or 'big books' can be used as a basis for exploring children's ideas about a range of phenomena, either in a small group or a whole-class discussion. Concept cartoons (Keogh and Naylor, 1998) are drawings of particular situations in which cartoon characters express, in speech balloons, different ideas about what is going on. These ideas are based on research of various ideas children are likely to hold and so enable them to identify with the characters. Children can discuss in groups the evidence for and against each suggestion, thus revealing their own ideas. They are particularly useful for initiating 'children-only discussion', where the teacher's absence 'removes from their work the usual source of authority' (Barnes, 1976, p. 29) and compels them to express and evaluate their own ideas. The outcomes of the groups' discussion are reported later to the teacher and other children.

Studying non-written products

There are often products or artefacts at several stages of children's activity and all have the potential to indicate children's ideas. For example, the way a bridge is constructed to support something, the shape of a boat moulded from plasticine, or the way in which fabrics were put together in piles in the fabric-sorting activity. These things alone may not provide very reliable evidence, but they alert the teacher to discuss with the children their reasons for doing things in certain ways and these reveal their ideas.

Children's drawing and writing

Children's drawing, which may not at first seem to give particularly rich information about their ideas, can be made to do so if they are asked to draw not just what they see, but what they think is happening or what makes something work. The drawing shown later, in Figure 10.10 (on p. 140), might well have shown just the container of water with the level going down had the children been asked to 'draw what happened', but instead the request was 'draw what you think made the water go down'.

Framing a drawing task in a way that requires children to express their ideas makes a very great difference to the value of the drawing to both pupil and teacher. Figure 10.1 shows a considerable insight into a child's ideas about the needs of living things through asking for a drawing of 'where you think would be the best place for a snail to live'.

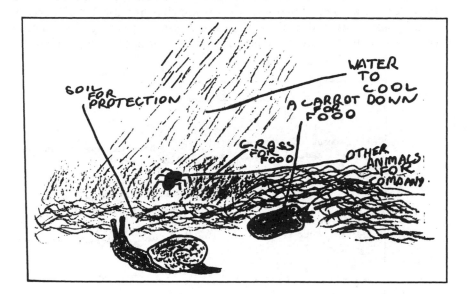

Figure 10.1 A young child's drawing (teacher annotated) of what snails need to live
Source: Unpublished SPACE research

For young children, expressing ideas through labelled drawings may not be easy, but it is then useful for the teacher to discuss the drawing with the child and to annotate it as a result of asking questions (as was done in Figure 10.1).

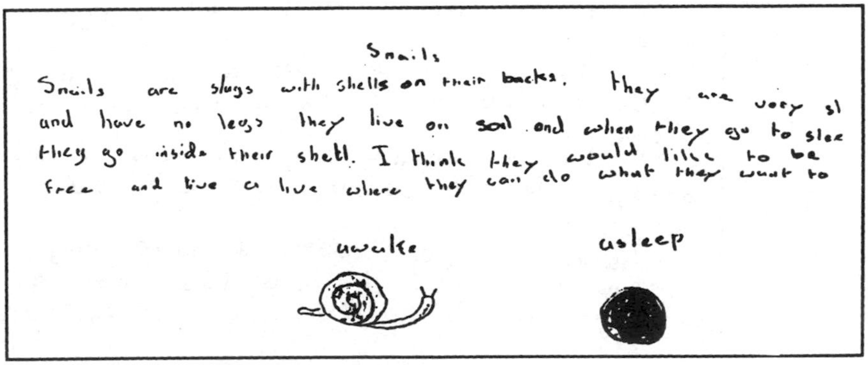

Figure 10.2 Ideas about snails and what they do

In the same way, children's writing may be made more productive for revealing children's ideas if the task requires ideas to be expressed. The same request that led to the drawing in Figure 10.1 led another child to produce the piece of writing in Figure 10.2.

Accounts of investigations also reveal information about ideas, providing the children are encouraged to reflect upon and not just report their findings. All too often, however, the account describes events somewhat uncritically. The account in Figure 10.3 by an 11-year-old, while it shows some understanding of insulation, makes no comment on the apparent rise in temperature during cooling of one of the cups.

> ## Water Experiment
>
> Donald, Sharon and I did an experiment to see which material could keep water hottest.
>
> We had four polystyrene cups and filled them with hot water. We put a different material over each one. We put polystyrene over one, polythene over another, cotton wool on another, and aluminium over the last.
>
> We left it for five minutes and checked the temperature with a thermometer.
>
> The foil was 50°, so were the polythene and the polystyrene, but the cotton wool was only 40°C.
>
> After another five minutes the cotton wool was the same, but the other three had fallen.
>
> We left them a further five minutes to get a final result.
>
> Aluminium foil came out at 41°C, the cotton wool had risen to 43°C and the polystyrene and the polythene were equal at 45°C.
>
> This shows that the polythene and polystyrene are best.
>
> I think polystyrene was best as it started off at 50°C and fell by only two or three degrees at a time.
>
> I think the polystyrene being best could of had something to do with the cups also being made from polystyrene.
>
> Insulation is good because it saves energy. If something isn't heated, it needs heated more often, but if something is insulated, heat can not escape so easily.

Figure 10.3 An 11-year-old's account of an investigation of insulation

Concept maps

Concept mapping has various meanings. In this context it is concerned with making links between concepts. As such it is a very direct way of gaining access to children's ideas, but needs to be carefully tailored to particular children to ensure that they are familiar with the words that are used. The approach is to represent relationships between words by means of arrows, thus 'ice' and 'water' are two words that can be linked to form a proposition that expresses the relationship between them, as in Figure 10.4.

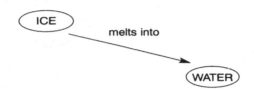

Figure 10.4 Representation of relationships used in concept maps

The arrow indicates the direction of the relationship; reversing it would mean 'water melts into ice' which does not make sense. When several concepts are linked together, the relationships form a web or map. The process is very easy even for the youngest children to grasp and the product gives some insight into the way they associate things together or see cause and effect. In some cases it helps to have the words written on cards so that they can be moved around. Arrows, also on cards, can be laid between words the children want to join. The linking words, written either by the child or by the teacher on behalf of the child, are important because it is the nature of the link that gives the clue to the way the child is making sense of the things.

The map in Figure 10.5 was drawn by 6-year-old, Lennie. After some activities about heat, the teacher listed words that they had been using and then asked the children to draw arrows to link them together and write 'joining words' on the arrows. From reading Lennie's map it would appear that he has useful ideas about the effects of heat but sees a thermometer as measuring both heat and temperature and has not distinguished between these two. Although this is to be expected from a child of this age, to be sure of the interpretation it would be necessary to talk through his map with him. As with drawings, the value of the product is greater if it is a basis for discussion between teacher and child.

Informal research reported by Atkinson and Bannister (1998) compared the information about their ideas from children's annotated drawings with that from concept maps. The study confirmed that concept mapping may be useful even with very young children. It also suggested that, in general, the older and more able children can express more ideas through concepts maps and the younger and less able express more ideas through annotated drawings.

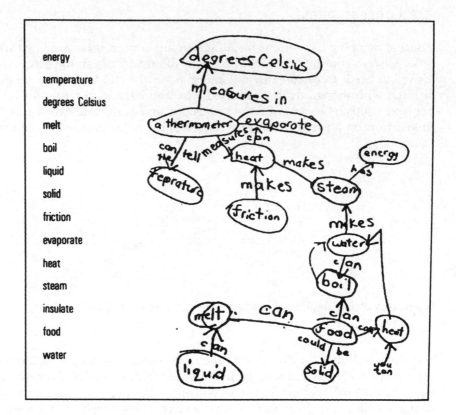

Figure 10.5 A 6-year old's concept map
Source: Harlen *et al.*, 2003, p. 128

SOME EXAMPLES OF CHILDREN'S IDEAS

These examples, covering the main ideas identified as goals of science education for 5- to 12-year-olds, come from research into children's ideas in various countries. Not all children will have the same ideas, of course, but teachers who have investigated their pupils' ideas in similar ways have found many of the same ideas. Being aware of the ideas children are likely to hold helps teachers to prepare to use these as a starting point for developing more scientific ideas.

Living things and the processes of life

The idea that there is a group of living things called 'plants' and another called 'animals', basic to biology, is not a simple matter of definition. Researchers who have interviewed children about what the word 'plant' means to them have found that it has a narrow meaning for many children. More than half of children up to the age of

10 in one study didn't consider a tree to be a plant; one 10-year-old explained 'it was a plant when it was little, but when it grows up it wasn't, when it became a tree it wasn't' (Osborne and Freyberg, 1985, p. 7). An even larger proportion considered that grass and dandelions were weeds, not plants, and that a carrot and a cabbage were not plants; they were vegetables.

In similar investigations of children's ideas about what are 'animals' it was found that many of the children considered only the larger animals, such as those found on a farm, in a zoo, or in the home as pets, to be animals. Research carried out by Bell and Barker (1982) involving interviews and a survey of children from age 5 to 17 years showed that children's initial idea of what is an animal is restricted to large land mammals. For instance, a high proportion of their sample of 5-year-olds recognised a cow as an animal and the proportion rose to 100 per cent by the age of 7 years. However, creatures such as worms and spiders were not considered to be animals by three-quarters of the 9-year-olds and only a slightly lower proportion of 12-year-olds. Only a fifth of the sample of 5-year-olds considered a human being to be an animal and this proportion rose to just over a half for 9- to 12-year-olds.

Research into children's ideas about the processes of life carried out by the SPACE project shows that young children become aware of the insides of their bodies, starting with the heart, as separate organs each with a single function. Later they come to perceive connecting channels between the organs which enable them to work together. When children were asked to draw on an outline of the human body what they thought was in their own bodies, it was found that children drew those parts that they could feel. For example, they identified the heart and bones. They also were aware of the brain. But in general they did not know about organs such as kidneys, lungs, intestines, which are not sensed (SPACE Research Report, 1992).

A further investigation by the SPACE team of children's ideas about the conditions that a plant needs to grow also showed the impact of their everyday experience. Children of 6 or 7 years indicated that the plant needed water or soil or Sun, with few mentioning all three. Older pupils tended to replace 'Sun' by light and heat and the number of requirements mentioned increased with age. The role of the soil in helping plants to live was regarded as simply being for support; very few children indicated that it would provide 'food' or substances needed by the plant.

Interaction of living things and their environment

In preparation for some work on camouflage some 12-year-olds were asked for their ideas about why brown bears are found in mountains in America and white bears in the Arctic. Many of the written answers used the word 'camouflage' (deliberately not used in the question) as if it were an explanation, for example, as in Figure 10.6. Those who attempted more of an explanation gave this in terms of human activity, as in Figure 10.7. However, a few mentioned climate and some, as in Figure 10.8, the predator–prey relationship.

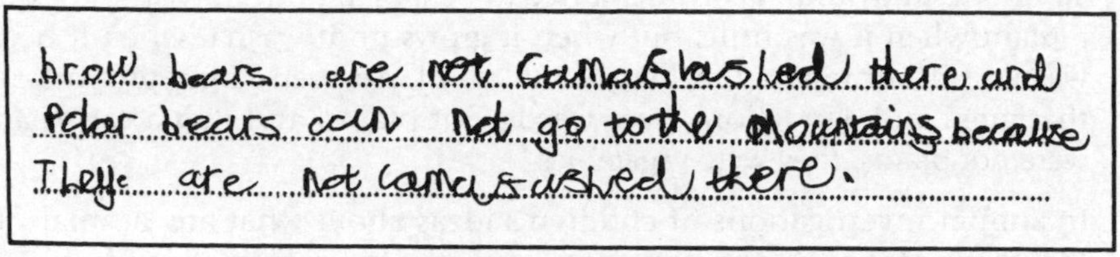

> brow bears are not CamaBlasled there and
> Pdar bears ccln not go to the ohauntains because
> Theye are not camasushed there.

Figure 10.6 A 12-year-old's answer to: 'Why do you think you don't find white bears in the mountains and brown bears in the Arctic?'

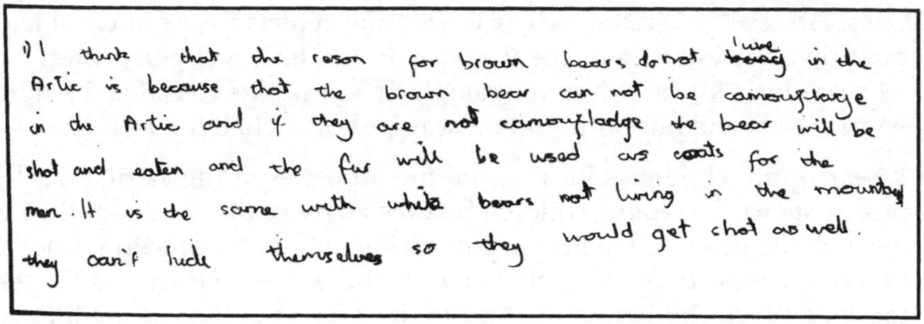

> 1) I think that the reson for brown bears do not luve in the Artic is because that the brown bear can not be camouflauje in the Artic and if they are not camouflaudge the bear will be shot and eaten and the fur will be used as coats for the man. It is the same with white bears not living in the mountay they can't hide themselves so they would get chot as well.

Figure 10.7 An 11-year-old girl's answer

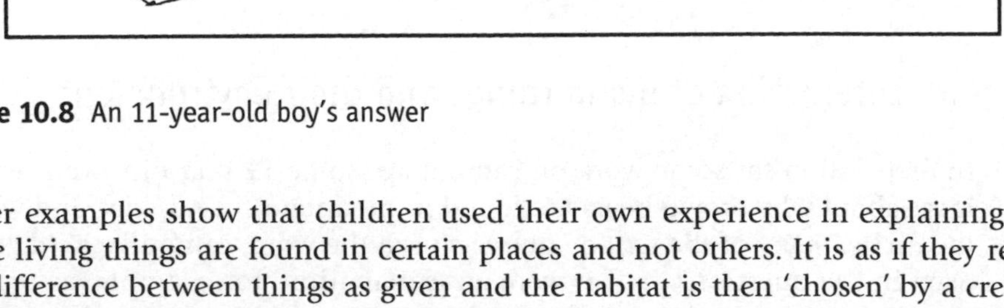

> 1 White Bears would show up very well on a mountain so their pray would no whole they were and Visa versa.
>   Example
> Brown Bear in arctic   White bear in mountams
>   White   Brown Bear in mountains.
>   Bear in arctic

Figure 10.8 An 11-year-old boy's answer

Other examples show that children used their own experience in explaining why some living things are found in certain places and not others. It is as if they regard the difference between things as given and the habitat is then 'chosen' by a creature to suit it.

Materials

The ideas children have about the use of materials for various purposes are at first circular: we use paper for writing on because paper is good for writing on. There seems to be no explanation needed in terms of properties of the material, just that it is chosen because it serves the purpose. Later the use of materials is recognised as being directly related to the children's experience of the properties required by various objects. For example: chalk is used for writing on the blackboard because it is soft and white; glass is used for windows because you can see through it; wood is used for doors and furniture because it is strong, firm, keeps out the rain and doesn't tear or bend (SPACE Research Report, 1991b).

In relation to changes in materials, too, there is a stage in which there seems to be no need for explanation. Children use their experience of finding rust under bubbles of paint on metal gates or bicycle frames to conclude that rust is already there under the surface of metal, hence there is no need to explain what causes it to form. For example, an 8-year-old wrote 'Screws are made of metal. Rust comes out of metal' (ASE, 1998).

Air, atmosphere and weather

Understanding of clouds, rain, frost and snow depend on appreciating that water can exist as vapour in the air. Without this, their ideas about clouds depend on some mechanism such as 'sucking up' water as in Figure 10.9. Here the 'reason' for rain is that 'the flowers need water'.

Figure 10.9 A young child's ideas about rain
Source: SPACE Research Report (1993, p. 67)

Young children do not see the need to explain why water dries up – 'it just goes by itself' (SPACE Research Report, 1990a). Later some recognise the effect of the Sun, but give it a very active role, such as in Figure 10.10.

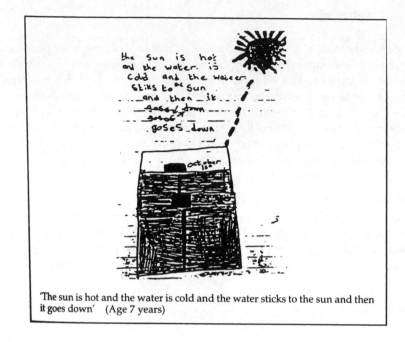

'The sun is hot and the water is cold and the water sticks to the sun and then it goes down'   (Age 7 years)

Figure 10.10 Evaporation according to a 7-year-old

Source: SPACE Research Report (1990a, p. 29)

Some children even included what looked like a drinking straw reaching from the Sun to the water! In the views of some children the clouds have this active role, being permanent features ready to receive evaporated water:

> When the water evaporates it goes on a cloud and then the cloud goes in any place and later it will go out as rain. It will keep going until it is all gone and then it will go to another place with water and do the same. The cloud is like a magnet so the water goes through the cracks and goes up, that is what I think.

(SPACE Research Report, 1990a, p. 30)

The use of the word 'evaporates' here is ambiguous (it seems to cover both evaporation from the ground and condensation in the cloud). It is common for children to speak of 'water rising' and the clouds 'bursting' to give rain without mentioning the processes of evaporation and condensation. Attempts to help children understand the water cycle can cause confusion if they do not take into account the ideas the children may have about evaporation and about clouds.

Rocks, soil and materials from the Earth

Quite young children are aware that rocks are found under and above ground. Their ideas are influenced by what they see around them and they often restrict the use of the word 'rock' to pieces that are jagged, not smooth, large, rather than small and usually grey but sometimes coloured. Younger children attribute changes in rocks to human action, while older children are more likely to recognise erosion by wind and sea, or just 'ageing'.

Children interpret the word 'soil' as material in which there are pieces of decayed plants and rock fragments, rather than seeing these as constituents. Soil is most commonly associated with growing plants, at first as a means of support and later as being the source of food and water. Clearly, understanding that water in soil dissolves material that is then taken up by plants is necessary if they are to recognise the need to replenish these nutrients and the effects of drought and water erosion.

The Earth in space

Children's early ideas about the movement of the Sun and Moon derive from their perceptions of the apparent rapid movements of the positions of these bodies caused by the children's own movement from one place to another. If they stand in the shadow of a tree the Sun appears to be behind the tree. If they move out of the shadow the Sun no longer appears to be behind the tree. The fact that they can see the Sun wherever they are gives them the idea that it follows them around. Older children can distinguish this apparent rapid and irregular movement from the regular patterns of movement day by day, although these will inevitably be interpreted as the Sun moving round the Earth.

In their drawings children represent the Moon and stars in conventional manner – a crescent moon and pointed stars – since they frequently see representations like this. They also see globes, drawings and even photographs from space, which show that the Earth is spherical and this experience is reflected in their drawings (SPACE Research Report, 1996). However, there is evidence that they may not really be convinced that this is the case and some ask: why don't we fall off the surface of the globe? This question in itself indicates the children's views of what causes things to fall and what 'down' means in the context of space. Ideas about gravity have to be brought in to give a convincing answer to this dilemma, illustrating yet again the interconnections between different ideas needed to explain the phenomena around us (Vosniadou, 1997).

Forces and movement

The relationship of forces acting on an object to its movement is a difficult area for primary science because so often the accepted scientific view is counter-intuitive. For example, it is a matter of everyday experience that a moving object such as a ball rolling along the ground stops moving apparently 'by itself' without any agent to stop it. But this ignores the forces exerted at the contact with the ground and with the air. Many forces like these are 'hidden', including the important one of gravity, and are ignored by children in making sense of why things stop moving. Thus a ball thrown upwards into the air will be thought to have an upward force on it when it is moving up, zero when it reaches its highest point and a downward force when it is moving down.

Gravity is a universally experienced force and it is perhaps because it is always present that children do not take it into account. Things that are dropped fall downwards 'naturally'. The SPACE research (SPACE Research Report, 1998) showed that various kinds of activities designed to help children to see gravity as a force acting towards the Earth from all directions, resulted in a large shift in primary children's recognition of gravity as a force pulling things down, although few described the force as being towards the centre of the Earth.

Gunstone and Watts (1985) identified some 'intuitive rules' from their review of research into ideas about force:

- Children identify force with living things – there is some intention involved.

- Objects in constant motion need a constant force to keep them moving in the same way.

- An object that is not moving has no forces acting on it.

- A moving body has a force acting on it in the direction of motion.

These are all ideas that have certain logic in relation to limited everyday experience and are held by many secondary school pupils and not a few adults. Their apparent 'common sense' makes them difficult to change.

Floating is a phenomenon depending on the balance of forces acting on an object in water, but children often consider that other factors are involved, such as the speed of movement of the object and the depth of water. Biddulph and Osborne (1984) asked children about a range of possible variables that might affect floating, such as the size of the object or the depth of water. The results show a definite trend with age. Only 10% of the 8-year-olds thought that a whole candle would float at the same level as a short piece of the candle. This proportion was 30% for 10-year-olds and 65% for 12-year-olds. Even at the age of 12 years, however, a quarter of the children thought the full-length candle would float lower than the short piece. To investigate the effect of changing the depth of water the children were shown a cross-sectional drawing of a boat being launched in shallow water and them moving to deep water. Half of the 8-year-olds said it would float lower in the deeper water; about a fifth of 10- and 12-year-olds also gave this answer.

Energy sources and uses

Light

Investigations of children's ideas about light have shown remarkable similarity in relation to the role of the eye in seeing things. Children who are past the stage of believing that objects no longer exist if they are hidden from view or if they close their eyes, nevertheless describe the process of seeing as if it is their eyes that produce the light that makes the objects appear. Figure 10.11 shows a 10-year-old's drawing of how you see a bottle standing on a table when the light is switched on.

Figure 10.11 The 'active eye'

It is perhaps understandable that the eye is seen as an active agent rather than a receiver, for this fits the subjective experience of 'looking'. When we choose to look at something we do feel our eyes turn as if we are the active agent in the process, and indeed the arrow from receiver to object does represent the line of sight.

A variation on this idea is to regard the presence of light as somehow activating the eye, as described in Figure 10.12.

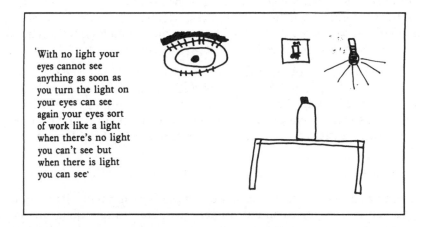

'With no light your eyes cannot see anything as soon as you turn the light on your eyes can see again your eyes sort of work like a light when there's no light you can't see but when there is light you can see'

Figure 10.12 The eye as activated by light

Figure 10.13 is typical of the responses from a class of younger children (7- to 9-year-olds). All but four of the 27 in the class showed light spreading to the eye and the bottle but nothing between bottle and eye. The children's interpretation of the situation does not take into account the need for light to fall on the object and to be reflected by it, or to be given out by it, for it to be seen.

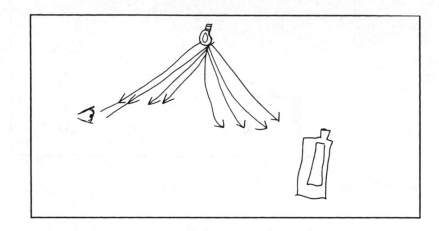

Figure 10.13 An 8-year-old's view of how we see

Sound

Ideas about the ear's role as a receiver in hearing sound are formed more readily than the equivalent ideas about the eye. This may be because the sources of sounds are more obvious than the source of light that enables objects to be seen by reflecting rather than emitting light. However, children have different ideas about the transmission of sound and the part played by 'vibrations'. Often vibrations are linked with the source when they are directly felt but not otherwise.

Many children do not identify vibrations with sound but make a distinction between them. Describing how a 'string telephone' made with yoghurt pots and string works, a 10-year-old wrote: 'The voices went to the string and were then transferred into vibrations which went down the string and when it got to the other yoghurt pot and were then transferred back into a voice' (unpublished SPACE research).

Electricity

Enquiries into children's ideas about simple electric circuits have shown that the representation of a single connection between battery and bulb, as in Figure 10.14(a), is persistent. It is even produced by pupils who have had experience that it does not work in practice (SPACE Research Report, 1991a). The representation in Figure 10.14(b) is arguably a more sophisticated view, but one which fails to recognise that there are two different connections to complete the circuit within the bulb. Figure 10.14(c) shows two connections but ones which would not work.

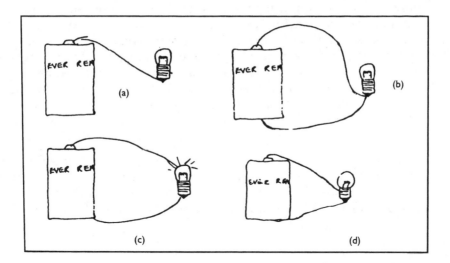

Figure 10.14 Children's ideas about connections in a simple circuit

The SPACE team reports a marked increase in the correct connections depicted following activities in which the children were asked first to discuss and draw how they would make connections, then to try out their plan.

GENERAL CHARACTERISTICS OF CHILDREN'S IDEAS

These examples have not been presented as a formal review of research but as indicative of findings of many different researchers working in a variety of contexts. The fact that similar ideas are found from working with children of quite different backgrounds suggests that the ideas are the product of children's reasoning about things that are experienced everywhere – the weather, the variety of living things, the materials and so on.

It is easy to see how, from a child's point of view, these ideas make sense of their limited experiences. Indeed they make more sense than the 'scientific' view, which is often counter-intuitive. The scientific view frequently makes use of ideas based on things that are not observable by children, such as water vapour, unseen forces, vibrations in air, etc. For example, the notion that moving things come to a stop if you stop pushing them suggests that it is 'natural' for movement to stop, whereas the scientific view is that there must be a force to stop the movement.

It also seems that the everyday usage of words has a considerable effect on children's concepts. This is particularly strong in the case of the concept of 'animal'. For example, notices in shops saying 'No animals allowed' would reinforce a narrow view of the notion of animal. So would the label 'animal house' in a zoo and the distinction between animals and fish which tends to be part of the common usage of the words.

These everyday ways of using the word conflict with the 'correct' use, based on the common features shared by all animals. The conflict can have serious consequences in children's misunderstanding if there is any uncertainty as to which meaning of the word is being used in a particular instance. A teacher can do nothing to prevent the word being used loosely in everyday situations, but can do something to find out what meaning the word conveys to the children. Teachers can help children to form the scientific idea (of 'animal', or 'energy' or other words having a scientific meaning different from everyday use) and at the same time make them aware that this is different from the everyday meaning. We discuss the use of words in Chapter 11.

Given the way their ideas are formed, it is not surprising that children's ideas have several shortcomings when compared with the scientific view, as the examples have illustrated. It is useful to examine these shortcomings since they give clues as to how to help children develop their ideas. Box 10.1 summarises the most obvious ones.

Box 10.1: Characteristics of children's own ideas

- Their ideas are based on necessarily limited experiences that provide only partial evidence (so they may well consider rust to be within metals if they have only paid attention to it when it appears under paint or flaking chrome plate).

- They are based on what children perceive through their senses rather than the logic, which may suggest a different interpretation (so if the Sun appears to move around and follow them, then they think it does move in this way).

- Younger children particularly focus on one feature as cause for a particular effect rather than the possibility of several factors (they identify 'Sun' or 'water' as the conditions needed for living things to grow healthily rather than a combination of factors).

- Some ideas are tied to a particular context, ignoring other contexts where the same idea may apply (they may explain evaporation of water from the tank in a different way from evaporation of water from washing on a clothes line).

- Some ideas are based on insecure reasoning not scientific reasoning (for example, if they made genuine predictions based on their ideas, these ideas would be disproved; instead they may 'predict' what they know to fit the idea).

- Some ideas are expressed in words without a grasp of their meaning (for example, 'floating', 'vibration' and 'evaporation').

- Some ideas are retained in the face of contrary evidence because no alternative view makes sense to them (they may adjust their idea to fit new evidence rather than give it up, as in the idea that 'light turns the eye on').

These characteristics give leads to ways of helping the development of ideas, so we will return to them in Chapter 11. At this point we turn to the interpretation of the children's ideas.

INTERPRETING EVIDENCE OF CHILDREN'S IDEAS

How can the evidence of the children's ideas be interpreted in terms of development towards the big ideas of science that are the goals of science education? How can we decide the next steps they need to take in this development? Answers to these questions depend on how we view progression in the development of ideas.

A progression in development or the sequence of teaching?

As in the case of process skills development, the question of progression is controversial, but for different reasons. For a start, however, we can get out of the way questions of whether, say, concepts concerning living things develop earlier or later than those about magnets or circuits. This will depend entirely on when and how these topics are encountered. Arranging them in a curriculum sequence is a matter of convention and convenience rather than of developmental considerations. Recalling Bruner's comment (Chapter 4, p. 46), all that is necessary to teach anything at any stage is to present the topic through activities that take account of children's ways of thinking.

However, development of ideas within a topic depends on more than the order in which they are taught. For example, ideas about sound are typically developed within the 5–12 age range in this sequence:

1 Sounds are heard through our ears.

2 Sounds are produced by vibrating objects.

3 Pitch and loudness depend on the way that the source vibrates.

4 Sound can travel through different materials and through some better than others.

5 Sound transfers energy and can be changed into other forms of energy.

The order of acquiring the first three of these ideas might well be a result of teaching in a particular sequence. Sequences that seem logical to adults are built into curriculum materials, and they ensure that there is some rationale for the order in which topics are encountered and thus for deciding appropriate next steps at a particular point. These sequences are no less useful for formative assessment within a topic on account of being the result of teaching rather than some underlying cognitive development. However, the fourth idea, the notion of sound travelling through different materials, brings together a number of ideas from difference experiences. The fifth one, 'sound as energy', is an even bigger idea that requires ideas about energy to be linked with earlier ideas about sound. Thus there is an overall sequence here in the degree of abstraction and breadth of application of the idea.

Similarly, looking across the various concepts discussed earlier in this chapter, the development can be seen as one of creating bigger, more encompassing ideas that explain a wide range of related phenomena from the earlier, smaller, ideas that explain only a few particular instances. It is this overall development that we should be seeking to describe and assist through formative assessment.

A general description of progression in ideas

This argument suggests that the progression in ideas can be expressed in general terms that can be applied to any specific ideas. Such generic indicators of progression are proposed in Box 10.2.

Box 10.2: Generic indicators of progression in ideas

Things that children do that are indicators of progression in ideas:

1. Offer a description only with no attempt to explain a situation.

2. Use a preconceived non-scientific idea to explain a situation or make a prediction.

3. Name a relevant idea (for example, 'friction', 'gravity') without explaining its relationship to the situation.

4. Use a relevant idea to explain a specific situation but not other situations where it also applies.

5. Use a relevant idea to explain several related experiences or situations.

6. Refer to a 'bigger' idea that explains a number of linked phenomena.

7. Use a bigger idea to predict events not yet encountered.

These generic statements can be 'translated' into a series of statements about the development of particular ideas that are the goals of work in certain topics. For example, if the goal is to develop ideas about condensation, the progression is likely to show in children:

1 just describing, for instance, 'mist' on a cold window when you breathe on it

2 saying 'it makes the window sweat'

3 saying 'its condensation'

4 explaining in terms of the window being cold and the breath warm, but unable to explain why a mirror mists over in a warm bathroom when someone takes a shower or bath

5 explaining that condensation may happen when a surface is colder than the air

6 linking condensation to water vapour in the air as well as the cooling of the air on a surface

7 predicting how condensation would depend on the water vapour in the air and on the temperature difference of air and surface.

Of course, a scientist will see that these ideas are still incomplete and need refinement. Further understanding of what is a complex phenomenon comes later, but developing ideas this far is a foundation for that further learning. Understanding is 'a continuous function of a person's knowledge' (White and Gunstone, 1992). It is not a dichotomy (not a matter of 'we either understand or we don't') nor a linear process (gradual advance from not understanding to understanding). Understanding grows as ideas become 'bigger', linking more phenomena, and thus being more powerful in explaining things. However, it clearly has to keep pace with experience and younger children are satisfied with 'smaller' ideas until their experience extends. We should not try to explain things that children have no knowledge of nor try to give ideas that they are unable to use. It is essential to safeguard children's enjoyment in understanding.

Using the generic indicators

For an example of the use of the generic indicators of progression in relation to specific ideas, we can look back at the evidence in Figures 10.6–10.8 of different children's ideas about camouflage. In Figure 10.6 the child writes about the bears being 'camouflaged' as if this were an explanation. The next steps for this child are first to try to explain how this idea accounts for the situation, then to apply it to other similar situations. In Figure 10.7 the idea of camouflage is explained in terms of the animals hiding themselves, but there is an indication of a conscious decision by the animal. The next step might be to clarify and if necessary challenge this view. Figure 10.8 gives evidence of using the idea of camouflage to explain both situations and of linking it to the animals being visible to their prey when hunting. The next step for this child may be to go further into considering the bigger idea about predators in which camouflage plays a part.

Attending to what children write and say

Before leaving the subject of interpreting evidence it is worth pointing out that using children's written work – and indeed their spoken words – requires attention to detail. Teachers have a great deal of work to look through and if they try to give attention to all of it, there may inevitably be some that is only read quickly rather than in detail. It's easy to miss a great deal of useful information because teachers have read so many similar things before. For the purpose of formative assessment, which we are considering here, tasks need to be set thoughtfully, as suggested on page 132, completed thoughtfully by the children and reviewed thoughtfully by both. Fewer pieces of work of this kind are more valuable than more routine tasks that are regularly marked and probably not used further. This is linked to the final topic of this chapter – planning to assess children's ideas.

PLANNING TO ASSESS CHILDREN'S IDEAS

When it comes to assessing children's ideas, the opportunities are far less frequent than the opportunities for assessing process skills, which are part of every activity to some degree. Ideas are linked to the subject matter and particular ideas will tend to be expressed in activities relating to the appropriate subject matter. Thus the opportunities to assess ideas have to be taken when they occur. This means assessing as many children as are working on that subject matter at any one time. Fortunately it is far more feasible to use the products of children's work for assessing ideas than it is for assessing process skills. Children's reports, other writing and drawing and other products can be collected and studied after the event. This is not to deny the importance of the context, which should be noted, and the added value that comes if the work can be discussed with the children. The type of feedback that is most helpful is discussed in Chapter 12. First, in Chapter 11, we look at how to help children to take the next steps that have been identified.

SUMMARY

In this chapter we have considered how, in the context of formative assessment, evidence of children's scientific ideas can be gathered and interpreted. Several ways of gathering evidence have been discussed and examples given of the ideas these are likely to reveal in children aged 5–12. Some general characteristics of children's ideas were drawn out from these descriptions and will be used in the next chapter to inform ways of helping the development of 'bigger' and more scientific ideas.

We have considered how the progression in children's ideas can be described and identified a set of generic indicators which can be applied to specific ideas that are the goals of children's science activities. Some examples of how these can be used have been given. Finally we noted the value of planning children's tasks so that they reveal their ideas and of scrutinising what they produce for evidence of their ideas.

FURTHER READING

Examples of children's concept maps, annotated drawings and other ways of gathering evidence about their ideas are given in:

Goldsworthy, A. (2000) *Raising Attainment in Primary Science*. Oxford: GHPD.

Chapter 11

Helping the development of scientific ideas

INTRODUCTION

Chapter 10 looked at how evidence of children's ideas collected for formative assessment can be interpreted to identify the next steps in learning. In this chapter we look at the teacher's role in helping children to take these next steps. This is at the heart of teaching and learning. Developing understanding of ideas, which is the focus of this chapter, has to involve the development and use of process skills and is influenced by attitudes. So the development of these skills and attitudes has itself got to be the focus of teaching, as we discussed in Chapter 9. In practice, developments of skills and ideas go on at the same time and it is only for clarity and convenience that we are treating them separately here.

We have argued that knowing what children's ideas are is essential to helping their learning, but it does not necessarily indicate what to do in specific cases. How to help children take forward their ideas depends on the particular circumstances and on what the ideas are. It is not often possible to prescribe in advance specific actions that will be effective. Therefore a teacher may have to decide this on the spot, drawing on a 'toolbox' of strategies. This chapter is about what is in this toolbox. It begins by deriving some general strategies from considering the characteristics of children's ideas. We then discuss and give some examples of these strategies in action, paying particular attention to the use of language and dialogue in science.

GENERAL STRATEGIES FOR HELPING CHILDREN TO DEVELOP THEIR IDEAS

In setting out a range of strategies teachers can use to help the development of ideas, we need to keep in mind the direction of the progression we are trying to encourage and the characteristics of the ideas children are likely to hold.

The overall direction of progression was suggested in Box 10.2 (p. 148). From ideas that can be shown to explain specific events or situations, progress is towards explaining a greater range of linked events, gradually forming ideas that are 'bigger', more widely applicable and useful in explaining new as well as familiar events.

The characteristics of children's ideas were summarised in Box 10.1 (p. 146). Each of the points made there indicates a limitation of children's experience or thinking and so provides a clue to helping development. Table 11.1 suggests action that can be taken in relation to each one.

Table 11.1 Action linked to the characteristics of children's ideas

Characteristic	Action to help progress in ideas
1. Based on limited experience	Provide experience of situations that help children to modify or extend their ideas by testing them. For example, give a range of large things that float and small ones that sink, to test their view that size determines whether objects float
2. Based on perceptions not reasoning	Help children to give attention to the processes of change, not just to the initial and final states. Ask them to draw a sequence of events or reverse a process, where possible; for example, pouring water into containers of different shapes and back again
3. Focused on one of several relevant features	Discuss all the things that might be relevant; have children listen to others' ideas; scaffold by asking about the possible effect of additional features; for example, whether the plant needs air as well as daylight
4. Linked to specific context	Ask them to consider whether the idea that explains one event might also explain another; for example, whether the idea of water condensing from their breath onto a cold window might explain the misting of a mirror in a bathroom
5. Based on insecure reasoning	Give help in developing process skills, as suggested in Chapter 9
6. Use words without understanding their meaning	Ask for examples of what they mean by words that are used incorrectly; for instance, 'melting', 'dissolving'. Explain scientific words using examples and link them to the 'everyday' words that the children use
7. Lack of convincing alternative ideas	Give access to alternative ideas from other children, books, and other information sources. Scaffold new ideas to explain events that their ideas don't explain

Looking across the types of action suggested in Table 11.1 it is possible to identify them as parts of four broad strategies:

- Extending children's experience (1, 4).

- Helping children to test their ideas. This includes linking together small ideas relating to specific instances to make bigger ones (2, 4, 5).

- Providing access to alternative ideas. These will come from a range of sources, including other children and the teacher; taking them on board may involve 'scaffolding' (3, 7).

- Promoting communication, dialogue and reflection. This involves the role of language in the development of shared understandings (3, 6).

We now consider what each of these mean in practice and give some examples of their applications in particular situations.

EXTENDING CHILDREN'S EXPERIENCE

Children's experience is clearly more limited than that of adults and a major role of science for younger children is to extend that experience so that they have more to draw upon in testing out and developing their ideas. For example, it is reasonable to hold the hypothesis that rust may originate inside the body of a metal if a child has only ever seen the exposed surfaces of metal objects. An 8-year-old girl interpreted her observations that the part of a nail that had been in water for a week went rusty as shown in Figure 11.1. Cutting through a rusted nail may be all that is needed to enable the girl to see that the evidence does not support this idea; noticing that the rust is only on the outside might lead her to another idea.

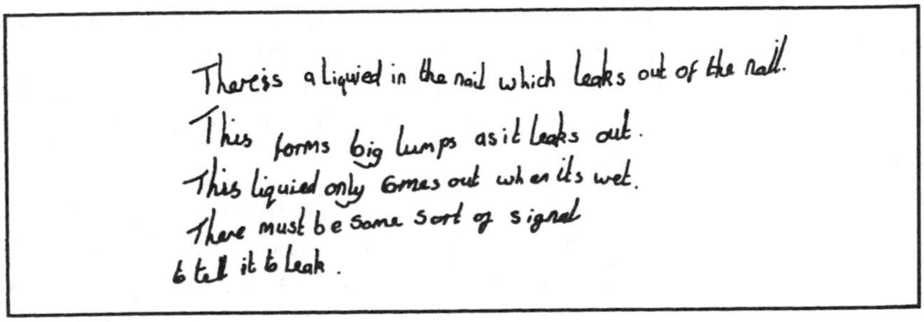

There is a liquied in the nail which leaks out of the nail.
This forms big lumps as it leaks out.
This liquied only comes out when its wet.
There must be some sort of signal
to tell it to leak.

Figure 11.1 An 8-year-old's writing about rust

Source: ASE (1998)

The teacher's role includes providing gradually extended experience as a matter of routine. This can be through classroom displays, which are added to as a topic proceeds: through posters and photographs mounted on the walls; information books at the right level for reference in the book corner; through visits, visitors and full use of the school buildings as resources for observation and activity; through film, CD-ROMs and other information technologies.

Against this background of regularly varied experience, teachers have to introduce specific information and activities in response to particular ideas, such as in the case of the rusting nails. In another example, after some children expressed the belief that plants do not grow during the day but only at night, their teacher introduced 'fast-growing plants' into the classroom. These plants grow so quickly that a measurable difference can be detected during a school day, so the children's idea could be tested. There was the further value that, because their life cycle takes only a few weeks, the change from buds to flowers and the setting of seeds can be experienced in a time-scale that has an impact on children's understanding of cycles of growth and reproduction.

HELPING CHILDREN TO TEST THEIR IDEAS

Extending children's experience helps them test their ideas, but sometimes they do not use information that is already available to them. If we think about how children arrive at their ideas, it is often the case that they have taken account only of certain evidence and ignored anything that is contradictory, or that they have not compared like with like. For example, as noted on p. 146, the children's idea that the eye is the active agent in seeing by sending out beams to what is seen is only tenable in relation to a limited range of experiences. It will not easily explain how the brightness and colour of things can be changed in different lighting conditions. Or, the idea that wooden blocks can be magnetic (Chapter 2) would hardly stand up to testing a prediction that, if magnetic, they should be able to attract materials that magnets attract.

An important part of a teacher's role in science is to set up the expectation that all ideas have to be tested, not just the children's but any the teacher proposes or those found in books. If this becomes routine then there will be no implied criticism in asking children to 'find a way to see if your idea works'. Once accepted, the teacher can help children to express their ideas in a way that can be tested and to gather and interpret evidence in a systematic way that ensures that ideas are properly tested. In other words, the focus is then on the way in which they use process skills and attitudes, as discussed in Chapter 9.

Not all tests of children's ideas will be of the kind suggested in books of scientific activities, and the teacher should be prepared to be as imaginative as the children in devising ways to address unexpected ideas. The example in Box 11.1 is a case in point.

We have described the development of ideas in terms of moving from small ideas that explain specific events to 'bigger' ones that can be used to explain a wide range of experiences. The change in thinking required is not just in the number of events that can be understood. There is also a qualitative change in ideas. In science, the aim is to arrive at ideas that are context-independent. This means, for example, an idea of what makes things float that can be used for all objects and all liquids, regardless of when or where. To move from realising why a particular object floats to the bigger idea of floating is a difficult transition, and if it is taken too far too quickly children will lose the link with their own ideas. So it is important that ideas are expanded in step with children's experience and do not run ahead of this.

Box 11.1: Children's testing of their own and others' ideas

A small aquarium tank was left uncovered to explore the children's ideas about evaporation. Among the children's suggestions for why the water level went down was that mice were drinking from their tank at night. Asked how they would test this, the children suggested leaving some cheese beside the tank. Evidence of nibbling of the cheese, they said, would be a test of their idea about the participation of the mice. The teacher helped them to carry out this test. Untouched cheese but continued loss of water forced them to consider an alternative explanation. The teacher helped them to do so by turning the children's thinking to water disappearing from clothes hung out to dry, asking the children to think about the similarities between the two events. Since they acknowledged that the water from the clothes went into the air, she helped them link this to the loss of water from the tank and consider whether the same thing could be happening. Further experimenting with dishes of water, covered and uncovered, provided evidence for the children to see that this was a possible explanation – although only after the demise of the hypothesis about mice, since this, too, would have explained the difference!

As a result of testing the idea drawn from other experience, the children developed an idea of how water can be taken into the air which was just a little broader than their initial one. The development of the bigger idea of water changing state into vapour would require further experience of the different forms of matter.

PROVIDING ACCESS TO ALTERNATIVE IDEAS

When no alternative that makes sense to the child is available, there is reluctance to give up existing ideas, even when these are shown to be inadequate. Children deal with the conflict of idea and evidence by making a small adjustment to their idea in order to reconcile the conflict. So, for example, the child who held a view that we see things because of light coming from our eyes, was able to explain why we cannot see in the dark (evidence that conflicts with this idea) by adapting his idea to include light 'switching on the eye' (Figure 10.12).

So how can children be made aware of alternative scientific ideas? It is not a simple matter of telling or explaining. It is all too easy to destroy children's confidence in their own thinking and reasoning if their ideas are swept aside by premature presentation of the 'right' ones. The best way of avoiding this is to ensure that more scientific ideas are introduced, not as being 'correct' but as alternatives worth considering, *and* that these are tested in terms of the evidence available so that everyone can judge the extent to which they 'work' in practice. Although there are many sources of alternative ideas, as already said, the two most readily available are other children and the teacher.

Ideas from other children

Discussion with other children is an important source of alternative ideas. It does not matter that these ideas are not necessarily more scientific. Becoming aware that there are other views different from their own helps to make children open to consider alternatives. As children progress in ways of thinking and experience they can be encouraged to seek alternatives, by argument and by information from secondary sources and not only from what they can experience directly.

When children hear ideas from other children they are less likely to accept them without question than if the ideas come from the teacher or other 'authority'. And, when their own ideas are challenged by others, they have to bring arguments or evidence that will convince others. Arranging for these things to happen requires planning and some structure, as in the example in Box 11.2.

Box 11.2: Moving towards 'bigger' ideas

A class of 10-year-olds had been investigating 'the best way of keeping a cup of soup warm', a fairly 'standard' activity that had involved children suggesting materials to use and then, in groups, carrying out investigations with containers of warm water. Groups had investigated the different materials that they had suggested. At the end of the practical work, the teacher arranged for them to combine their findings by reporting in a whole-class discussion. So they identified several materials that were good for retaining heat and others that were not so good.

It could have been left there – as often is the case – but there was more understanding to be built from this activity. The teacher asked the children to think about why some materials were better than others – what did some materials do that others did not? These were quite challenging questions, so the children were asked to consider them in their groups for ten minutes and come back together to report their ideas. This produced some quite contradictory ideas, for example:

- that the materials that were best for keeping things warm were warm themselves

- that the ones that were best were colder than the others.

In discussion it was found that the group who came up with the first of these ideas had compared how the materials felt before they were wrapped round the container. The other group had felt the outside of the materials when they were wrapped round the containers and noticed that they were cooler than others. The discussion led them to check each other's findings and was significant in leading all the children to the idea that when the water stayed warm, the heat was not getting away through the sides.

The teacher challenged them to predict which material would be best for keeping cold things cold. Not all the children were able to apply their ideas successfully in answering this, but they were all able, later, to test their ideas. These activities took the children beyond the knowledge that materials vary in the extent to which they allow heat to pass through them and towards some more widely applicable ideas about heat transfer.

Ideas introduced by the teacher: scaffolding

Teachers are often unclear about how, when or whether to introduce the scientific view of things. There is often fear that the children will not understand and will be more confused, or that the teacher will not be able to explain it in ways that the children can understand. Consequently children may be left with their own 'everyday' way of thinking when in fact they could be trying out ideas that expand their understanding. 'Scaffolding' is a term used to describe the introduction of ideas at a time and in a way that helps children to advance their ideas towards the scientific view.

The theory behind scaffolding derives from the views of the psychologist Vygotsky (1962) who suggested that, for any learner, there is an area just beyond current understanding (where a person is in conscious control of ideas and knows that he or she is using them) where more advanced ideas can be used with help. Vygotsky called this area the 'zone of proximal (or potential) development'. It is, in essence, what we have called the 'next step' that the child can be expected to take, identified in the cycle of formative assessment.

The teacher's role in scaffolding is to support children in using an idea that they have not yet made 'their own'. For example, Figure 11.2 shows what a teacher of 7- and 8-year-olds did to help the children to develop their understanding of light being reflected, using a football. The children did not make this link for themselves but were able to learn from it. They transferred the idea to a mirror, using the hole in unifix cubes to fix their line of sight (Figure 11.3).

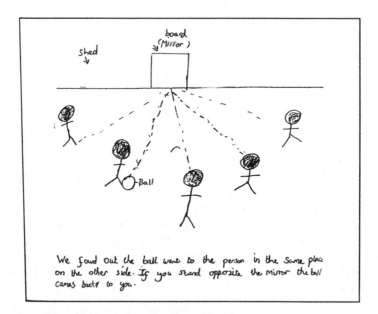

Figure 11.2 Using analogy to scaffold understanding of reflection of light
Source: ASE (1998)

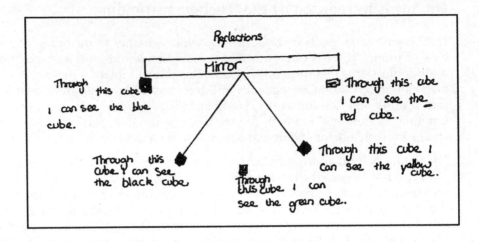

Figure 11.3 Applying the idea of bouncing to the reflection of light

Source: ASE (1998)

Examples of scaffolding are readily found in helping learners with skills such as knitting, weaving, playing tennis and even using a word-processing package on a computer. The learner first needs to be shown how to do things, then later may need to be reminded of what to do, and at all times needs encouragement, until eventually the actions are carried out without external help. In much the same way, help with understanding can be given by suggesting ways of thinking about events in terms of ideas different from the children's own. For example:

- About gravity – 'Suppose the Earth is trying to pull everything on it towards itself . . . what would happen to something that you let go of?'

- About forces and movement – 'Suppose something was moving across a surface that was very, very slippery . . . when do you think it would stop moving?'

- About the apparent movement of the Sun – 'Suppose the Earth was turning and the Sun was in the same place . . . where would we see the Sun at different times?'

The teacher need not be the source of the information, which could come from books or other sources. Models of the solar system can be used to introduce explanations of the apparent movement of the Sun and Moon, which can override the naive interpretations of direct observations. But whatever the source of information, it is the teacher's role to bring the ideas to the children in a way that allows them to try them out, rather like trying on new clothes for size. The analogy is quite apt, since new clothes for growing children are always chosen to be just a little larger, but not too much.

A warning has to be given about scaffolding, however. Research on the effects of introducing scaffolding in professional development, by Askew *et al.* (1995, p. 216) found that 'teachers could "talk scaffolding", but appeared to implement it only marginally'. Similarly Scott (1998, p. 69) warned about the 'casual use' of the term and pointed out that what scaffolds new ideas for one child might not work for a whole class. So we should be wary of assuming that an idea that is a good fit for one child will 'fit all'. Moreover, scaffolding is not an excuse for telling children the 'right answer'. It enables children to advance their ideas but it remains essential that they work out for themselves that these ideas make sense of their experience.

PROMOTING COMMUNICATION, DIALOGUE AND REFLECTION

Language, thought and knowledge

Different schools of thought exist about the relationship between language and thought. On the one hand is the view that speaking is a means of communicating thoughts that have been developed through actions and interaction with things in the world around. On the other hand is the view that thinking and speaking are virtually the same, that language and social interaction have key functions in *developing* ideas not just in communicating them. This is taken further in the view that regards picking up language and ways of representing things from a community of learners to be an important part of learning. Some key ideas around the role of language in learning are summarised in Box 11.3.

Box 11.3: Key views about language, thought and knowledge

For Piaget, the development of knowledge is tied to physiological development of the brain and learning is brought about by direct physical activity with things around. Thoughts are internalised actions not words, and language a means of sharing thoughts, not of developing them. Construction of ideas is within the individual; this is 'personal constructivism'. Until the child reaches the stage of formal operations (Piaget, 1964), usually after the age of 13, the role of the teacher is seen mainly as facilitating first-hand interaction with materials and social interaction with peers.

Bruner emphasises the role of language in translating experiences into a symbolic form in the mind. The development of language in the child opens up the possibility of direct input into a child's thinking through language and the reordering by the child of experience by using language 'as a cognitive instrument' (Bruner, 1964, p. 12).

Vygotsky shares Bruner's view that language is a means of reinterpreting the world: 'Speech . . . does not merely accompany the child's activity; it serves mental orientation, conscious understanding: it helps in overcoming difficulties' (Vygotsky, 1962, p. 20). In this view ideas are constructed through social interaction rather than by the individual alone.

Box 11.3: Continued

In **Ausubel's** theory of 'meaningful learning', the role of firsthand activity is subordinated to the role of giving meaning to verbal statements. Ausubel, like Bruner, believes that any scientific idea can be made accessible to children in some form. He does not believe that learners invent ideas but learn them from others. What is needed is that the idea or theory to be learned is broken down and expressed in language appropriate to the learner, then illustrated by practical activity. The significant point is that he regards verbal statements as the source of knowledge and the role of practical activity as giving meaning to them (Ausubel, 1968).

In recent thinking about learning there has been a perceptible shift away from the view that ideas are formed by individuals in isolation, that is, 'individual constructivism', towards 'socio-cultural constructivism', which recognises the impact of others' ideas on the way learners make sense of things (Bransford *et al.*, 1999). This means that there is greater emphasis than before on communication through language, on the influences of cultural factors and on linking in to a 'community of learners'.

Developing shared understanding

It is through language that we develop a shared understanding of ideas. The ideas that we may form from direct experience have to be communicated and this involves trying to find words that convey our meaning to others. In this process our own ideas often have to be reformulated in ways that are influenced by the meaning that others give to words. This is not the same as saying that learning science is learning the 'language' of science, or just understanding the commonly accepted definitions of words. But it does mean that an important element of learning is 'negotiating meaning'.

In the case of children in school, negotiation provides children with assurance that they have reached a way of understanding something that is shared by their teacher and other children (Sutton, 1992). The process requires some 'give and take' as children reflect on and reconstruct their own ideas in response to others'. When ideas are changed, it is important for there to be some review of how earlier experience was understood. Without this there may be a residue of naive ideas that continue to be used to explain previous experience. For example, we can all probably recall believing in something like 'the man in the Moon', but recognise that this belief was overtaken by more rational views. It would be illogical to believe both in a man in the Moon and the Moon as understood more scientifically. To avoid the equivalent in children's growing ideas the teacher should help them to reflect on previous experience in terms of new ideas. It is helpful to be quite explicit about 'how your ideas about . . . have changed' for this legitimises changing ways of understanding things, which is essential for the continued development of ideas.

The role of discussion

Discussion plays a central role in both negotiation of meaning and reflection on thinking. Douglas Barnes drew attention to this role through studying children's speech when they were involved in group tasks. Barnes showed how individuals contribute to an understanding of an event (or process or situation). An idea of one child is taken up and elaborated by another, perhaps challenged by someone else's idea, and leads them back to check with the evidence or to predict and see which idea stands up best to testing. With several minds at work there is less chance of ideas being tested in a superficial manner than there is if one child does so with no one to challenge how it is done. The challenge can only be made if the thinking is made open and public through the use of language.

Thus Barnes argues that talking is essential to learning. By 'talking' he does not, however, mean the formal reporting or answering of teachers' questions which in some classrooms is the only speech officially sanctioned. Barnes lays particular emphasis on the value of talk among children with no adult authority present. In such situations children with a problem to solve use non-formal speech: they interrupt each other, hesitate, rephrase and repeat themselves. Barnes sees this hesitant or 'exploratory' talk as signifying the openness of the situation and constituting an invitation to all involved to throw in ideas.

The opportunity for exploratory talk of this kind comes only when the children are in charge of the situation. Generally, this does not happen when the teacher is present, for his or her presence provides an authority which children expect to be greater than their own views. As Barnes says:

> the teacher's absence removes from their work the usual source of authority; they cannot turn to him to solve dilemmas. Thus . . . the children not only formulate hypotheses, but are compelled to evaluate them for themselves. This they can do in only two ways: by testing them against their existing view of 'how things go in the world', and by going back to 'the evidence'.

(Barnes, 1976, p. 29)

It is not difficult to see that learning through talking is exposing children not only to different ideas but compelling them to think about how those ideas relate to previous and new experiences. In other words they are finding better ways of dealing with ideas and checking them against evidence; they are developing the mental process skills. Hence what Barnes has to say, while relevant to all learning, is particularly significant for science. In making this point, he goes further in proposing a role for language in helping children to reflect on the way in which they have processed the ideas and information available to them:

> Much learning may go on while children manipulate science apparatus, or during a visit, or while they are struggling to persuade someone else to do what they want. But learning of this kind may never progress beyond manual skills accompanied by slippery intuitions, unless the learners themselves have an opportunity to go back over such experience and represent it to themselves. There seems every reason for group practical work in science, for example, normally to be followed by discussion of the implications of what has been done

and observed, since without this what has been half understood may soon slip away. Talk and writing provide means by which children are able to reflect upon the bases upon which they are interpreting reality, and thereby change them.

(Barnes, 1976, pp. 30–1)

It is possible that by following the ideas of Piaget, mediated through educators who have translated his views of learning into classroom experiences, there has been an overemphasis in primary classrooms on activity at the expense of discussion. Moving from one activity to another without pause for thinking and reflection is not an effective learning experience. Children need not only to have direct experience but to develop their understanding of it through negotiation – exchanging views with others. It is important, therefore, to plan time for discussion into practical work. It also helps to structure that time so that ideas are shared and used to take the understanding of all beyond what each could achieve individually.

Dialogic teaching

The role of talk in learning has been taken further in the concept of dialogic teaching, described by Alexander (2004) as 'a distinct pedagogical approach'. He writes:

Dialogic teaching harnesses the power of talk to stimulate and extend children's thinking, and to advance their learning and understanding. It also enables the teacher more precisely to diagnose and assess. Dialogic teaching is distinct from the question-answer-tell routine of so-called 'interactive' teaching, aiming to be more consistently searching and more genuinely reciprocal and cumulative.

(Alexander, 2004, p. 1)

As Alexander points out, the process of dialogic teaching is very similar to that of formative assessment. It aims to engage children and teachers in listening carefully and responding to each other, asking and answering questions, expressing and explaining and evaluating ideas, arguing and justifying. In this process teachers can both gain and use information about how children's learning is progressing. Box 11.4 gives the principles of dialogic teaching as expressed by Alexander.

Box 11.4: The principles of dialogic teaching

Dialogic teaching is

- *collective*: teachers and children address learning tasks together, whether as a group or as a class;

- *reciprocal*: teachers and children listen to each other, share ideas and consider alternative viewpoints;

- *supportive*: children articulate their ideas freely, without fear of embarrassment over 'wrong' answers; and they help each other to reach common understandings;

- *cumulative*: teachers and children build on their own and each other's ideas and chain them into coherent lines of thinking and enquiry;

- *purposeful*: teachers plan and steer classroom talk with specific educational goals in view.

(Alexander, 2004, p. 27)

Introducing scientific words

Some of the questions that concern teachers of 5- to 12-year-olds revolve around the use of a scientific vocabulary: when should teachers introduce the technical language of science and expect children to use it correctly? Should this be done, as it were, from the beginning? Or should we allow children to describe things in their own words even though more precise terms are available? What do we do about those words which have both an 'everyday' and a 'technical' meaning, such as 'work', 'force', 'power', 'condensation'? These are not separate but interconnected problems and opinions differ as to how to deal with them.

Words used in science label a related set of ideas or characteristics. But the same word can be used with a 'big' meaning or with a meaning that is locally applicable, or 'small'. In Box 11.5 we consider different meanings of the word 'solution'.

Box 11.5: Small and big meanings of 'solution'

- *Big meaning*: for the scientist a solution means a system in which one substance is distributed at the molecular level in another without being chemically combined with it. It includes the solution of solids in solids as well as in liquids, liquids in liquids and gases in liquids.

- *Smaller meaning*: for the secondary school pupil the meaning will be much less extensive, probably being restricted to solids in liquids but still bringing with it the notion that there is a limited amount of solute that will dissolve in a given amount of a solvent, that solutions are clear but may be coloured and are different from suspensions.

- *Small meaning*: for younger children it will have an even more restricted meaning. It may not include a coloured solution or a solution in which some solid remains undissolved.

For all, however, a solution is also the answer to a puzzle or crossword clue!

It would be unreasonable to insist that the word 'solution' should only be used with its full scientific meaning (indeed, it would never accumulate this meaning without being used in a more restricted sense first). But it is equally unreasonable for the word to be used the first time a child experiences a solid disappearing into a liquid.

There is probably no single guideline that can be used for all children and all words. The decision about introducing a special word depends on:

- whether the child needs the word, that is, has had relevant experiences that require a label

- whether it would add to the understanding, for example by linking to other experiences and ideas.

If these things apply it may be the right time to introduce an appropriate word. A simple example is of supplying the word 'sinking' to a young child who is describing an object as 'falling to the bottom' of the bowl of water. The word 'solution' might be offered to the older child, with plenty of experience of putting various solids in water, who wanted to describe how the liquids 'that you can see through' are different from the liquid before any solid was put in. Feasey (1999) proposes that teachers scaffold the use of new words by using both the everyday and the scientific word together (for example, 'see-through' and 'transparent') until the new word can be used confidently.

The most persuasive argument for waiting until the child seems to need the word before introducing it is that there is then more chance that the 'package of ideas' that it represents to the child will not be too far away from what it represents for the teacher, or the author of the books the child might read or other people with whom the child may communicate. It does children no service to provide words that they cannot use to convey meaning because they do not realise what meaning the word has. Of course, we cannot prevent children collecting words, like stamps, and showing off their trophies by talking about black holes, radioactivity, cloning and such. But we accept this for what it is, mere imitation of adult language, not intended for communication.

The same argument can be the guideline for the words that are used not only in science but have a more precise meaning when used as a scientific term than when used in everyday life. It is pointless to try to prevent the word 'work' being used for occupations, like thinking, which involve no 'work' in the physicist's understanding of the word. When the word is required in its scientific meaning, that is, when children have some notion of the concept, then is the time to say 'the word "work" is used for this in science and not for other things that are called work'. The everyday use of the word can be discussed as well as the scientific use to clarify the distinction and help children form the scientific idea at the same time as the awareness that this is different from the everyday use. Thereafter, the teacher should be careful to notice how the children are using the words, by listening and reading what they write, so as to find out the concept that is conveyed by the children in the words they use.

Concern about the special vocabulary of science should not take all the attention. Normal non-scientific words can also present a barrier to communication if they are put together in complex structures. When we say warm air is 'rising' (instead of going up), light is 'travelling' (when we could say that it is going from one place to another), a balloon is 'expanding' (rather than getting bigger), we should stop to ask ourselves: do we really need to use these words? Do they help the children's understanding or are they just another layer of verbal wrapping paper?

When a new word is introduced it will be necessary to spend some time discussing with children their view of where it fits their experience. Asking for examples and non-examples is a useful way to approach this. For instance, in the context of introducing the word 'dissolve' where children had been using 'melt', can they give examples of things dissolving and examples of things becoming liquid which are not dissolving? Children need time and encouragement to reflect on earlier ideas and to ask themselves, for example, 'is this, that I used to call melting, what I now know to be dissolving?' Reflection on earlier experience is necessary so that this is taken into ideas as they expand and so that ideas called forth by words bring with them all the relevant experience.

SUMMARY

In this chapter we have continued the focus on children's scientific ideas, by considering how teachers can help this development. We noted that it is not possible to anticipate precisely what to do in particular circumstances, but teachers can be prepared with a range of strategies to select according to the children's ideas. Four general strategies were identified:

- Extending children's experience.

- Helping children to test their ideas.

- Providing access to alternative ideas.

- Promoting communication, dialogue and reflection.

Each of these has been discussed and some examples given of what they mean in practice in the primary classroom. We have given particular attention to the role of talk and dialogue in learning. Feedback to children also has an important role in helping children develop their ideas, but since it is also relevant to process skills and other aspects of development it is considered in the next chapter.

FURTHER READING

Ideas for linking literacy development and learning science can be found in:

Feasey, R. (1999) *Primary Science and Literacy*. Hatfield: Association for Science Education.

The following materials from the Qualifications and Curriculum Authority/Department for Education and Skills (QCA/DfES) relate to the role of dialogue across the primary curriculum:

QCA/DfES (2003) *Teaching, Speaking and Listening in Key Stages 1 and 2*. London: QCA/DfES.

QCA/DfES (2004) *Teaching through Dialogue* (video with handbook). London: QCA/DfES.

Teachers wishing to develop their own understanding of scientific ideas can find accessible explanations in:

Wenham, M. (2005) *Understanding Primary Science: Ideas, Concepts and Explanations.* (second edition). London: Paul Chapman Publishing.

Chapter 12

The children's role in using assessment for learning

INTRODUCTION

In this chapter we look at the children's role in assessing their own and others' work. Putting children at the centre of the formative assessment framework, in Figure 7.3, signals the importance of their role not just as objects of the teacher's assessment but as active participants in all the stages of the cycle. So, after briefly discussing the reasons for involving children, we look at what it means in practice. The first step, on which all later stages depend, is the communication of the goals of an activity or series of activities on a particular topic. We then consider the children's role in the stages of making judgements, for which they need to know what standard or quality of work to aim for. In the last section, we show how children can participate in deciding and taking next steps, using feedback from their own self-assessment, from the teacher and from other children. We consider the nature of the feedback teachers give through marking work and suggest ways of ensuring that marking has a role in advancing learning. In this section we also discuss the particular value of peer-assessment in providing formative feedback.

WHY INVOLVE CHILDREN IN THE FORMATIVE ASSESSMENT OF THEIR WORK?

Answers to this question come both from the theory of learning and from evidence about practice. The theory relates to the kind of learning we are trying to bring about, described in Chapter 1 as learning with understanding, in which learners have an active role. In Chapter 2, also, we have seen children 'doing the learning' by constructing meaning from their experiences using existing ideas and mental models. When learning is understood in this way, the learner is at the centre of the process. It follows that the more learners know about what it is intended should be learned – the learning goals – about where they have reached in relation to these goals, and about what further needs to be done to reach the goals, the more the learners can direct their effort usefully for learning. Teachers themselves plan with both medium-term and short-term objectives in mind, so why do they not share these with children? The objection that children will not be able to understand the goals has now been met by a good deal of development and the publication of examples showing how goals can be expressed in child-friendly ways (see, for instance, Clarke, 1998; Goldsworthy *et al.*, 2000).

In terms of practice, the empirical research reviewed by Black and Wiliam, outlined in Chapter 7, identified the involvement of children in self-assessment as a factor that contributed to improved levels of attainment. This should not come as a surprise since it was recognised by inspectors in the early 1990s that effective practice included 'the involvement of pupils both in setting their learning objectives and assessing their achievements' (DES, 1991, p. 10).

The experience of teachers who have developed self-assessment skills in their pupils is that it has many advantages, as summarised in Box 12.1. These far outweigh the effort that is required initially to implement new practices.

Box 12.1: Benefits reported by teachers from implementing self- and peer-assessment

- Children take ownership of their learning.
- Children see assessment as a process in which they are involved and to which they can make a contribution.
- Children have control over their learning and see themselves as partners in the teaching–learning process, raising their self-esteem.
- Teachers gain greater insight into children's understanding by reflecting on the children's assessment of their work.
- Children can use the skills of self-assessment in a variety of learning contexts.
- Self-assessment can clarify ideas for the children, helping them to refine and question their own concepts.
- Children become more self-critical and pro-active as learners.
- Children focus upon the next goal in their learning. They feel that the next target is being set by themselves, rather than being externally imposed.

SHARING GOALS OF LEARNING

As for any learners, children direct their effort more effectively if they know what they are trying to achieve in terms of thinking and learning, rather than just knowing what they have to do. The difference is between

> 'today you are going to wrap these ice cubes in different materials and see which ice cubes take longest to melt'

and

> 'today you are going to find out which materials keep ice from melting longer than others and think about why some are better than others'.

Of course children do need to know how to go about things, although they generally learn more if they are expected to think this out for themselves, but if this is all they are told they are likely to miss the point of the activity. When asked what they have learned following the first of the two introductions above they will probably reply 'about how to keep ice from melting' rather than referring to the properties of materials, which was actually the teacher's goal for the activity.

Communicating goals to students is essential for learning and for self-assessment, but it is not easy – particularly for young children. It certainly can't be done in the terms that are used to communicate goals to teachers in standards documents or curriculum statements or even teachers' guides. This is not only because of the language used but also because they are stated in terms of concepts that students cannot understand until they have investigated the phenomena for themselves. For instance, the teachers could not express the goals for the ice-cube activity in terms of 'insulation properties of materials' prior to children having experiences that make these terms meaningful.

The goals that are useful to children have to be specific to the particular activity and should be the same as the teacher's goals. If they are not, and the teacher has 'hidden' goals not shared with the children, the children are not able to focus their activities to achieve what is intended. Stating goals at the start of the lesson is not the only way of communicating them. Indeed it is unlikely to be really effective by itself. Other strategies that teachers have used are:

- Writing the goals on the board or a poster left visible throughout the relevant activities as a reminder.

- When children are discussing what they will do in an investigation, asking them what they think they will be learning.

- Checking with groups or individuals to find out if they know the reason for their activities in terms of what they are learning.

- Commenting on the procedures and the outcome of the activities in ways that reflect what they are learning.

Usually a combination of some or all of these is more effective than one only. However, including a statement about intended learning as part of the introduction to a lesson or activity is clearly a key factor. This means 'translating' the goals from the teacher's language to language that communicates with the children. Table 12.1 gives some examples of how this might look for some goals relating to development of ideas and others relating to process skills.

Table 12.1 Communicating goals of learning to children

Teacher's goal of learning	Words used with children
To learn that the pitch of a sound depends on how rapidly it vibrates	When you make different sounds with these things, I want you to see if you can find out what makes the sound higher and what makes it lower
To plan an investigation that will be a fair test of which material will keep an ice block from melting for the longest time	When you test these materials I want to see if you can do it in a way that the test is fair and you are quite sure that it is the material that is making the difference
To learn that pushes and pulls can make things start or stop moving	When you make these toy cars go and then make them stop, think about what you are doing to make them go faster and then slow down
To learn to use a table to set out results, from an investigation of materials	When you put down your results, see if you can use a table to make it easy to see which material was best

Although the initial statement is important, reinforcement during the activity is also necessary, particularly if children seem to be straying from the goal. This might be by asking 'can you explain how doing this will help you . . . (for example, find out what makes the sound higher and what makes it lower)?'

HELPING CHILDREN TO KNOW WHAT STANDARD TO AIM FOR

As well as knowing the goals, children also need some idea of the standard or quality of work to aim for. That is, they need to share the teacher's understanding of what is 'good work'. For instance, if they are to make a report of their investigation, it is not just any report that will achieve this goal but one that meets certain criteria, reflecting what can be expected of children at a particular stage. Similarly, what they say they find out about the properties of materials or how to make sounds of different pitch, should meet expectations about being based on reasoning about evidence.

It's not that children don't make judgements about the quality of their work, but that they do not necessarily apply the criteria that are appropriate to their science work. For example, when teachers ask children to select their 'best work', what they choose reflects how they are judging their work (see Box 12.2). This may well indicate to the teacher that, for instance, work is being selected on the basis of being 'tidy' or 'good writing' rather than in terms of its content. Telling the children directly the criteria on which they should be judging their work is not the most effective way of helping this aspect of self-assessment. They will still need to know what the criteria mean in terms of examples. Better ways of going about this are to involve children in thinking about what makes a piece of work 'good' in a discussion in which the teacher can also contribute ideas. Some examples are given in Box 12.2.

Box 12:2: Helping children to recognise good standards of work

Using examples

One teacher of 10-year-olds spent some time at the beginning of the year discussing with her class what made a 'good' report of a science investigation. She gave each group of children two anonymous examples of children's writing about an investigation from children in the same class in earlier years. One was a clear account, well set out so that the reader could understand what had been done, although the writing was uneven and there were some words not spelled correctly. There were diagrams to help the account, with labels. The results were in a table, and the writer had said what he or she thought they meant, admitting that the results didn't completely answer the initial question. There was a comment about how things could have been improved. The other account was tidy, attractive to look at (the diagrams were coloured in but not labelled) but contained none of the features in the content shown in the other piece.

The teacher asked the children to compare the pieces of work and list the good and poor features of each one. Then they were asked to say what were the most important things that made a 'good' report. She put all the ideas together and added some points of her own, to which the children agreed. She later made copies for all the children to keep in their science folders. But she also went on to explore with the children how to carry out an investigation in order to be able to write a good report. These points too were brought together in the children's words and printed out for them.

Brainstorming

A variation on the above is for the children to brainstorm ideas about, for example, how to conduct a particular investigation so that the children are sure of the result. The list of what to think about can be turned into questions (Did we keep everything the same except for . . .? Did we change . . .? Did we look for . . .? Did we check their results? etc.). Before finishing their investigation they check through their list, which becomes a self-assessment tool for that piece of work.

Discussing 'best work'

This approach can be used with children from about the age of 8. It begins with the children selecting their 'best' work to put into a folder or bag. Part of the time for 'bagging' should be set aside for the teacher to talk to each child about why certain pieces of work have been selected. During this discussion the way in which the children are judging the quality of their work will become clear. These are accepted without comment, whether or not they reflect the teacher's view of good work.

To clarify the criteria the children use, the teacher can ask: 'Tell me what you particularly liked about this piece of work?' Gradually it will be possible to suggest criteria without dictating what the children should be selecting. This can be done through comments on the work: 'That was a very good way of showing your results, I could see at a glance which was best', 'I'm glad you think that was your best investigation because, although you didn't get the result you expected, you did it very carefully and made sure that the result was fair'.

CHILDREN'S ROLE IN DECIDING AND TAKING NEXT STEPS: USING FEEDBACK

The examples in Box 12.2 show that the process of helping children to understand the quality of work that they should be aiming for, through looking at their own work, is already involving them in assessing it. The aim of judging the work is not to decide whether or not it is 'good', or 'correct', but how it can be improved. Having multiple and detailed criteria helps to avoid an overall judgement, which would leave children either satisfied and uncritical, or dissatisfied and demotivated. The fact that the children themselves identify where their work falls short means not only that they understand what else they need to do but that they are also committed to doing it.

However, we are not suggesting that children be left to themselves to decide their next steps and what they should do. Clearly the ultimate responsibility for ensuring opportunity for learning is the teacher's. But, as we have said before, teachers can't do the learning for the children and a key part of their role is to bring about commitment to learn. Participation in decisions about what to do is central to enlisting this commitment. It also ensures that children know what they have to do if they have shared in deciding it.

Feedback into learning is the determining feature of formative assessment. Unless the process leads to changes that help learning, either by direct feedback to the children or indirectly through influencing the teacher's planning, then it is not formative. Feedback to help in deciding and taking next steps can be from three sources:

- the child's own self-assessment
- the teacher
- other children.

We now look at ways of ensuring that these can be carried out so that they are genuinely effective in helping learning.

Self-assessment

Once children understand the goals of their work and the quality criteria to apply to it, they need practice in self-assessment and time to do it. Both of these are included in what Clarke (2001) describes as training children in self-assessment. She suggests that teachers begin this training by displaying in the classroom some questions to promote self-assessment and spending some time at the end of lessons for a few weeks 'modelling' how to answer them. Examples of the questions (2001, p. 41) are:

- What did you find difficult while you were learning to . . .?
- What do you need more help with about learning to . . .?
- What are you most pleased with about learning to . . .?
- How would you change this activity for another group/class who were learning to . . .?

The 'modelling' includes asking children to think and not answer straight away. Once the idea has taken root, Clarke suggests asking self-assessment questions linked to the goals of the lesson as a routine, so that children always have the opportunity to reflect and think about their learning.

Clarke also makes a useful point about encouraging children to be candid about being 'stuck', by welcoming this as an essential step in getting help. She even suggests the teacher might tell children who report no problems that this might mean that they are not learning anything new. She comments that this approach 'eliminates the culture of striving for work to be easy' (Clarke, 2001, p. 44), a point which accords with Dweck's (1999) view that we should encourage children to feel that they can overcome problems by effort, rather than that they succeed because they are clever and don't need to make an effort (see Chapter 6).

'Traffic lighting' is an approach to self-assessment developed by teachers of lower secondary children. Black *et al.* (2003) give several examples of the use of this technique in which traffic-light icons are used by children to indicate where they need further help. Children are given red, green and yellow spot stickers, which they attach to their work when they have finished it and have considered whether they understand and are satisfied with what they have done (green), are unsure about part of it (yellow) or feel that they need more help (red). This is useful feedback for teachers in planning whether to spend more time on a particular topic but, unless followed up, lacks potential for children to identify what they can do to improve.

Feedback from the teacher

Apart from on-the-spot comments, the most common form of feedback from teachers to learners is through marking. The importance of different ways of providing this feedback has been underlined by research. What has been found is that not all feedback has a positive impact on children's learning (Kluger and DeNisi, 1996) and indeed some can be quite demotivating, particularly if every small error is pointed out.

A study that has had particular influence on thinking about feedback is summarised in Box 12.3. What this study reveals is that if children are given marks or brief judgemental remarks such as 'good work' or 'well done' they then seize upon marks and ignore any comments that are intended to help further learning. They look to the marks for a judgement rather than help in further learning. When marks are absent they engage with what the teacher wants to bring to their attention. The comments then have a chance of improving learning as intended by the teacher. In order to do this, of course, the comments should be positive, non-judgemental and, where possible, identify next steps.

Here positive and non-judgemental mean that the comments:

- focus on the work, not on how good the children are
- encourage children to think about particular aspects of the work
- suggest what to do next and give some ideas about how to do it.

Box 12.3: Research into different kinds of feedback

In a study by Ruth Butler (1987) the effect of different types of feedback by marking were compared. Using a controlled experimental design she set up groups which were given feedback in different ways. Children in one group were given marks, or grades only; those in another group were given only comments on their work and the third group received both marks and comments on their work. These conditions were studied in relation to tasks, some of which required divergent and some convergent thinking. The result was that, for divergent thinking tasks, the pupils who received comments only made the greatest gain in their learning, significantly more than for the other two groups. The results were the same for high and low achieving pupils. For convergent tasks, the lower achieving pupils scored most highly after comments only, with the marks only group next above the marks plus comments group. For all tasks and pupils, comments only led to higher achievement.

Judgemental feedback has the contrary features and focuses attention on how well the child has done rather than on how well the work has been done. Box 12.4 describes a teacher's experience of using non-judgemental comments.

Box 12.4: Formative feedback

The teacher noticed a considerable change in her children's motivation once she avoided giving any indication of judgement in her written comments on their work. She now keeps all judgemental comments in her own records and feeds back to the children suggestions as to what to do next or writes questions that help them link what they found to other experiences. The children's work then becomes a medium for genuine communication between teacher and child.

For example, Andrea's account of dropping balls of plasticine of different weights (in Figure 12.1) seemed to leave some ambiguity in the mind of the teacher. The question 'How were you convinced?' was written to remind both of them to clear this up.

In other parts of Andrea's work there are several examples of the teacher's question being answered in writing. Part of Andrea's report of testing several materials in a simple circuit is shown in Figure 12.2, including the teacher's question and Andrea's answer.

Falling Plasticine

We dropped four different weights of plasticine two at a time. The weights weighed 50g, 100g, 150g, 200g.
First we dropped the 50g and 100g from a height of 1m 64cm. Then we did the same with the 150g and 200g balls.

Results

We found that the balls dropped at the same time.

What I Decided

At first I thought that the heaviest would hit the ground first but after a while Mrs Griffithes convinced Robert and I that they hit the ground at the same time.

How were you convinced?

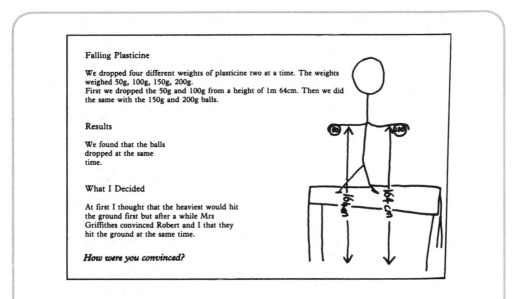

Figure 12.1 Andrea's report with teacher's question

We found that all the metal like things allowed electricity to pass through to the bulb and all the things that didn't have any metal in didn't allow electricity to pass thou through to the bulb.
What general names do we give these two groups of things? conductors and insulators

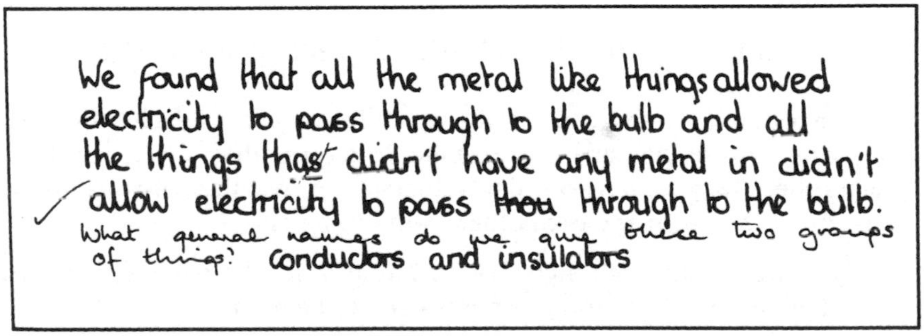

Figure 12.2 Question and answer on Andrea's work

Many of the points about good practice in marking were brought together in a list of 'dos' and 'don'ts' by Evans (2001). The things 'to do' include the following:

- Comment only on certain features, relating to the goals of the work, telling children that this is what you are doing.
- Consider carefully whether to comment on neatness, spelling, etc. unless these were specifically goals of the work.
- Emphasise how to improve by pinpointing aspects that need attention.
- Give time for children to read comments, reflect on them and respond as necessary.

Marking in this way takes more time and thought than just giving a tick or grade. So one of the ways of compensating the extra time on some pieces of work is to be selective in what is marked in detail. Evans suggests concentrating on work that is worth attention because of its potential for learning science and not wasting time on tasks that are mainly about reinforcement. Such other work can be acknowledged by a signature.

If this represents a considerable shift in marking policy then it will be important to explain the reason for the change to those (parents, children, other teachers) who expect every piece of work to be meticulously marked, and to point out the advantages of providing formative feedback. However, Black *et al.* (2003) found that teachers' worries about the reactions of the children or their parents were largely unjustified. One teacher reported that 'At no time during the first 15 months of comment-only marking did any of the students ask me why they no longer received grades' (2003, p. 45).

There are others advantages, too. Black *et al.* (2003) report that teachers themselves began to be more thoughtful about the work they marked and how they could encourage the children to improve. In turn this led them to reconsider some of the tasks that they were giving to the children. Some tasks provided opportunity for children's understanding and skills to be revealed and thus helped their learning, while other tasks involved conveying information and were less useful in developing understanding and skills. Realising this, teachers spent more time devising activities that gave opportunities for development.

Feedback from other children: peer-assessment

Peer-assessment, in this context, means children helping each other with their learning, by deciding the next steps to take. It is quite different from children marking each other's work. It has several advantages. For instance, when children are asked to talk about their own and each other's work in pairs:

- children go through their work again and use the criteria of quality that enable them to see where improvements need to be made

- they express this in words that they understand

- they are more likely to take seriously criticism from a peer (Sadler, 1989)

- it requires less one-to-one attention by the teachers compared with other approaches to self-assessment.

Just as important as the time saved, however, is that the assessment takes place without the pressure that comes from the unequal relationship between the child (novice) and the teacher (expert). It is also consistent with the understanding of learning as being the development of ideas through social interaction as well as through interaction with materials. It can help children to respect each other's strengths, especially if pairs are changed on different occasions.

The paired discussion needs to be structured, at least when it is new to the children. For example, the children can be asked to exchange work and then come up with two or three questions about it reflecting the criteria of quality. If the work describes a conclusion from something that has been observed or found from an investigation, the questions might be 'Can you tell what was found?', 'Does the conclusion help to answer the question that was being investigated?', 'What would help to make it clearer (a diagram, or series of drawings)?' After such a discussion one child said about having her work assessed by another:

> She said it was hard to understand my investigation so I asked her what sort of thing I should have put to make her understand. Next time I will make sure that I describe things more clearly.

This approach to peer-assessment clearly requires a class atmosphere where co-operation and collaboration, rather than competition, are encouraged. When they have confidence in gaining help from a structured exchange with a peer, children begin spontaneously to ask each other for their opinion. The recognition of being able to help themselves and each other enables learning to continue when the teacher is occupied with those who need extra help.

SUMMARY

This chapter has set out some advantages of involving children closely in decisions about their work. It has looked at what this means in relation to sharing goals of activities with the children, and helping them to recognise the standard or quality of work to aim for. With this knowledge the children are in a better position to realise what they need to do to improve their work and are more likely to be committed to doing it. Feedback from the teacher is most likely to support further learning when it is non-judgemental and indicates the next steps. Some ways of making marking of children's work more productive for their learning have been suggested. Children can also help each other through peer-assessment. A class climate of co-operation and collaboration is needed to support the learning through social interaction which is possible when children are given a role in using assessment to help learning.

FURTHER READING

Practical strategies for communicating goals, pupil self-assessment and marking are given in:

Clarke, S. (2001) *Unlocking Formative Assessment*. London: Hodder and Stoughton.

Discussion of feedback and peer-assessment particularly applicable for older children is given in:

Black, P. and Harrison, C. (2004) *Science Inside the Black Box*. London: NFER-Nelson.

Part IV

MANAGING LEARNING IN SCIENCE

Chapter 13

Summarising and recording learning

INTRODUCTION

In this fourth part of the book we turn to matters that involve decisions at the school level rather than those that are the concerns mainly of individual teachers. These include how and when children's achievement is recorded and reported, relating to communication about children's learning within the school and to parents and governors or school boards, as well a decision about learning resources, whole-school planning and how provision for science is kept under review.

This chapter begins by placing summative assessment, for reporting the achievement of individual children, in the context of other purposes of assessment. Chapters 7–12 have been devoted to the important use of assessment to help learning, so here we consider other uses. We then look at different ways of providing summative assessment of children for internal purposes. The third section addresses issues relating to the use of summative assessment, particularly in the form of tests results, for the high-stakes purposes of evaluating the effectiveness of teachers and schools. By drawing attention to these problems it is hoped that the negative impact of such tests on teachers and children can be minimised. In the fourth section we consider ways of record-keeping in the school and finally discuss the nature of reports to children's parents or carers.

THE PURPOSES OF ASSESSMENT

Part III of this book has been framed by the use of assessment to help learning, or formative assessment. But this is only one of several purposes for which we assess children's learning. In Chapter 7 we looked briefly at summative assessment, or assessment *of* learning, mainly to contrast it with formative assessment and point out how the characteristics of assessment relate to its purpose. In addition to these two purposes, children are also assessed, particularly towards the end of schooling, for certification and selection for employment or higher or further education. Another purpose, that probably looms largest in the minds of primary children and their teachers, is for monitoring achievement year on year at the school, local or national level, using national tests. To bring these together, the main purposes of assessment are:

- Formative – to help learning.

- Summative – to record and report achievement and progress of individual children, for school use.

- Summative – to recognise learning through awards and certification used in selection beyond school, for uses external to the school.

- Evaluative – to evaluate the effectiveness of teachers, schools and systems.

At primary school level the summative assessment we are mainly concerned with is for keeping records of progress and reporting achievement at certain times to parents, children and other teachers. We describe these uses of summative information as being 'internal' to the school and certification and selection as 'external' uses.

SUMMARISING ACHIEVEMENT FOR INTERNAL SCHOOL PURPOSES

The use of assessment for recording and reporting achievement requires information on each child's achievement to be available at certain times and in forms that make it useful to other teachers and meaningful to parents and to the children themselves. For these purposes, evidence has to be judged by the same criteria for all children, since comparisons between children may be made and performance may be aggregated across children. The information also needs to give an overall picture of achievement and much of the detail has to be summarised. This will inevitably mean bringing together aspects of achievement that are best kept separate for formative assessment purposes. A further difference from formative assessment is that those receiving the report on achievement generally want to know where a child has reached in relation to expectations set for all children, indicated for the sake of convenience by standards or levels.

Figure 7.4, in Chapter 7, set out the procedures for summative assessment. It indicated that the evidence collected by the teacher is interpreted and summarised in terms of achievement of goals. There are three ways of doing this, depending on the type of evidence gathered, which are:

- summarising evidence gathered during regular activities

- checking up using special tasks or tests

- using special tasks or tests in addition to evidence from regular activities.

Using evidence from regular activities

This means that evidence collected and used for formative assessment may also be used for summative assessment. This is an ideal situation in theory since the evidence will be rich and reflect all the aspects of children's learning. But it is important to remember that the two purposes require different interpretation of the evidence. For formative assessment the evidence is interpreted in relation to the progress of a child towards the goals of a particular piece of work, next steps being decided according to where a child has reached. The interpretation is in terms of what to do to help further learning not what level or grade a child has reached. There are two related but different matters to be considered in moving from using evidence in this way to using it to summarise what has been learned. These are the goals involved and the basis of judgement of the evidence.

From lesson goals to levels of achievement

First, the goals of a lesson, shared with the children, will be specific to the subject matter of the lesson. Addressing these specific goals will contribute to the development of a more general understanding or improved skill, that is, to goals at a more generic level than the specific lesson goals. For example, the goals of a specific lesson might include the understanding of how the structure of a snail is suited to the places where snails are found. This will contribute to an understanding of how animals in general are suited to their habitats, but achieving this will depend on looking at a variety of animals, which will be the subject of other lessons with their own specific goals. Similarly skills such as planning a scientific investigation are developed not in one lesson, but in different contexts in different lessons.

Relating the achievement of particular lesson goals to the progression towards more general goals is where the indicators of development, described in Chapters 8 and 10, come in. But these are still too detailed for most summative uses. For instance, for reporting to parents or to other teachers, what is required, at most, is an overall judgement about what has been achieved in terms of, for instance, 'knowledge and understanding of life processes and living things' or 'scientific enquiry skills'. So a further aggregation of evidence is needed relating to the range of ideas and processes that are included in these global terms. So we have, for instance, evidence from several lessons in which a goal is to help students plan scientific investigations, leading to identification of where students are in planning investigations. This skill in turn is part of a broader aim of developing enquiry skills, a target of the National Curriculum on which teachers provide a summary end of year or key stage report. Figure 13.1 attempts to depict this three-stage relationship.

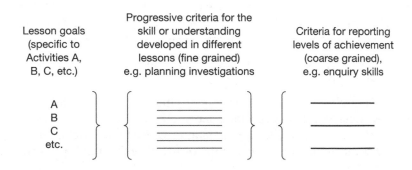

Figure 13.1 Goals at various levels of detail (from Harlen, 2005)

From child-referenced to criterion-referenced judgements

Second, we turn to matters concerning the basis of judgement. In formative assessment, when evidence is gathered in various activities (A, B, C, etc., in Figure 7.3 for example) it may be used on the spot or later to help students or groups achieve the lesson goals. In doing this the teacher will interpret the evidence in relation to the progress of the individuals involved, so the judgement will be child-referenced (or ipsative) as well as being related to the criteria. However, if the evidence is also used to report on achievement of broader aspects of skills or knowledge, moving from left to right across Figure 13.1, then the evidence must be evaluated according to the criteria only. Thus the evidence can be used for the two purposes providing it is *reinterpreted* against criteria that are the same for all children. This means that if the information already gathered and used formatively is to be used for summative assessment it must be reviewed against the broader criteria that define levels or grades. This involves finding the 'best fit' between the evidence gathered about each child and one of the reporting levels.

In practice, reviewing children's work and teachers' notes to decide the best fit with reporting criteria is not as easy as it sounds. There is always room for personal interpretation and differences among teachers will inevitably arise. No criteria in a list of manageable length can be so specific that they can be used with total agreement. Useful criteria have to be couched in general terms so that they can apply in the wide variety of contexts in which learning takes place and this means that they are inevitably ambiguous to some extent. For example, it could be said that 'notices patterns in findings', could apply as equally to a research scientist as to an 8-year-old. The same could be said of almost any statement that uses the word 'appropriate' or 'relevant'. In using such statements, therefore, there must be some consideration of what it is reasonable to expect of children at certain ages. Thus an element of norm-referencing intrudes into a criterion-referenced judgement.

Moderating teachers' judgements

Clearly it is essential for there to be as near uniformity as possible in the interpretation of criteria if they are to be useful in practice. Ideally one teacher's judgement of whether a child has achieved, say, level 2 or the standard expected at 5th grade must be the same as another's. In practice it is very difficult to achieve this and even to find out the extent to which there is agreement. However, there are various steps that can be taken to help to align, or moderate, teachers' judgements. Among these are:

- Collecting examples of work, which can be judged against the criteria by several teachers independently.

- Discussing published exemplars. This can be valuable as a basis for helping teachers to adjust their judgements to be in line with official views on the meaning of standards. QCA's 'Assessing Progress in Science' materials (QCA, 2003a), and the Performance Standards for the New Standards published in the USA are examples.

● Individual teachers can use the examples given in some curriculum materials which are designed to help teachers to summarise achievement in terms of national standards.

● Groups of teachers meeting face to face to discuss their own pupils' work.

The disadvantage of using published examples is that they rarely evoke the context, background and conditions in which the work was done – all of which influence judgements in real situations. However, teachers discussing the work of their own children can describe the goals and context more precisely. Moreover, such discussion has added benefits in enabling teachers to share ideas about how to achieve certain goals. This adds formative value to the summative assessment process.

It is important in using all examples that it is the *work* that is described in terms of the levels and not the child, since a child's level should be judged from a number of pieces of work.

Teachers can find some help in using the review of children's work formatively as well as judging it summatively from the QCA (2003a) materials. In this resource, the National Curriculum level statements have been supplemented by adding other statements that help teachers identify the level at which children are working, thus forming a bridge between the progressive criteria and the reporting levels. The additional statements extend the description of progression and make it possible to see the difference between children who have mastered what is required at a level and those just approaching it. Teachers have various ways of indicating these degrees by using signs for 'approaching', 'attempted', achieved', or similar.

Another example of enabling teachers to use evidence from ongoing work with children is provided by the 'Foundation Stage Profile', which replaced statutory baseline assessment in 2003 (QCA, 2003b). The profile, completed in the final term of the reception year, serves a double purpose, providing information about the strengths and needs of new entrants to school and of constituting a baseline from which to measure the improvement in achievement at a later stage of schooling. Teachers make judgements about 13 aspects of learning, assigning a point from 1 to 9. The process of collecting and judging the information helps practitioners to see where children need help to achieve early learning goals, while the scores on each of the 13 scales are used for reporting to parents as well as being collected by local education authorities.

● Using special tasks or tests

Assessment for summative purposes needs to be reliable, that is, as free as possible from error and bias. With this in mind, there is an attraction in using special tasks or tests, because they can be specified and controlled and presented to children in the same way, and marked using the same rubrics or criteria. Thus they appear to give children the same opportunities to show what they can do at a particular time. However, giving children the same tasks is not the same as giving them the same opportunities and when, in the interests of 'fairness', children are constrained in what is more like a test situation, this has all the disadvantages of tests that we discuss in the next section.

Many of these disadvantages are avoided when teachers who wish to check up on children's progress through giving special tasks embed these in children's usual work rather than presenting them as formal tests. Examples of such tasks were provided by the work of the Science Teaching Action Research (STAR) project and published in Schilling *et al.* (1990). The materials are described in Box 13.1 with some example questions on leaves in Figure 13.2.

Box 13.1: An example of embedded tasks

The materials devised and used in the STAR project take the form of a small class project about an imaginary 'walled garden'. The children were introduced to various features of the walled garden – water (in a pond with a fountain), walls, wood, minibeasts, leaves, bark, sundial. For each of these seven features a poster was produced, to be displayed in the classroom, giving suggestions for activities and posing some questions. Children worked on one poster at a time and answered the questions in the answer booklet linked to the activities for that feature. Pupils could carry out the activities in any sequence and so a whole class could be working at the same time without interfering with each other's work. The questions were designed for written answers, but the element of active exploration in arriving at the answers extended the range of skills tested. The questions were process based and the different content provided by the seven features created opportunities for the skills to be used in different contexts and so avoided to some extent the problem of validity which arises when skills are used on limited content. Since the activities were well designed, attractively presented and intriguing to children there was no problem in children engaging with the tasks as if they were normal work.

When tests are more overt, teachers can still do much to avoid the disadvantages by ensuring that they:

- discuss with the children the purpose of the tasks and why they are being assessed

- explain the criteria that will be used in assessing their answers

- encourage them to focus on their own progress, not on comparison with others

- avoid a test atmosphere that will make some children nervous

- give feedback that enables children to know how to make further progress.

The last of these points refers to making formative use of summative assessment as far as possible. This can be done when tests are in the hands of teachers. Some teachers have helped children to learn from testing by asking them to create tests for each other. They find that the tasks are far harder than the teacher would have given, and that both those setting and taking the tests learn from them. Others involve students in marking each other's tests, in some cases after devising the mark scheme.

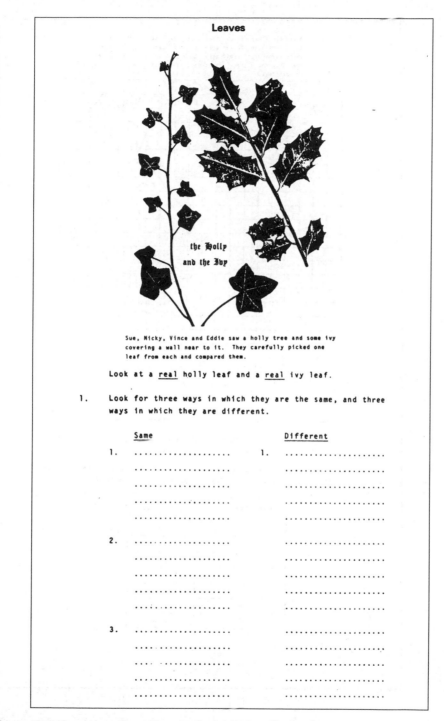

Leaves

the Holly
and the Ivy

Sue, Nicky, Vince and Eddie saw a holly tree and some ivy
covering a wall near to it. They carefully picked one
leaf from each and compared them.

Look at a <u>real</u> holly leaf and a <u>real</u> ivy leaf.

1.   Look for three ways in which they are the same, and three
     ways in which they are different.

<u>Same</u>   <u>Different</u>

1.   ....   1.   ....
     ....
     ....
     ....
     ....

2.   ....
     ....
     ....
     ....
     ....

3.   ....
     ....
     ....
     ....
     ....

Figure 13.2 Examples of questions in the 'walled garden' tasks

2. Nicky and Vince noticed that there were lots of different
    sized leaves in the ivy growing up the garden wall. They
    asked everyone in their group to pick a leaf. Back at school
    they drew round their leaves on squared paper to find the area
    of each leaf.

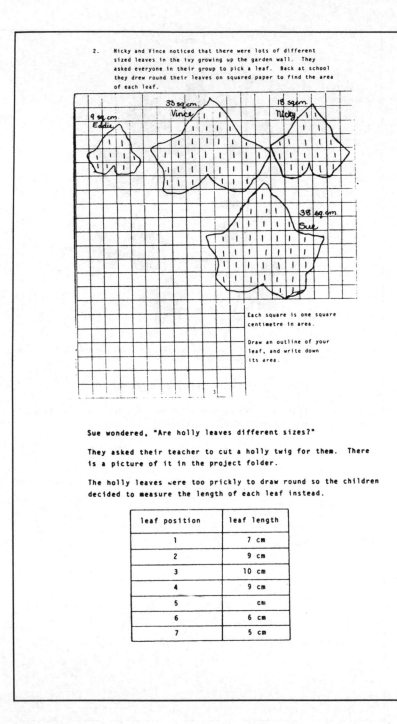

Sue wondered, "Are holly leaves different sizes?"

They asked their teacher to cut a holly twig for them. There
is a picture of it in the project folder.

The holly leaves were too prickly to draw round so the children
decided to measure the length of each leaf instead.

leaf position	leaf length
1	7 cm
2	9 cm
3	10 cm
4	9 cm
5	cm
6	6 cm
7	5 cm

Figure 13.2 Continued

3. a) The children had found that the IVY leaves were larger the further they were from the tip of the twig.

Are HOLLY leaves arranged that way? What do you notice about the length of the leaves and the distance from the tip of the twig?

....

....

....

b) What do you <u>think</u> the length of leaf 5 might have been?

.... cm. (The picture is NOT the right size.)

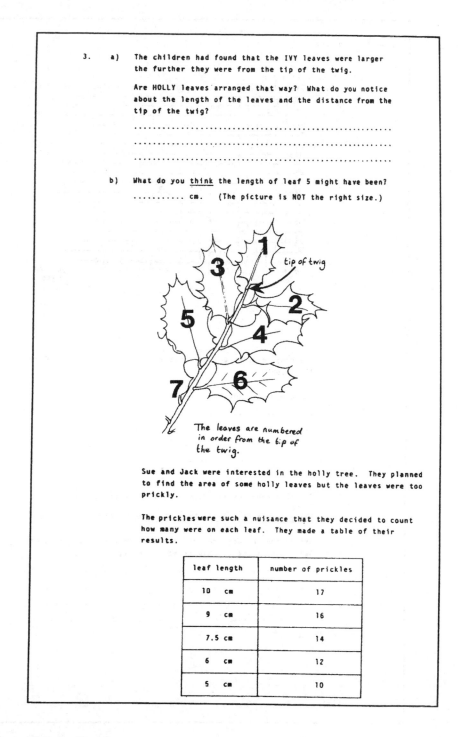

The leaves are numbered in order from the tip of the twig.

Sue and Jack were interested in the holly tree. They planned to find the area of some holly leaves but the leaves were too prickly.

The prickles were such a nuisance that they decided to count how many were on each leaf. They made a table of their results.

leaf length	number of prickles
10 cm	17
9 cm	16
7.5 cm	14
6 cm	12
5 cm	10

Figure 13.2 Continued

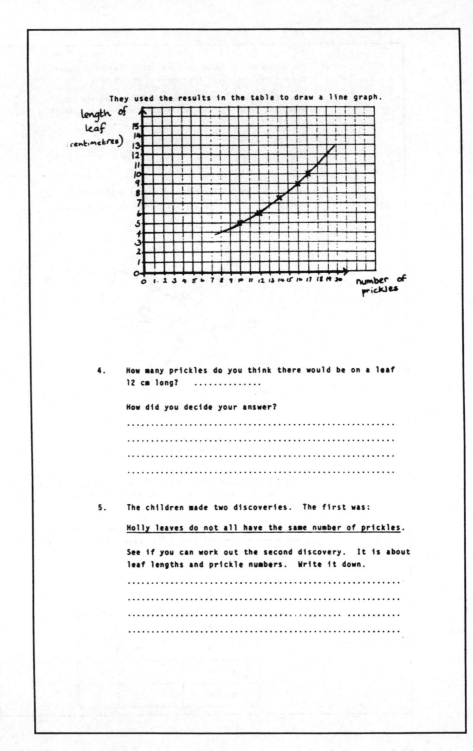

They used the results in the table to draw a line graph.

4. How many prickles do you think there would be on a leaf
    12 cm long?   ....

    How did you decide your answer?

    ....
    ....
    ....
    ....

5. The children made two discoveries. The first was:

    Holly leaves do not all have the same number of prickles.

    See if you can work out the second discovery. It is about
    leaf lengths and prickle numbers. Write it down.

    ....
    ....
    ....
    ....

Figure 13.2 Continued

A combination of special tasks and teachers' judgement

There are some good reasons why teachers' judgements might need to be supplemented by special tasks or tests. If summative assessment is based solely on evidence gathered within the context of regular classroom activities, this evidence will be limited by the range and richness of the educational provision and the efficiency of the teachers in collecting evidence. In some circumstances the evidence required to summarise learning may need to be supplemented by introducing special tasks if, for instance, the teacher has been unable for one reason or another to collect all that is necessary to make judgements about all the students. Further, for formative purposes it is often appropriate to consider the progress of groups rather than of individual students. Additional evidence may then be needed when making judgements about individual students.

The more weight that is given to the summative judgement, the more stringent the quality assurance needs to be, possibly including some inter-school as well as intra-school moderation of judgements of evidence. Having access to children's performance in some common tasks can help to align judgements.

Using two sources of evidence raises the question of how the two are combined. If one acquires the role of the determining factor – and in general that one is the test result – then it will be regarded as the more important and what it assesses is likely to be emphasised. Further, since the ongoing evidence is gathered and interpreted by teachers, while the tasks or tests and their marking schemes are usually externally set, the relative value given to each could be seen as a reflection of confidence in teachers' judgements as compared with external tests.

In some systems the two are combined in a given proportion (e.g. 50:50 or 30:70) to give the overall result. Numerical scores are needed to make such calculations and the result lacks meaning in relation to criteria. An alternative way, that preserves this meaning, is used in the Scottish system. Teachers use their accumulated evidence to decide when a child has achieved what is specified at a certain level. The teacher then administers an externally produced test for that level. If the test is passed (i.e. a cut-off score achieved), the child is confirmed as having reached that level. If not, then the teacher uses the test results to identify weaknesses and, after a minimum period, can retest the child using a different but equivalent test. This procedure ensures that children only take tests when they are expected to succeed, but it still gives the test a determining role.

So, for a variety of reasons, combining judgements from teachers' assessment and from tests, although attractive in principle, is difficult to implement in practice without incurring some disadvantages. Having tried various ways of combining the two in the English National Curriculum, it was decided to report teachers' assessments and test results separately and not to combine them. This acknowledges that the different procedures mean that slightly different things are assessed: teachers' assessment is based on a broad range of evidence, but gathered in non-standard situations; tests provide standard situations for all children but are based on a narrower range of evidence and the more easily tested aspects of performance. The difference needs to be understood by those receiving the information.

THE IMPACT OF NATIONAL TESTS

Although not a matter that schools can control, it is important to consider the evaluative use of assessment through testing. The reason for this is that, where they exist, external tests have a stranglehold on classroom practice, making the kind of teaching and learning we have discussed in this book difficult to implement. One way of resisting this constriction is to understand how it arises.

The use of frequent summative assessment in the form of tests to monitor and evaluate the performance of schools has increased over the past 15 or so years – to epidemic proportions in parts of the UK (particularly England) and the vast majority of states in the USA. The rationale for this policy is based on a claim that testing raises standards of achievement. It is indeed the case that when testing programmes are first introduced levels of performance on the tests of successive cohorts of children do tend to rise. This happens, it is claimed, because teachers and pupils are motivated by the rewards of high scores, or more often by the penalties attached to low ones, to put effort into passing the tests (Kellaghan *et al.*, 1996). Such arguments underpin most of the state-mandated testing programmes in the USA and the national tests for students at ages 7, 11 and 14 in England.

Flaws in the theory of the impact of tests

However, there is evidence to show that these arguments are flawed. We have to look carefully at the evidence before accepting that the claims on which they are based have substance. Box 13.2 outlines three serious problems with these claims.

Box 13.2: Flaws in the arguments for raising standards by testing

First, we should ask: 'standards of achievement' in what? The answer is to be found by looking at what is tested. Is it the full range of goals of education so that the results really reflect the skills, understanding and values that we try to help our children develop? In the case of the national tests in science in England, the assessment of enquiry skills is notable by its absence, so many teachers feel they need to focus on the knowledge that is tested and minimise the opportunities for children to develop investigative skills. In countries and states where there is mandatory testing of mathematics and English only, science is a neglected area, as are many other subjects.

Second, in practice, any rise in test scores lasts for a year or two, but then tapers off. For example, the proportion of 7-year-olds reaching level 2 in mathematics rose from 84% in 1998 to 90% in 2000, but did not change in the next four years. The same was found for 11-years-olds, in both English and mathematics, with the plateau starting at 2001 (Toynbee and Walker, 2005). A widely expressed view of educators who have conducted research into summative assessment is that the initial increase in test scores is due to greater familiarity of teachers and children with the type of tests rather than increasing learning.

Box 13.2: Continued

Third, in relation to motivation we have to ask: what kind of motivation? As discussed in Chapter 6, all learning is motivated in some way, but motivation to do what is needed to pass a test is not the same as motivation to learn. There is firm research evidence that repeated testing and practising for tests is damaging to motivation to learn. Moreover, it is particularly damaging to lower achieving children and has the result of increasing the gap between higher and lower achievers.

Perhaps these flaws would not matter if the tests were treated as routine necessities, taken only at the end of the year by children of certain ages, with little impact at other times. But that is not how they are treated. Because the results are used to compare school with school and rate schools according to whether they achieve certain target levels of test scores, they have important consequences for schools and teachers. These 'high stakes' attached to the tests mean that teachers do all they can to ensure that their children pass, by giving them more tests and practising test-taking. As a result, the introduction of national tests brought with it an increase, not a decrease, in the use of other tests (Harlen and Deakin Crick, 2003).

The response to 'high stakes'

High-stakes tests are inevitably designed to be as 'objective' as possible since there is a premium on reliable marking in the interests of fairness. This has the effect of reducing what is assessed to what can be readily and reliably marked. Generally this excludes many worthwhile outcomes of education such as problem-solving and critical thinking. However, even when test-constructors do try to include higher-level thinking skills, the pressure on teachers of the high stakes attached to test scores can lead to training for the test, to the extent that students can pass any kinds of test, even those intended to assess higher cognitive skills, when they do not possess these skills (Gordon and Reese, 1997).

Even when not teaching directly to the tests, research shows that teachers report changing their approach. They adjust their teaching in ways they perceived as necessary because of the tests, spending most time in direct instruction of facts to be tested and less in providing opportunity for students to learn through enquiry and problem-solving. The research outlined in Box 13.3 conducted in Northern Ireland, where tests are used for selection to grammar schools, shows the impact that tests have on teaching. Research in primary schools in England also shows that when teachers and schools are in the grip of summative testing, teachers make little use of assessment formatively to help the learning process (Pollard *et al.*, 2000; Osborn *et al.*, 2000). In other words, high-stakes summative assessment squeezes out formative assessment as teachers emulate the tests in their own assessments. Moreover, the classroom climate becomes one of competition, where achievement is valued more than effort.

Box 13.3: The impact of tests on teaching

A study by Johnston and McLune (2000), conducted in Northern Ireland, indicated how the impact of high-stakes tests on teachers' teaching style can affect children's feeling of themselves as learners. These researchers used several instruments to measure children's learning dispositions, self-esteem, locus of control and attitude to science and related these to the transfer grades obtained by the children in the 11+ examination. From the measures of how children preferred to learn in science they grouped children according to their learning dispositions. These showed a strong preference for learning through firsthand exploration and problem-solving. The researchers also observed in classrooms to identify the teaching style of the teachers. They found a high proportion of teaching through highly structured activities and transmission of information and very little opportunity for children to learn 'hands-on'. In interviews the teachers indicated that they felt constrained to teach in this way on account of the nature of the tests. This meant that many children were not able to learn in the way they were disposed to learn and as a result felt inadequate and demoralised as learners.

In a later unpublished survey, conducted in 2004, of experience and opinions of primary teachers in relation to science, teachers in a Northern Ireland focus group commented:

> I think in P7 and in P6 [the final two years of primary school, for ages 10 and 11] we are bound by the dreaded Transfer [11+]. There is just no getting away from it and you end up giving them information, not having time to do the practical work . . . The problem is that the content becomes boring for the children at the end of P6 and beginning of P7.

> Investigative work stops halfway through P6 and it doesn't start again until halfway through P7.

What are the alternatives?

The first thing to note is that it is not necessary to assess every child in order to monitor performance at the national level. This approach means that the national picture is based on the aggregation of test results based on the relatively small number of items that individual children can be given in a test. It gives a far more restricted picture than was provided, for example, by the APU (see page 104), which monitored achievement in England, Wales and Northern Ireland between 1980 and 1985, the Scottish Survey of Achievement in Scotland and the National Assessment of Educational Progress in the USA. In these programmes, only a sample of children is assessed and each child takes only one or two of a large number of tests. These surveys provide detailed pictures of performance over a wide range of outcomes, including practical investigations in science. The results are only meaningful when brought together across the whole sample and no results for individual children are given. Consequently these tests do not have high stakes and do not disrupt all schools every year, as does the blanket testing of all children.

For evaluation of schools, the use of assessment of children's achievement is controversial, because pupil performance is a product not just of the school, but also of out-of-school influences, such as the social and educational home background of the children. One approach to allowing for this is to take into account children's achievement on entering school and calculating a measure of 'value added' by the school, but this requires a measure of earlier achievement and leads to more testing. In any case, the research evidence referred to above shows that the national tests just do not give the information that they purport to give (that is, they have low validity) because:

- children are drilled in passing them even when they don't really have the understanding being assessed

- they are too narrowly focused to give information about what children can do

- testing disadvantages some children, particularly the lower achieving ones and those who become anxious about tests.

This points to the desirability of a change in policy in relation to assessment, away from dependence on testing and towards making greater use of teachers' assessment. The advantages put forward in favour of this are summarised in Box 13.4 (based on Working Paper 2 of the Assessment Systems for the Future project (ASF), 2004).

There are some indications that the arguments in Box 13.4 are being accepted by policy-makers, as evident in the removal of tests for 7-, 11- and 13-year-olds in Wales and the proposals for assessment of 14–19-year-olds emerging from the curriculum review for that age group. In Scotland, teachers' assessment remains the main source of evidence with teachers able to call on tests to support their judgement.

Box 13.4: Arguments in favour of using assessment by teachers for summative assessment

- As part of their regular work, teachers can build up a picture of children's attainment across the full range of activities and goals. This gives a broader and fuller account of achievement than can be obtained through tests, which can only include a restricted range of items.

- There is less pressure on children and teachers compared with external tests and examinations; freedom from test anxiety means that the assessment is a more valid indication of children's achievement.

- There can be greater freedom for teachers to pursue goals in ways best suited to their children, rather than being constrained by what is perceived as necessary in order for children to pass tests.

- There is the potential for information about children's ongoing achievements to be used formatively, to help learning, as well as for summative purposes.

- Assessment by teachers can facilitate a more open and collaborative approach to summative assessment in which children can share in the process through self-assessment and derive a sense of progress towards 'learning goals' as distinct from 'performance goals'.

MAKING AND USING RECORDS

It is important to distinguish between three kinds of records that teachers need to keep:

1 Records of children's activities and experiences.

2 Records of children's day-to-day achievements.

3 Records of what individual children have achieved at certain points.

The guiding principles in keeping records are that the information should have clear purposes and that it is used for those purposes (see Box 13.5).

Box 13.5: Records for different purposes

1 Records of activities should not be confused with records of what has been achieved through them. The purpose of recording what children have experienced is to inform the teacher's future planning; this kind of record is often kept by annotating short-term plans.

2 Information about day-to-day achievements is used formatively by the teacher. Any records that are made are essentially for the teacher to remind him or herself of children's progress, and the amount of detail and the exact form are individual matters. Circumstances and experience as well as personal preference influence the amount of information teachers can keep in their heads and what it is essential to put down on paper. Unnecessary recording and transcribing from one form to another must be avoided.

3 Summary records are made for communication with others and so it is usual for the format and structure to be agreed within the school. Records of what children have achieved may attempt to capture the richness and variety of their performance through description and collection of examples of work, or it may take the form of symbols representing the achievement in relation to certain criteria (for example, those signified by levels or grades). It is important for any symbols or summary phrases that are used to be interpreted in the same way by the teacher who makes the record and others who will receive and use it. The form of record is an integral part of an assessment. It is in making the record that the actual performance is replaced by some representation of it.

Most teachers now include intended outcomes as well as learning activities in their scheme of work and these form a focus for recording achievement. The scheme of work for Key Stages 1 and 2 science published by the Department for Education and Employment (DfEE, 1998) makes a distinction between learning outcomes for specific activities and 'end of unit expectations'. For example, in a unit of work on 'using electricity' (for Year 2, or 6–7-year-olds) there are six activities, each with identified learning outcomes, extending over about eight hours of work. It would probably be unnecessary as well as far too time-consuming for teachers to record achievement for each child in relation to each activity. Notes about any child with particular problems would be sufficient as a reminder to give help later in the unit.

It is at the end of the topic or unit of work that it is helpful to make a record since that topic may not be revisited before the end of the year or the time when reports are given to parents. This could be done in relation to the 'unit expectations'. However, in the DfEE scheme these refer only to the knowledge developed in the unit and a more comprehensive record of progress would include process skills and attitudes. Figure 13.3 gives an example of how a cumulative record might be kept using the indicators of development in Chapter 8 (Boxes 8.4 and 8.5). Each number represents a particular indicator. Some achievements could be represented by a single line across the appropriate box, with a second line being added when there is more evidence leading to greater certainty about what the child can do. For conceptual understanding, titles are written in according to the topics or units being studied. Extra boxes for further areas of knowledge and understanding can be added. Such records create a cumulative summary automatically and can be passed from class to class with the child.

Child s name . . . .
Dates of records . . . .   - - - - - - - - -

Investigative skills

Raising questions	Hypothesising	Predicting	Using observation	Planning and Investigating	Interpreting evidence	Communicating and reflecting
1 ☐ 2 ☐ 3 ☐ 4 ☐ 5 ☐ 6 ☐ 7 ☐	1 ☐ 2 ☐ 3 ☐ 4 ☐ 5 ☐ 6 ☐ 7 ☐	1 ☐ 2 ☐ 3 ☐ 4 ☐ 5 ☐ 6 ☐ 7 ☐	1 ☐ 2 ☐ 3 ☐ 4 ☐ 5 ☐ 6 ☐ 7 ☐	1 ☐ 2 ☐ 3 ☐ 4 ☐ 5 ☐ 6 ☐ 7 ☐	1 ☐ 2 ☐ 3 ☐ 4 ☐ 5 ☐ 6 ☐ 7 ☐	1 ☐ 2 ☐ 3 ☐ 4 ☐ 5 ☐ 6 ☐ 7 ☐

Knowledge and understanding

Ideas about	Ideas about	Ideas about	Ideas about	Ideas about	Ideas about	Ideas about . . . .
1 ☐ 2 ☐ 3 ☐ 4 ☐ 5 ☐ 6 ☐ 7 ☐	1 ☐ 2 ☐ 3 ☐ 4 ☐ 5 ☐ 6 ☐ 7 ☐	1 ☐ 2 ☐ 3 ☐ 4 ☐ 5 ☐ 6 ☐ 7 ☐	1 ☐ 2 ☐ 3 ☐ 4 ☐ 5 ☐ 6 ☐ 7 ☐	1 ☐ 2 ☐ 3 ☐ 4 ☐ 5 ☐ 6 ☐ 7 ☐	1 ☐ 2 ☐ 3 ☐ 4 ☐ 5 ☐ 6 ☐ 7 ☐	1 ☐ 2 ☐ 3 ☐ 4 ☐ 5 ☐ 6 ☐ 7 ☐

Figure 13.3 Using progressive indicators for recording achievement

Involving children in summative assessment

The characteristics of summative and formative assessment (Chapter 7) bring out the greater need for reliability and judgements against common criteria in summative compared with formative assessment. This suggests that there might be less room for children to assess themselves for summative than for formative purposes. Some attempts have, however, been made to involve children and to express the criteria in terms that children are likely to understand. For example, the Association for Science Education (ASE) published a document designed to be used with children. It comprises a series of statements relating to attainment of the knowledge targets of the National Curriculum, expressed in language easily understood by children. For example: 'I have made a circuit with a bulb and a switch to control it. I can put the switch in different places in the circuit. I can make a circuit diagram containing a battery, bulbs and wires' (Willis, 1999, n.p.). The statements are arranged as 'bricks' in a wall and a brick is coloured in when the teacher and child feel that it has been achieved. This is a cross between a record of activities and a record of achievement and it only relates to the knowledge outcomes of the curriculum. However, it does allow children to take part in building a record of their work and is something they could show to, and talk about with, their parents.

Most approaches to involving children emphasise the formative rather than the summative role of assessment (for example, the London Record of Achievement, described in Johnson *et al.*, 1992). This is important because we want children to know how to improve and, where to direct their effort. Summative assessment shows some children that they have not achieved as much as others, which can be damaging to their self-esteem. While we should be honest with children it is also important that they see this information as helping them, not labelling them. The process of summative assessment needs to be handled so that 'when they don't have skills or knowledge, or they're behind other students, this is not a sign of a deep, shameful deficit. It's a sign that they need to study harder or find new learning strategies' (Dweck, 1999, p. 129). It is not only tests that can damage children's motivation to learn (see Chapter 6).

Reporting to parents or carers

What is appropriate for within school records is not likely to be a friendly way to report to parents, who need to know what symbols, 'levels' and words such as 'approaching' mean in terms of what their children can do. Parents also have to take in information about their children's achievements and progress in all areas of the curriculum and so a balance needs to be struck between reporting too little and too much detail. Box 13.6 shows an example of a science report that, while using some National Curriculum language, adds examples which bring it to life.

Communication with parents through a written report is made easier if this is not the only contact with the school science activities. Parents' evenings, where teacher and children show and explain their work, science fairs, participation in visits to science centres, and so on, are all ways of helping parents to understand the aims of science education and their children's progress. Parents unable to visit may keep in touch with such activities though the school website. Understanding what the school is aiming to achieve in science is important when children are asked to carry out some science activities at home or given science homework.

Box 13.6: A science report to parents or carers

Science

Throughout the year David has participated in a range of scientific activities. He under-stands that scientific ideas are based on evidence. He is willing to change his ideas when the evidence suggests it. He is usually able to carry out a fair test. When writing up his investigations he can suggest a number of ways of presenting information and usually chooses a good method of recording information.

He has gained a good knowledge of life processes and living things. He can name the major organs in the human and can show where they are in the body. He can describe feeding relationships using food chains and knows what words such as 'predator' and 'prey' mean. He made an excellent poster about food chains with his group which is still on display in the corridor.

He describes differences between properties of materials with confidence and can explain how we use these differences to classify materials. He can describe a number of methods to separate mixtures. He has a good level of knowledge and understanding of the physical processes.

Next steps

In the next term we will be carrying out more investigations. David should concentrate on fair testing and thinking about the best way to record information. He might like to take home the activity box 'Inventors and inventions' as I am sure he would enjoy it.

Next term our topics will be 'Sound and Music' and the 'Earth, Sun and Moon'.

(From Harlen and Qualter 2004, p. 269)

SUMMARY

We have discussed here two further purposes of assessment to add to the discussion of using assessment for learning, which was the focus of Part III. Assessment for summarising learning for school records and reporting to parents and others can use evidence already available from ongoing assessment of regular activities, from special tasks or tests, or a combination of these. Reference has been made to various ways of establishing levels of achievement that are embodied in national curricula, guidelines or benchmarks. We have discussed ways of increasing the dependability of teachers' judgements by various kinds of moderation.

We have also pointed out the research evidence of the detrimental impact on teachers and children of using children's test results for 'high stakes' evaluation purposes, where important decisions for teacher and schools depend on whether children reach certain test scores. The impacts include teachers focusing narrowly on what is tested, restricting opportunities for investigative work and smothering the use of assessment to help learning.

We have noted that it is important to distinguish between records of activities and of learning. Children are often given a role in the former, but in relation to assessment their role is more appropriately in assessment that is used to help learning. Finally we have briefly considered how individual achievements in science can be reported to children's parents or carers.

FURTHER READING

ARG (2002b) *Testing, Motivation and Learning*. Available from the Institute of Education, University of London and the Assessment Reform Group website: www.assessment-reform-group.org

Schilling, M., Hargreaves, L., Harlen, W. with Russell, T. (1990) *Assessing Science in the Primary Classroom: Written Tasks*. London: Paul Chapman Publishing.

Chapter 14

Resources for learning science

INTRODUCTION

Investigation of things in the natural and made world is at the heart of science education. Although we can learn a great deal by looking, listening and talking about observations, the development of understanding through enquiry generally requires some equipment, materials, information sources and other resources. In this chapter we don't attempt to cover all aspects of selection, purchase, maintenance and storage of resources but provide an overview of the principles that can guide decisions about these matters. In the first section we look at the purposes of resources. We then consider the important subject of safety and briefly discuss principles relating to selection and storage of equipment. The subsequent three sections then consider in turn resources for three main purposes: as objects of study; resources that are needed to support study; and ones that are sources of information.

THE PURPOSES THAT RESOURCES SERVE IN PRIMARY SCIENCE

It is useful to think of resources as serving three main purposes:

- As objects of study; these can be living or non-living, inside or outside the classroom.
- As the means to aid study, such as measuring instruments, containers, computer programs.
- As sources of information, including books, CD-ROMs, the Internet, visitors and other links.

Figure 14.1 sets out the main types of resources that serve each of these purposes.

As we see, some resources serve more than one purpose, but the divisions serve well enough to provide a structure for discussion. First, however, there are general points to consider about safety and about selection and storage.

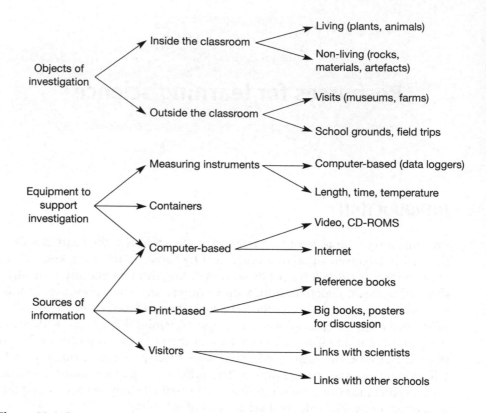

Figure 14.1 Purposes and main types of resources for primary science

SAFETY FIRST

Children's natural curiosity may lead them to try certain things which could be dangerous or to pick up objects outside the classroom which may harm them, or collect things which may harm the environment. So it is essential for teachers to be aware of potential dangers, and, without confining children's activities unnecessarily, to avoid situations that could lead to injury. There is comprehensive advice available in the excellent booklet *Be Safe* published by the ASE (2001). This covers use of tools, sources of heat, chemicals, food and hygiene, micro-organisms, suitable and unsuitable animals for keeping in the classroom, poisonous plants and work out of doors. It contains several safety 'codes' which usefully summarise precautions that teachers should take in certain situations. It suggests that children should be taught to recognise and observe warning symbols, and be encouraged to consider safety when they plan and carry out investigations.

Working safely should not be presented in a way that controls children but as a positive aim of science education. Helping children to act responsibly in matters of safety is part of helping them to take responsibility for their learning. In particular, Borrows points out in an article in *Primary Science Review* that 'science in primary schools is very safe' (Borrows, 2003, p. 18). In similar vein *Be Safe* points out that:

> Children are much safer in school than they are at home or when travelling between home and school. Within school, science is one of the safest activities – far more accidents occur in the playground or during PE lessons. Minor accidents, which result in scratches, bumps and cuts, are an acceptable part of growing up and a necessary part of the learning process.

> (ASE, 2001, p. 4)

Nevertheless it is important for teachers to assess the risks, if any, in science activities. These may vary according to the children involved and the timing of the activity. Children with behavioural difficulties may be at greater risk in some activities than other children and when children are excited or tired may not be the time for activities that require particular care and concentration. All education departments in the UK have endorsed the ASE's *Be Safe* and it is recommended that relevant points are included in schools' schemes of work.

SELECTION AND STORAGE OF RESOURCES

Rarely does a school have the task of drawing up a shopping list of requisites for science starting from scratch. Almost always it is a matter of augmenting an existing collection that has often been assembled in an unplanned way. However, listing and keeping a catalogue of equipment is essential and, with the help of a simple computer database, is not as arduous a matter as it used to be. Whenever the school programme for science is revised it is important to carry out an audit of the equipment needed to support it. Unless the school policy is to follow a particular set of curriculum materials, it will be necessary for the school to draw up its own list of resources to support its own programme.

Equipment used in science falls into three main categories:

- materials and equipment that are generally available in every classroom (glue, Plasticine, string, scissors, rulers, etc.) plus some items used mainly in science but which are of the 'everyday' kind, such as transparent plastic containers, rubber bands, boxes
- large and expensive items used in other subjects, such as computers, interactive whiteboards, cameras, video-players
- science-specific equipment such as magnifiers, measuring instruments for mass, time, temperature, and bulbs, wires, living things, etc.

Here we are concerned with the third of these only. The list of science-specific equipment is not in fact very long, for many activities can be carried out with materials already in the classroom. For example, no specialised equipment is required for the wide range of activities young children can engage in that help their awareness that there is air all around. They can 'feel' air moving as they rush through it or fan it on to each other, make paper gliders, parachutes, kites, windmills, make bubbles in water, try blowing a pellet of paper into an 'empty' bottle – all without using any materials other than those which can be collected at school or brought from home. Similarly, there are many activities concerning sound and hearing which make use of everyday objects or containers, rubber bands and any musical instruments already in the school.

Keeping it simple

There is virtue in keeping the specialised equipment to a minimum and not merely on grounds of economy. As mentioned in Chapter 4, special equipment that is used only in science and not found in other parts of children's school or everyday experience can isolate science from the 'real' world around children. If a special set of instruments has to be used for weather observations, for example, the impression may be given that useful measurements depend on that set. It can come between the things being measured and the child. Research has shown that this is often the case in secondary science (Woolnough, 1997). A better understanding of what is being measured may come from a home-made rain gauge, a windsock made from a stocking and an anemometer made with yoghurt containers rather than from more sophisticated equipment. These will be designed by the children to do the job that they have defined; they will not be starting with an instrument whose function they have to learn. Using more sophisticated equipment later will make more sense with this foundation. The more children help in designing the ways they interact with their surroundings the more they will realise that they can investigate and learn about the world around through their own activity.

There are many publications which provide help with the selection of science equipment. Lists of items, advice about obtaining and maintaining it and useful addresses can be found in publications from the ASE, such as *Primary Science Resources* (Feasey, 1998a) and *Be Safe* (ASE, 2001). Curriculum materials invariably list the equipment needed for the units or activities they suggest and the *Scheme of Work for Science at Key Stages 1 and 2* (DfEE, 1998), produced by the QCA, lists the materials and resources needed for each unit.

Storing equipment

Storing equipment centrally in the school is an obvious way to make best use of items that have to be purchased. Items such as hand lenses, mirrors and magnets need only be obtained in sufficient quantities for one class, or for two in a large school. There are obvious disadvantages of this, arising when items are mislaid, not returned to the store or not returned in good condition. So it requires careful labelling and indexing, keeping records of replacements needed and the provision of easy access and ways of transporting equipment around the school. It is the responsibility of the science subject leader to set up a system that all teachers find workable and to ensure its operation.

Organising the store

The organisation of equipment in the store depends to some extent on how science is organised in the school. The notion of 'topic boxes' has been adopted in some schools, particularly where the work is organised round units of work used through-out the school. It seems wasteful, however, for materials to lie in boxes when they could well be of use in topics other than the one for which they are earmarked. Further, this organisation would not suit more open-ended activities where equip-ment demands cannot be anticipated. The opposite extreme is to have all items stored in separate sets and for the collection needed at any time to be gathered by the teacher. This could be wasteful of time, too, since it could be anticipated that bulbs, bulb holders, wires and batteries would probably always be used together.

A compromise is probably possible, in which some equipment is kept in topic collec-tions and other more general equipment kept in separate sets. Careful cataloguing is the key to the success of this, or indeed any other, system. A listing of every item should be available to all staff showing where it can be found, if stored as general equipment, or in which topic box it is stored.

When boxes are used for storage, the contents and storage position of each topic box should be listed. This may seem a great deal of cataloguing but this is no problem once a computer database has been set up. The database can be designed to enable items to be viewed alphabetically, by shelf or whatever variable is appropriate. It should be accessible to all teachers and, in some cases, children, who can help to organise the equipment. In large schools the computer may also be used to 'book' equipment at certain times, so that a planned lesson involving the microscope, for instance, is not frustrated by finding it already in use in another classroom. The database would also have a section for ICT hardware, where this is shared among classes and for software, such as CD-ROMs and videos.

Accessing the store

For transporting equipment a trolley, or preferably more than one, is almost a neces-sity. If several can be obtained, some can be converted as the permanent and mobile store for certain commonly used materials, or for particularly heavy topic equipment. Most often, though, a teacher will load the trolley with the collection needed at a particular time. When a chosen collection is in use in a classroom for a few days or longer, details of what is there should be left in the store.

Anticipating expansion

In setting up a store it is as well to remember that collections of material generally grow quite rapidly, they rarely diminish. Items brought to school to add to a display or to the range of materials being investigated are generally donated. In this way useful items such as an old camera, clock, clockwork or battery-driven toys, metal and wood off-cuts are added to the store and room has to be available for them. The store should also house a range of containers and other general equipment that is extra to that required in each classroom for activities other than science.

This collection can swell quite quickly, too, once parents are aware that squeezy bottles, yoghurt pots, foil pie-tins and plastic bottles are all useful for school activities.

Display

Although it is essential to be able to store equipment and materials tidily away, not all of it should be always out of sight. As mentioned in Chapter 9, displays can provide starting points for activities and give children a useful way to pass odd moments. Displays can feature anything from a collection of tools, measuring instruments, or materials taken from the store, to special items on loan from the museum, local craft centre or industry. There should always be information provided about the exhibits in a suitable form and, if possible, invitations for children to handle and explore them or to enquire further in other ways.

RESOURCES FOR STUDY

Things to study in the classroom

At various times children should have the opportunity to study and investigate a wide range of living and non-living objects and materials. Non-living objects will include, for instance: bulbs, batteries, switches, buzzers, etc; collections of common materials, such as stone, wood, metal, plastic, glass, rubber, paper and objects made from them; toys that move, some with wind-up mechanisms; musical instruments; springs. They will also include things of particular relevance to children, such as food and ingredients for cooking, from which there is a great deal to learn, not just about changes in materials but about why food needs to be handled hygienically. If children are to taste what they produce in studying food, it is essential to ensure that at all stages surfaces, utensils, aprons and hands are clean and that items used in food preparation are not used for other purposes. Children should be helped to understand the reasons for these precautions.

Studying 'ourselves'

Some of the living things studied in the classroom are always present – the children themselves. Such study needs particular care, however, and *Be Safe* (ASE, 2001) includes a 'safety code' for investigating ourselves, of which the main points are summarised in Box 14.1.

Studying other living things

Other living things brought into the classroom to be studied may be kept there for short periods or can be given more permanent lodging, in which case they will need specialised housing and regular care. It is worthwhile planning the provision of these non-human members of the school so that they make the most contribution to children's experience of the variety of living things. In one school there were salamanders in one classroom, fish in another, gerbils in another and so on. Each year the children changed classroom, so that they lived with each type of animal in turn. In other cases an agreed rota for exchanging classroom animals might be more appropriate, with teachers planning children's activities to suit the animals in residence at different times.

Box 14.1: Safety code for investigating ourselves

- Be sensitive to the differences between children.

- Avoid putting individuals into situations of physical or emotional stress.

- When foods are used for investigations into the sense of taste, ensure that children do not share spoons or cups. Wherever possible use disposable items, e.g. straws.

- When smelling things put them in containers covered with muslin or similar, so that they cannot be eaten by mistake.

- In work on sound and hearing tell children that loud sounds can damage their ears; if speaking tubes are being tested, warn children not to shout or blow down them.

- Disinfect mouthpieces and any object put into the mouth.

- Tablets that disclose plaque, while safe, may encourage children to eat 'pills'.

- Teeth brought to school for study should be sterilised before handling.

- Measure body temperature on the forehead or under the armpit rather than in the mouth.

(Based on ASE, 2001, p. 24)

As well as captive animals in the classroom it should be possible to provide access to animals in natural habitats set up in the school grounds. Many schools are now using a small part of the grounds for an outdoor study area, where plants are grown and where birds, insects or other 'minibeasts' can find food and shelter. Few schools are unable to find the few square metres where plants can be grown, even if it is only in a chequer-board garden formed by taking up one or two patio slabs. Generally, much more can be done, so that nesting boxes can be provided, shrubs planted to attract butterflies, a bed for planting seeds with larger areas of garden for planting out seedlings and, quite important, a semi-wild area where wild flowers and grass can grow up round a pile of stones, giving shelter to a range of insects and other invertebrates. An outdoor resource area provides a valuable opportunity for children to study creatures without disturbing them too much. But if brought into the classroom for further study, temporary housing can be improvised from a variety of clear plastic containers.

Safety aspects of keeping and studying living things are well covered in *Be Safe* (ASE, 2001), which advises on suitable plants for growing in the classroom and on poisonous ones that should be avoided when exploring outside. With regard to animals in the classroom there are, in addition to *Be Safe*, a number of guides produced by animal welfare organisations.

Visits

Visits to places of work or visitors' centres provide opportunities for children to experience things that can't be brought into the classroom. They are highly motivating to children, who bring back to school many vivid impressions which often persist over several weeks and sustain follow-up work in other areas of the curriculum as well as science. A most successful teacher of primary science always began every topic with a visit; he said it was the equivalent to charging a battery, giving energy and vitality to the work for the next five or six weeks. Each visit was chosen to suit the programme planned and to provide opportunities for children to develop science concepts during follow-up investigations. It is not difficult to select a site for a visit in this way since most venues provide opportunities for development of any of a whole range of ideas. Figure 14.2 illustrates this, showing just some of the links between the possibilities for visits and the main areas of basic science concepts. The list in Figure 14.2 does not include museums or special exhibitions which could relate to any or all of the concepts; these have a valuable role in children's learning in addition to and not as a substitute for visiting places which are more a part of everyday life.

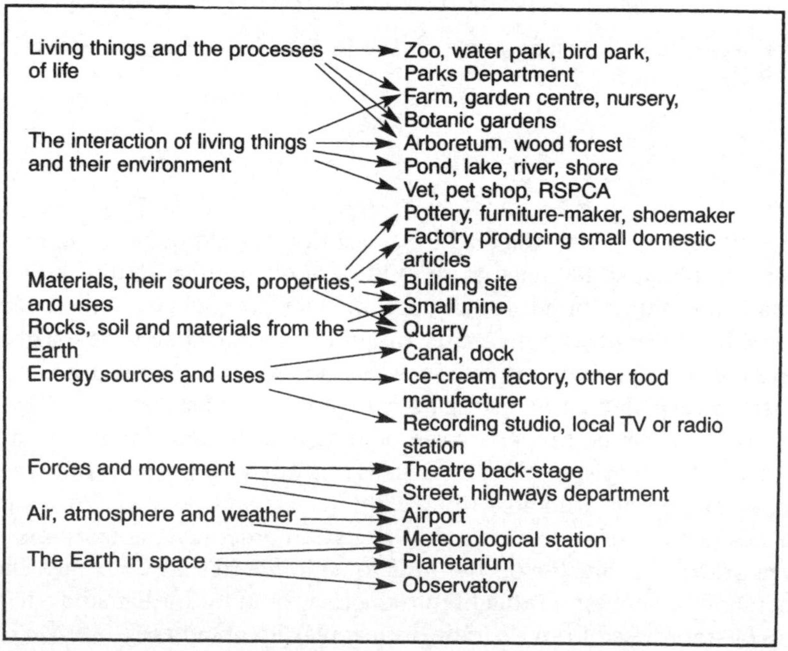

Figure 14.2 Places to visit and ideas that can be developed

Planning a visit

A considerable amount of work for the teacher is involved in planning and organising a visit, but this is rewarded several times over by the quality of the ensuing work of the children. The necessary preparation varies according to whether the visit will be entirely under the control of the teacher (as in fieldwork at a pond or in a wood) or whether people at the site will be involved in giving access and information (as in a visit to a workplace).

Where the teacher is the sole person involved in planning (even if parent-helpers or others accompany the party), the preparation must involve an initial survey of possibilities, having in mind the characteristics of the children who will be visiting. For example, 5- to 8-year-olds will want things to watch, touch, smell, handle and so there should be plenty of opportunity for being able to do these things safely; children need to be shown very clearly any dangerous plants or objects that should not be touched. Eight to ten-year-olds will not be satisfied with just looking and feeling; they will want to explore how things are related, to make more systematic observations in which patterns can be detected. Ten to twelve-year-olds are capable of concentrating on a particular question and can use the visit to gather evidence systematically, for example about the different communities of plants and animals to be found in different habitats.

Preparing the children

Once the teacher has seen what a site offers, the particular aspects to be observed or investigated have to be fully planned, possibly involving another visit. Preparation of the children then begins. The visit will be more fruitful if children begin studying the materials, equipment, plants or animals, etc. that they will see beforehand so that the visit is part of the study of a topic rather than a stand-alone event. Children should help in identifying beforehand questions that they want to answer during the visit.

The question of worksheets for the children to use during the visit is likely to arise in the context of planning. If these are detailed and require children to look for specific things, they may end up focusing their attention too narrowly and spending their time with their head buried in their notebooks. It is, however, important for the children to be prepared beforehand so that their attention will be focused on the main areas of interest and enquiry. They may also give some prior thought to what information they should aim to collect, in whatever form, so that they can discuss and review it afterwards.

Preparing those to be visited

Where the visit will involve those at the site, then the preparation must involve correspondence and close communication between the school and those who will be involved in the visit. A prior visit by the teacher is essential, not only for the teacher to find out what the children may experience and what safety precautions need to be made beforehand, but to tell those in the place to be visited, who may be acting as guide, demonstrator or informer, something about the children. In some cases those involved may have little idea of the level of background knowledge, length of attention span and interests of primary school children. The teacher can help them with their preparation by suggesting some of the questions the children might ask and the sorts of things that will need to be explained in simple terms.

It may also be helpful to invite someone from the industry back to the school to talk to the children some time after the visit. This gives the children an opportunity to pose questions that have occurred later during reflection on the visit. The double benefit here is that the representative from the industry has the chance to learn about the children's work and the school environment, which can improve school–industry communication to the good of later visiting groups.

This suggests that a visit to a site is not an isolated event, but part of a more enduring link with an industry. Feasey (1998b) gives some good advice on developing successful school–industry links. Among the variety of forms that the links can take are:

- a scientist or industrialist having an extended relationship with a school, so that they are able to visit classrooms, talk to children and teachers and help to plan lessons and visits

- teacher placements in industry, so that teachers can experience for themselves how industry works, for as short a time as one day or for a week or two

- the production of materials for classroom use, in partnership with teachers

- a supply of material discarded in production that the school can use, for example off-cuts of wood or metal, paper, plastic sheeting

- children communicating with industry through fax, e-mail and letter.

Visiting farms

Farm visits are particularly rich in opportunities for learning about living things, food and the use of the environment. Richardson (2000) sets out the precautions that need to be taken to avoid the very rare, but serious, infections that can be picked up from direct contact with animals. Other aspects of the topic, and a list of useful resources, is included in the same issue of *Primary Science Review* (Issue 62, 2000).

Visits to natural sites

Natural sites, such as a wood, hillside, riverside or the sea shore, are particularly valuable if they are close enough to the school to be visited regularly at different times of the year. Some schools are fortunate enough to have such opportunities within their schools ground, if developed as suggested earlier. Some of the opportunities that such sites provide are indicated in the quotation in Box 14.2.

In order to derive the benefit from study of natural sites that Box 14.2 describes, it is necessary to start with a small piece – either a limited area, often described as a 'minifield', or a transect. A 'minifield' is a small piece of ground, of about one square metre, marked out by using pegs and string or a hoop or frame of any shape. It should be an area chosen as likely to be interesting. Attention is focused by limiting the area. Children, in groups of about three for each minifield, look at what is there and gradually begin to identify different plants and creatures within it, map it and then ask and answer questions such as: which kinds occur most? Which least? Do some crowd out others? Are some being eaten by some creatures? A transect is defined by a line across several metres of ground, rather like an elongated minifield. The main difference is that it cuts across different kinds of terrain, so changes can be seen along its length. Again children can start by identifying what is there and then begin to hypothesise and investigate why there are changes along the length of the transect.

Box 14.2: Relevance of studying natural locations

Living and growing, while we often regard it as commonplace, is quite an extraordinary process. Anything that lives and grows is confined to some specific place and depends on the local conditions prevailing there; on the soil and what it is composed of, on weather and climate and the amount of exposure to, or shelter from, sunshine, wind and other disturbances. Nothing lives entirely alone. There are the eaters and there are the eaten; some creatures encroach on others and displace them, or given them shade or provide protection. Others move, lift, trample or nibble. Every surviving living thing has adapted itself to some extent to conditions of mutual dependence in its own community. That is why the study of fellow creatures should not stop at their 'external and internal features' or appearance, and even less at the names we have given them. The creatures around become more fascinating if studied in the wider context of their community, however small, where every creature acquires its own singular significance. Moreover, the concept of 'community' will gain greater depth of meaning for the children, which is a prerequisite for mature insight into the wider relationships within our larger environment of the Earth.

(Elstgeest and Harlen, 1990, p. 30)

RESOURCES TO SUPPORT INVESTIGATIONS: USING ICT

Figure 14.1 lists resources to help investigation as including measuring instruments, containers and computers. We have discussed the first two of these under the heading of selecting resources, so here we will deal with the use of equipment that involves computers and other forms of ICT.

One of the criticisms of practical work in science, at primary as well as at secondary level, has been that the procedures of handling equipment and of recording results, particularly drawing graphs or charts, often becomes the main focus of attention, while the meaning of the results assumes a minor role. For example, the simple investigation of the cooling of warm water in different containers involves using a thermometer (and so knowing how to read it), taking down readings at particular times (and remembering to do this – or risk dubious results) and then drawing a graph or displaying the results so that comparisons can be made. This takes much time and energy and although it is useful to learn how to do these things, if the purpose is to understand something about cooling, there is too much activity intervening between asking the question and obtaining the answer.

The use of sensor probes and data-logging using a computer removes these intervening steps and enables children to focus on their results. Portable and hand-held (pocket-book) computers enable this kind of work to be carried on outside as well as inside the classroom. Data-loggers can be used in the field and then connected to a computer on return to the classroom. The experience of two teachers described in Box 14.3 illustrates these advantages.

Box 14.3: Comparing experiences with and without data-logging

Two teachers described the effect this had on a project involving taking various measurements in a woodland (Baume and Gill, 1995). Some children (10- and 11-year-olds) had to use conventional instruments while others used a portable computer and temperature and light probes. The teachers reported that 'those using the probes were able to gather data and very quickly see a graph, or graphs, appearing on the computer screen. Without any prompting, the children commented on what appeared on the screen and immediately began to ask questions such as, "What would happen if?" The emphasis changed from collecting data to working in the field, analysing, predicting, moving probes and testing what we had discussed. Dynamic thought and action had replaced mundane recording. Science sprang to life. (Baume and Gill, 1995, p. 14). They also reported that the children were motivated to test ideas about temperature and light levels in other locations such as the stream, the football pitch and the playground. 'The tools were in our hands. Ideas could be quickly tested. We were in charge?' (p. 15).

Using computers not only takes the drudgery out of some practical work, but can extend the range and sensitivity of information that pupils can use in their science investigations. Sensitive and rapidly responding detectors of temperature, light, sound, rotation, position, humidity and pressure, linked to the computer via a universal interface, can become the means for pupils to investigate phenomena to which the tools previously available to them were quite insensitive. For example, a probe that can measure temperature precisely can be used to test the idea that dark surfaces heat up more quickly than light ones when exposed to sunshine, or to find out whether the skin on different parts of the body is at the same temperature, or whether metal objects that feel cold really are at a different temperature from their surroundings. Light-sensitive probes can be used to compare intensities associated with changes in the size of the pupil of the eye, to investigate regular and irregular reflection from surfaces, the effect of placing a filter between a light source and the probe, etc. In all cases the measurements can be displayed in numerical, symbolic or graphical form.

These are just some examples of the wealth of possibilities opened up by using the computer to extend the senses, to help in measurement and recording data. Such uses increase dramatically children's ability to use evidence in testing ideas, both their own and others'. The speed with which the computer accomplishes the drudgery of measurement, tabulation and display enables children's attention to be focused on the interpretation of data, on making sense of what they are finding. This is just the aspect of investigating which is neglected in the absence of this help, when obtaining results seems an end in itself, the climax of the work rather than the beginning of thinking, as should be the case. The construction and testing of ideas by children can become more central to their scientific activity when they control the technology and are not confined by it. Of course, children have to become used to using the technology – although one suspects that this is far easier for them than their teachers.

Using interactive whiteboards

The use of interactive whiteboards was mentioned briefly in Chapter 10 in relation to the teacher recording events and displaying the images later for discussion with the children. Another example of using this technology is for improving investigative skills and helping the interpretation of data. Software enables children to write directly on the boards, to enter data in a combined record, for example, or to interact with each other in graphing and interpreting data and save work to be followed up later. Earle (2004) describes an example of such work and lists many advantages for both teacher and children, in terms of saving time, ease of reviewing and changing earlier work, collaborative learning and motivation.

Keeping the link to real life

In relation to using computer programs a warning has to be sounded in relation to ensuring that the 'real world' is not replaced by the vision on the computer screen. This is less likely to happen when computers programs are used for data-logging and display, where the sensor is clearly in touch with the situation being investigated, than when a progam is used to simulate reality. Simulations enable children to investigate situations that they may not be able to explore directly. They enable users to test out the effect of changing certain variables, but only the ones built into the program. Even with older children, there is a danger that simulations give the impression that variables in physical processes can be easily and independently controlled, and can represent a caricature of reality rather than a representation of it. Thus computers are probably best used as tools in children's investigations of the real world rather than as a replacement of the real world.

Using live video images

One way in which the link to real life can be just that is the use of what is in practice closed circuit TV to spy on wildlife in the school garden. The equipment needed is a video camera, microphone, cable and TV receiver, which can be purchased as a purpose-built package at a cost well within the budget of most schools. An account of how this equipment enabled 5- to 7-year-olds to observe the behaviour of blue tits from inside a nesting box, as they nested and laid eggs, is given by Barker and Buckle in an article in *Primary Science Review* (2002, p. 8). The authors give details of cost and sources of information about the equipment (now becoming more widely available) as well as a deeply engaging description of the range of learning experiences of the children.

SOURCES OF INFORMATION

Children's experience can be extended not only through direct interaction with the world around but also through information provided in books, CD-ROMs, television, video and film. These may provide information about the natural world, scientific ideas, suggestions for enquiry and, in some cases, data that can be used by children to test their own and alternative ideas. Some of these resources are used individually by children and some in groups. In all cases it has to be emphasised that these resources have an important role in learning science, but they must be regarded as supporting and not replacing children's first-hand enquiry.

CD-ROMs

More and more information is being provided in CD-ROM form, some including video, sound and animation as well as text and graphics. Navigation through such a resource may absorb much of children's attention when they first use it and teachers need to ensure that this is not so demanding that little thought is given to the subject matter. In general, if the CD-ROM is well chosen for the children, they quickly become adept at exploring the material. The chief problem then becomes selection, since there is so much information available, and so it is particularly important to ensure that the children have a clear purpose in mind and are able to use the resource selectively. The criteria for choosing CD-ROMs will include the reading level, the ease of exploring and the extent of interactivity that is possible.

By providing information in a visual and easily accessible form, CD-ROMs allow children to seek answers to their own questions, test hypotheses and make connections between different pieces of information, as in the example in Box 14.4.

Box 14.4: Using information on a CD-ROM to test a hypothesis

Govier (1995) recounts how children new to using CD-ROMs chased down information to test their hypotheses about the position of the eyes of various animals. Some, like lions and cheetahs, have forward-facing eyes, while others, like horses and deer, have side-facing eyes. Having rejected the idea that this difference was associated with the speed of the animals, the children considered the predator–prey difference. The CD-ROM helped them to test their suggestion that the predators have eyes at the front and the preyed-upon have eyes at the sides:

> Even before they had looked at lots of examples to test this hypothesis, some of the children were postulating an explanation. The hunted animals need side-facing eyes so that they can keep a good look out all around. Explaining the eye position of the hunters was more difficult. But a few experiments on binocular vision, in particular the difficulty of judging distances or looking at stereoscopic pictures with only one eye open, pointed to a possible answer. Several video clips on the CD-ROM showed predators making a kill, and the importance of being able to gauge distance accurately could clearly be seen.

(Govier, 1995, pp. 16–17)

Using the Internet

The potential of the Internet as a source of information is enormous, but it is not always easy to realise in practice. The Internet provides materials that are more up to date than textbooks and reference books and creates the links with the real world which give the much valued relevance to classroom work. However, searching can also be frustrating and time-consuming, so children need to be trained in how to do it efficiently, just as for using CD-ROMs. Some schools have an intranet which gives access to a restricted range of sites and can be a useful starting point for learning how to search, select key-words and follow links from one site to another.

Schools' access to the full World Wide Web is invariably limited by blocking unsuitable sites to minimise the chance of children stumbling on inappropriate material and so make it safe for them to use without constant close supervision. Using the Internet and search engines gives children opportunity to find information, test hypotheses and explore different environments as long as they have a clear idea of what they are looking for and are selective in what they download. The sites set up by museums and science centres are particularly appropriate for science work and are generally easy for children to use. A single address (www.24hourmuseum.org.uk) gives links to a range of museums, science centres and galleries in the UK.

Books for children

Children need access to reference books for information beyond that which a teacher can supply, to satisfy their curiosity and sometimes their appetite for collecting names and facts. Information books for young children are difficult to write. Finding a way to present information in simple understandable terms requires an expert in the subject matter; the best such books are written by scientists or doctors (for example, the award-winning books by Balkwill and Rolph, 1990a and 1990b). Introducing fantasy as a vehicle for telling 'the story of a meal' or 'the life of a drop of water' does not necessarily aid understanding.

In choosing reference books for children the criteria are not very different from those for good reference books for adults – large, clear, coloured photographs, with straightforward text and an easily used index or other way of locating information. However, modern reference books, as in the case of web pages, now use more complex formats, than straightforward blocks of text with linked illustrations. There are more often diagrams where the layout is part of the message, arrows, icons and most text spread out in boxes or labels. Children need to learn how to take the messages from these more varied ways of presenting information. Peacock (2004, p. 7) gives the following advice:

> Children tend to look first at blocks of text, but it is usually more helpful to encourage them to look first at captions, icons, questions or pictures. When the child has identified the page they need to use, you can help by 'teaching the page'. This means asking questions as the child tries to 'navigate' around a page, such as: What is this (pointing to heading, picture, icon, caption, etc.)? What does it tell you? What else tells you about …?

Reference books can usefully be kept together in a central school library and borrowed by classes, perhaps for an extended time such as half a term, on those occasions when they are likely to be in constant demand for the topic in hand. With this type of use in mind it may be preferable to purchase smallish books restricted to one topic (such as Observer's Books published by Warne) rather than large encyclopaedic volumes.

Wallcharts and big books

Not all reference material is in standard book form. Wallcharts, although less durable than books, have some advantages over them. Several children can consult them at one time and each can see all the information available: useful either for identifying a specimen by matching or for seeing the parts of a process linked together in a large flow diagram.

'Big books' are large-format books, usually on board and about 600 by 450 mm, with large print and illustrations which can be seen by a group of children. They are particularly useful with the youngest children, as part of discussion between the teacher and a small group of children. The teacher may cover some of the written information at the start and question children about what is shown in the illustrations to gather ideas and gradually reveal the text so that there is not too much to take in all at once. Used in this way they can provide a stimulus to investigation, but without an active follow-up there may be little scientific understanding developed.

VISITORS AND LINKS

Links with scientists

There are schemes that link individual scientists with schools with benefits for both parties in this relationship:

The research scientists offer:

- Up-to-date information, resources and expertise

- Classroom support and ideas

- Role models which can help to dispel the usual stereotypes.

The teachers and children offer the research scientists an opportunity to:

- Share their ideas and interests

- Develop interpersonal skills

- Develop communication skills

- Gain insight into primary children's ideas.

(Feasey, 1998a, p. 109)

Many schools have scientists among the children's parents, who would be happy to visit and share some of their experience and expertise with children. This is what happened in a Cambridge school (Quail, 2001), when children found out more about the work of a GP, an astronomer and an Antarctic researcher. Other schools have invited environmental scientists to talk about work in testing water and air for pollutants. These are people who are not generally identified by children as scientists. Such visits help in countering the usual white-coated image of scientists and emphasise the role of science in everyday life.

Two initiatives of the Centre for Science Education at Sheffield Hallam University aim to develop links between schools and scientists. Although developed for secondary schools, the Acclaim Project (www.acclaimscientist.org.uk) can be adapted for older primary children. It aims to enthuse and inform children about the work of leading scientists, through talks, videos about scientists and curriculum materials. The Researchers in Residence (http://extra.shu.ac.uk/rinr) project prepares and then links cutting-edge scientists working at PhD level with a host school. What they do in school is negotiable between the host school and the researcher; there are clearly possibilities for primary schools.

Links with other schools

Other links that are fruitful in relation to science education include links with schools in other parts of the world. Children can communicate from school to school electronically and sometimes via video-link. They can exchange data about, for example, the weather, the locality, what they eat and wear and, most importantly, undertake collaborative investigations, pooling data and adding to what each class could achieve alone. The project 'Science Across the World' puts teachers and pupils in touch with each other to exchange information, opinions and ideas on a variety of science topics, via the website www.science-across.org

SUMMARY

We have discussed a range of resources that help learning in science in different ways – as objects of study, as equipment to help study and as sources of information. Frequent reference has been made to safety precautions, although the point has also been made that primary science is a very safe activity. We have suggested that equipment used in carrying out investigations should be as simple as possible, using everyday objects in preference to science laboratory equipment. As well as living and non-living resources to be studied in the classroom, attention has been given to taking children out to visit workplaces and natural sites. Visits provide opportunities for enquiry and motivation for continued study later in the classroom. The importance of preparing children for visits and embedding such work in relevant topics has been emphasised.

In relation to the use of ICT, the use of probes and data-logging devices for collecting information and computer programs for displaying data helps to ensure that children reach the point of interpreting their findings and are not held up by the mechanics of collecting data manually. Sensors also extend the range of data that children can collect to test their ideas. Interactive whiteboards facilitate collaborative work and class discussion of findings.

Children need information sources to answer some of their questions and test their hypotheses and these can be provided in the form of books, CD-ROMs, the Internet and people – people visiting the classroom or at places visited by the children. The value for learning science of links with industry, with scientists and with other schools has also been mentioned.

FURTHER READING

Primary Science Review, Issue 69, September/October 2001 contains various articles on learning about science and scientists.

A range of ways of using computers is given in:

Frost, P. (1999) *IT in Primary Science: a Compendium of Ideas for Using Computers and Teaching Science*. Hatfield: Association for Science Education.

Three chapters in the *ASE Guide to Primary Science*, third edition (2005) are relevant:

Dunne, M. and Lakin, L. (2005) Obtaining and managing resources. In W. Harlen (ed.) *ASE Guide to Primary Science*, (third edition). Hatfield Association for Science Education.

Mitchell, R. (2005) Availability and use of ICT. In W. Harlen (ed.) *ASE Guide to Primary Science*, (third edition). Hatfield: Association for Science Education.

Peacock, A. and Dunne, M. (2005) Learning science outside the classroom. In W. Harlen (ed.) *ASE Guide to Primary Science*, (third edition). Hatfield: Association for Science Education.

Chapter 15

Managing science at the school level

INTRODUCTION

In this final chapter we look at ways of ensuring that the school has an agreed programme for science that provides breadth, balance, continuity and progression in children's learning experiences. Setting this up requires planning across the school and, once in place, requires maintenance to ensure that individual class programmes are consistent with the overall objectives. This will involve monitoring and evaluating and using the findings formatively to provide any professional development or resources that are found to be needed. The work involved in planning, implementing and evaluating provision for science falls upon the teacher with special responsibility for science – who may be called the science subject leader or co-ordinator – in collaboration with the headteacher or principal.

The role of the subject leader has dramatically grown in extent and importance since the later 1980s and in England is now underpinned by the specification of national standards (TTA, 1998). This chapter is, therefore, in one sense, all about the role of the science subject leader, since all the topics discussed relate to the tasks that are likely to be part of this role. In the first section we review the responsibilities and tasks of the science subject leader. We then consider aspects of developing a school programme, involving long-term and medium-term planning. The third section considers what is involved in auditing or monitoring the programme in action in order to decide what support is needed. In the final section we consider support in terms of professional development.

In discussing evaluation the concern here is limited to evaluation for formative purposes, for improving science education in the school. The concern is not with evaluation by external agents such as inspectors. Inspections of science are described by Oakley (1998), while the role of the subject leader in preparing for such external evaluations is discussed by Bell and Ritchie (1999). To try to avoid confusion in the use of terms, the word 'evaluation' here is used in relation to programmes, practices and learning experiences, while 'assessment' is used in relation to children's achievements.

THE ROLE OF THE SCIENCE SUBJECT LEADER

In schools where teachers teach all, or almost all, subjects to their own classes, and there is no specialist teaching, the responsibility for co-ordinating the teaching of particular subjects is generally assigned to particular teachers. There has been a change in the title of the teacher who takes such responsibility, from co-ordinator to subject leader. This change signifies a change in the range of tasks undertaken and, to some degree, of emphasis within them. As Bell and Ritchie (1999) point out, when described as a 'co-ordinator', the role is reactive, while the title of 'subject leader' is associated with a more pro-active role. The latter may extend to appraising other staff in relation to their teaching of the subject and involves greater emphasis than before on monitoring, evaluation and target-setting.

The National Standards for Subject Leaders, set out by the Teacher Training Agency (TTA) in England, are couched in terms that can apply to any subject. Interpreted in relation to science, they describe a set of responsibilities set out in Table 15.1.

Table 15.1 The responsibilities of the science subject leader

Key areas	Responsibilities	Tasks
Strategic direction and development of science in the school	• Develop and implement a a science policy • Create and maintain a climate of positive attitudes and confidence in teaching science • Establish a shared understanding of why teaching science is important and of its role in children's education • Identify and plan support for underachieving children • Analyse and interpret appropriate data, reserach and inspection evidence • Establish short-, medium-, and long-term plans for developing and resourcing science in the school • Monitor progress in implementing plans and achieving targets and evaluate effects to inform further improvement	• Auditing provision for children's learning in science • Analysing and evaluating audit evidence • Communicating information about science teaching in the school to management and other staff • Seeking advice as necessary • Agreeing aims, targets, criteria for success and deadlines • Preparing action plans in relation to science • Documenting policies and plans

▶

Table 15.1 Continued

Key areas	Responsibilities	Tasks
Teaching and learning	• Ensure science curriculum coverage, continuity and progression for all children • Ensure teachers understand and communicate objectives and sequences of teaching and learning • Provide guidance on teaching methods to meet the needs of all children and the requirements for understanding science • Ensure that science contributes to the development of literacy, numeracy and ICT skills • Establish and implement policies and practices for assessing, recording and reporting learning in science • Set expectations for staff and children and evaluate achievement • Evaluate teaching, identify good practice and act to improve the quality of teaching in science • Establish partnership and involvement of parents • Develop links with the community, business and industry	• Preparing and documenting schemes of work, assessments, records and reports for science • Advising colleagues on science activities and lessons, and providing ideas and starting points • Helping colleagues to develop their own understanding in science • Mounting displays relating to science • Keeping up to date with new ideas in the teaching of science • Checking links with other areas of the curriculum • Being the link between the school and outside contacts, such as zoos, museum services, industry
Staff management	• Audit staff needs for professional development in science • Co-ordinate provision of professional development • Ensure that trainees and newly qualified teachers are supported so that they reach appropriate standards in teaching science • Work with the school co-ordinator for special needs to develop individual plans for some children	• Planning, arranging and running professional development • Working with colleagues in classrooms • Keeping the schools in touch with new thinking and developments in science

Table 15.1 Continued

Key areas	Responsibilities	Tasks
Resource management	• Establish needs for resources of all kinds for teaching science • Ensure effective organisation and use of resources for science including ICT • Maintain existing resources and find out about new ones • Create a stimulating and safe environment for learning science	• Selecting and ordering materials and equipment • Organising storage and efficient access for resources • Finding out about new equipment and materials for teaching science • Making proposals for enriching the school environment as a resource for scientific investigation • Assessing risks in using equipment and ensuring safety precautions are observed

Source: Based on TTA (1998)

The opportunities for subject leaders to carry out all of the responsibilities indicated in Table 15.1 are in practice limited by having too little time released from teaching his or her own class to help others. So the situation that Ritchie (1997) found in research a decade ago reflects what is still the norm. He found that science subject leaders were most frequently involved in developing the school policy, preparing schemes of work, obtaining and managing equipment and materials and giving advice to colleagues. Few were teaching science to other teachers' classes or worked in other classes to provide support for colleagues. However, this may well change as more emphasis is given to school self-evaluation within the context of school improvement, in which subject leaders will have a key role in evaluating teaching and learning in the school.

CURRICULUM PLANNING AT THE SCHOOL LEVEL

Planning at the school level should provide a framework within which each teacher can produce his or her class programmes of work with confidence that there is progression and no unintended overlap across the years. Schools may not wish to adopt, in its entirety, an official scheme of work such as that proposed by the QCA (DfEE, 1998), but such documents do provide useful examples of what needs to be set out in a school's scheme if it is to provide a basis for continuity and progression. The QCA document is also helpful in defining three levels of planning as quoted in Box 15.1.

The long-term plan

The overall long-term plan for the school should set out how the parts of the curriculum are divided across the years so that there is a balance of topics within each year and progression from year to year. How the topics are described reflects the school's view of science and how it relates to other areas of learning. General topics (such as 'transport', 'clothing', 'festivals') combine objectives of learning science with those of other subjects. Science-focused topics (such as 'water', 'the sky', 'the weather', 'stopping and starting') concentrate on the objectives of learning science and are usually designated as science lessons or science activities. There are values in both forms of curriculum organisation. Integrated topics or themes allow work to follow children's interests and can extend across timetable and subject boundaries. Science topics, on the other hand, have the advantage of providing opportunities for in-depth study of particular ideas and provide for explicit attention to process skill development. They also enable children to test their own ideas and identify science activities as such.

Box 15.1: Long-, medium- and short-term planning

Long-term planning for science is undertaken in the context of each school's overall curriculum plan which reflects the needs of all children. All staff need to agree which parts of the programmes of study are drawn together to make coherent, manageable teaching units. The long-term plan shows how these teaching units are distributed across the years . . . in a sequence that promotes curriculum continuity and progress in children's learning. The units for each year should reflect the balance of the programme of study. They may be linked with work in another subject.

A medium-term plan identifies learning objectives and outcomes for each unit and suggests activities enabling these to be achieved. A medium-term plan usually shows a sequence of units that will promote progression and an estimate of the time each unit will take. In many schools all staff are involved in the production of the medium-term plan, with the science co-ordinator ensuring there is consistency within the units and that they promote progression.

Short-term planning is the responsibility of individual teachers, who build on the medium-term plan by taking account of the needs of the children in a particular class and identifying the way in which ideas might be taught to the children in the class.

(DfEE, 1998, p. 12)

In practice, the integration of science with other subjects is extremely difficult. When not done well it has been criticised by school inspectors for leading to fragmentation of the subject and comprising activities that do not justify the label of 'science activities'. Integrated topics that do lead to good science require 'outstanding knowledge, expertise and insight from the teacher' (DES, 1989, p. 18). In the past the publication of the work of the few outstanding teachers may have given the impression that this approach to science is much easier than is really the case.

The overall plan, probably drawn up by the science subject leader, has to be agreed by all teachers and is probably best expressed in terms that leave some flexibility for individual teachers, through medium-term planning, to teach them as science-focused topics or to weave them into broader topics if preferred.

Medium-term plans

As Box 15.1 indicates, medium-term planning sets out what is to be taught during a block of time spread over several weeks. The plan is often worked out by the class teacher and science subject leader together. The plan for a class will take into account the particular needs of a class and their previous work and experiences. It will set out:

- the learning objectives and how progress towards them will be identified
- the activities to be undertaken by the children and the assessment opportunities they provide
- the resources that will be required, including use of ICT
- the background knowledge required by the teacher
- any special activities, such as visits or events in school, that require information being sent to, or permission sought from, parents or carers.

The amount of detail included is an individual matter for the teacher, depending on his or her confidence in understanding and teaching the subject involved. Some will need more help than others from the science subject leader in relation to background information and appropriate resources.

The extent to which the teacher integrates science with other subjects is also a matter where there is room for individual choice within the overall policy of the school. The criticism of broad topic work has already been mentioned. But the opposite – strict subject teaching – has also been criticised as unproductive. Inspectors in England have noted that schools adopting a flexible approach to the organisation of children's work are more likely to achieve higher standards than those sticking rigidly to subject teaching. The Primary Strategy (DfES, 2003) urges schools to feel free to organise the curriculum and timetable as they find best for their children and teachers.

Links between subjects add to the relevance of what is learned, particularly important in science where understanding the world around is the aim. Linking subjects also helps in dealing with what is widely perceived as an overloaded curriculum. The overload appears greatest when every item is seen as having to be taught separately, whereas learning can be maximised by carefully planned topics bringing appropriate subjects together. Medium-term planning should result in setting out the learning goals and types of activity so that the meaning of the topics is clear enough to prevent repetition or gaps across children's experiences.

KEEPING THE PROGRAMME UNDER REVIEW

An important part of the science subject leader's role is monitoring and evaluating the learning and the provision for learning in science. To use the term 'evaluation' makes it sound very formal. Formality is not necessary but the process does need to be rigorous, with everyone involved agreeing to the criteria being used in deciding whether or not action needs to be taken to improve the teaching and learning.

Evaluation is the process of gathering and using information to help in making decisions or judgements. The distinction between the *evidence* and the *criteria* used in judging it is important. Making explicit the criteria on which the judgement is based identifies evaluation as quite different from passing an opinion, which does not need to be justified. Nevertheless evaluation is by no means the value-free process that some might have supposed and others would wish it to be. The selection of criteria, the kind of information and the way the two are brought together will all affect the judgement that is made. Indeed it might well be said that understanding the nature and limitations of evaluation is essential to its usefulness. Naive assumptions as to what can be achieved by evaluation, what faith can be placed in its results, have to be avoided.

There is a close parallel between the process of assessment of learners' achievement, in which evidence is judged in relation to criteria (see Chapter 7), and the process of evaluation. There is also a parallel in relation to the different purposes of making the judgements, which can be formative or summative. The concern here is with formative evaluation, conducted for the purpose of improving the educational provision. Nevertheless, to be useful the process has to be carried out with rigour and this means identifying the criteria to be applied in making judgements and using them systematically.

Formative evaluation

The parallel with the formative assessment of children's performance extends to the representation of the process of evaluation as a repeated cycle of events, as in Figure 15.1.

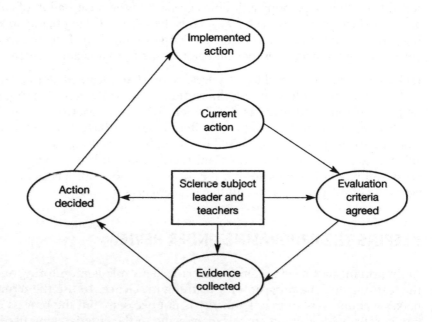

Figure 15.1 Formative school evaluation cycle

It is not necessary to take on the whole of the curriculum, learning and provision for science in the evaluation at a particular time. What is indicated as the 'action' in Figure 15.1 could be, for example, one or more of the following:

- the science provision for children with special educational needs
- the use of ICT in science
- the children's achievement of process skills
- the nature and use being made of the school's policy for science
- the extent of continuity in pupils' experience from class to class
- the adequacy of resources and equipment
- the support and development of staff
- the assessment and record-keeping in science.

Identifying criteria

The choice of focus might be made by the teachers or the science subject leader, or might be in response to a report from external advisers or inspectors. Once it is decided, the first step is the identification of criteria. This comes before collection of evidence, since the criteria determine the evidence that is relevant. Identifying criteria means asking and answering questions such as:

- How would we identify good . . . (provision for children with special educational needs)?
- What are our aims in making use of . . . (ICT in science)?
- What are the indications of satisfaction . . . (with the school's policy for science)?

Some examples of possible answers to some of these questions are suggested in Box 15.2.

Collecting evidence

Sources of evidence are signalled in these criteria. Teachers are clearly a major source. Their records and opinions need to be collected and reviewed systematically. In addition, their views on the adequacy of support, equipment, professional development, etc. can be sought by questionnaire (in a large school) or interview. Documents provide a second source of information. School programmes and procedures and national or regional curriculum standards and assessment requirements or guidelines have to be analysed and compared. Then there are the perceptions of pupils, parents and others, such as governors, local inspectors or advisers, which can be elicited by questionnaire or interview. Where time allows, semi-structured interviews held with a well-selected sample are probably most helpful, since they can probe reasons for satisfaction or dissatisfaction and so suggest action to be considered. The science subject leader has a key part in collecting these data and in evaluating how well the criteria are met.

Box 15.2: Some examples of criteria for judging various aspects of provision for science

- Teachers are aware of and use the school policy on science.

- Teaching methods are consistent with those agreed and expressed in the school policy.

- The children's work is marked according to the school's policy.

- The programmes of individual classes cover the relevant part of the requirements of national or regional guidelines without gaps or unnecessary repetition.

- Records of children's experiences and learning are kept consistently in every class.

- Teachers are satisfied with the amount, quality and accessibility of equipment.

- Teachers can find the help they need in planning and teaching their science programmes.

- Teachers are satisfied with provision for professional development in science.

- Children's performance shows regular progress at the levels expected.

- Children are enthusiastic about science.

- Parents are satisfied with their children's experiences and performance in science.

In relation to children's learning experiences, the children's written work provides a useful source and one that may be the easiest to access by the science subject leader unless time is reserved for observing and interviewing colleagues. Wright (2003), from long experience as an adviser for science, gives advice on the process of scrutiny of children's work. She suggests that looking through children's work can provide evidence of whether children's experiences truly reflect teachers' plans or whether 'some colleagues are spending a long time on topics they like and feel secure with and whizzing through the unfamiliar. Are the children getting the breadth and balance that the long- and medium-term plans are meant to ensure?' (2003, p. 8). She notes that obvious features, such as whether the work is dated or has a title, may indicate the value to children of recording their work. Further useful points about work scrutiny are quoted in Box 14.3.

Deciding action: using the criteria

Some measure of the extent to which the criteria are met is needed in deciding whether action is required. In some cases information will come from several sources, and so it is probably best to take the criteria one at a time and to scan across all the relevant information in order to make the judgement. This procedure may seem rather rough and subjective, as indeed it is, but in practice greater refinement is not needed for the purpose being considered. It is usually the case that in the areas where there is a gap between what we would like to be happening (as represented by the criteria) and what is happening (evident in the information gathered) it is likely to be large and obvious. Evaluation in this context is not intended to produce fine judgements of the extent of success, but to the make the work of the school more effective. The process of gathering information and sifting it systematically is likely to be of more value in bringing shortcomings to the attention and in suggesting ways of improvement than the end product. Indeed the end product is only the beginning of the next cycle in what should be an ongoing review.

Box 14.3: The evidence from scrutiny of children's work in science

Looking through a collection of work also gives a good idea as to whether the pace of lessons is appropriate. A lot of unfinished work may indicate a mismatch between tasks and the pupils' interest and abilities, particularly for the lower attaining pupils. Are the children putting enough effort into it so that it reflects care and pride in their work? In some science activities, such as observing seeds, drawings are probably more important than words. Are drawings and diagrams large enough, neat enough and correctly labelled? Do they show what they are supposed to show?

. . . Without scrutinising work, it can be quite difficult to get an accurate idea of the balance of recording methods used across the school. There is nothing wrong with worksheets, but if every lesson is recorded on them, have the children enough opportunity to express their own thoughts and ideas fully? Sometimes older children record science as dictation, copying from the boards or as a cloze procedure. Again, is there enough chance for the children to describe and explain their own developing science ideas? The scrutiny will provide a check that in each class children have the maximum opportunity to learn by using an increasingly wide range of appropriate recording techniques. These should reflect not only what they know and understand, but also how their science skills are developing. Is there clear evidence of investigative activities?

(Wright, 2003, p. 9)

Ideally these are tasks that science subject leaders should be able to undertake, since the process would add to the richness of their overview of science provision in their schools. However, this is clearly time-consuming and also depends upon subject leaders acquiring the necessary skills.

Note that if the purpose of the evaluation is summative, to report to others how well the school is doing, or to set targets or add to the picture across schools in an area or system, then the evidence will need to be more quantitative, less impressionistic, and relate to widely agreed criteria.

Self-evaluation by teachers

While evaluation at the school level can improve overall provision for science, the quality of individual children's experience is ultimately dependent on their teacher. Self-evaluation by teachers, with the support of the subject leader, is a process that should be directed at answering the question: how can the children's learning opportunities be improved? The intention is formative, for the teacher to judge how well he or she is doing and what changes might be made. It is not so that others can judge how well the teacher is doing.

Information about the children's activities and what they have achieved will in any case be recorded, as suggested above. To find out how to improve learning this needs to be supplemented by information about how the children go about their activities and what they feel about them. For example, have the children:

- talked to each other and listened to others' ideas?
- talked freely to the teachers about what they think?
- explained certain words they have used?
- suggested ways of testing ideas?
- used sources of information to gain information or test ideas?
- been absorbed in their work or shown in other ways that it is important to them?
- shown understanding by readily linking new ideas to previous experience or applying ideas to new situations?

To answer these questions (which are criteria in a different form, embodying value judgements about how children best learn) teachers will need to gather information during lessons, which can be reviewed later. Ways of doing this include making brief notes during lessons, holding discussions with groups of children about their preferences and how they feel about certain activities and sometimes tape-recording discussion among children during their group activities. There is perhaps more value, however, in having the help of a colleague, particularly the science subject leader, to give an alternative view and advise on change that may improve the quality of the children's learning experiences.

PROFESSIONAL DEVELOPMENT

Evaluation at both class and school levels is likely to identify staff development needs. These are liable to vary over time, but generally include the need to increase teachers'

- own understanding in certain areas of science
- confidence and ability in facilitating children's investigations
- implementation of formative assessment and all that this means in terms of questioning, feedback, discussion, pupils' self-assessment.

Research studies provide ample evidence that 'increasing teachers' own understanding is a key factor in improving the quality of teaching and learning in science' (Harlen, 1999, p. 80). Classroom observations by inspectors (OFSTED, 1994) and by researchers (Osborne and Simon, 1996) show a close relationship between teachers' own understanding and the understanding of the children they teach. It is, however, important to recognise the role of teachers' subject knowledge in teaching science, which is not so that teachers can convey factual information didactically to pupils. Rather it is so that teachers can:

- ask questions that lead children to reveal and reflect on their ideas
- avoid 'blind alleys'
- provide relevant sources of information and other appropriate resources
- identify progress and the next steps that will take their children's learning further.

These things cannot be done if teachers do not understand the ideas they are aiming for. At the same time, knowledge of the scientific ideas is not enough. As Shulman (1987) has pointed out so effectively, teachers also need:

- general pedagogical knowledge – about classroom management and organisation
- curriculum knowledge – about national requirements and materials that are available
- pedagogical content knowledge – about how to teach the subject matter, including useful illustrations, powerful analogies and examples
- knowledge of learners and their characteristics
- knowledge of educational contexts
- knowledge of educational goals, values and purposes, including the history and philosophy of education.

So it is important that subject knowledge is acquired as part of a wider discussion of children's learning and how to facilitate it. Recent publications that do this rather than presenting science in a textbook style have been produced by Wenham (2005) and the Nuffield Primary Science Project (1997).

Opportunities for staff development that can be provided in school

In-school workshops or meetings can be better tailored to the help needed by a school than attending courses at centres, although they provide less opportunity for sharing ideas and solutions across schools.

Use of ICT enables science subjects leaders to have access to information about available resources of all kinds and to the professional development that need to spearhead the development of science education in their schools. CD-ROMs are particularly flexible sources of ideas and information, as they can be used with groups in school, and by individual teachers at school or at home. The ASE (2002) and QCA have produced CD-ROMs including material relevant to the use of formative assessment, among others.

The Internet has been used to enable teachers to access information and share ideas with others at any time and from any location with an Internet link. For example, the 'Science On-Line Support Network' (Plowman et al., 2000), developed in Scotland, provides teachers with four facilities:

- an e-mail connection to science educators who act as 'helpers' and respond to questions put to them by teachers

- a 'library' of selected documents which can be read on the screen or downloaded as required

- a 'notice board' where messages and information (about new sources of equipment, for example) can be posted and which provides the facility for teachers to add comments to notices

- a 'preparation room' where teachers can share schemes of work, children's work and methods of assessment.

The Teachers TV channel provides what teachers most value, the opportunity to see other teachers in action in their classrooms. Again, these programmes can be recorded and discussed at a school professional development session or studied by teachers at home.

The ASE's Continuing Professional Development Programme is particularly aimed at the needs of science subject leaders. Its key characteristic is flexibility so that it matches the needs of the science subject leader and the school (Haigh, 2003). A mentor is assigned to each teacher and the first step is for the mentor and teacher together to diagnose the areas where development is most needed. Specific tasks are then identified – real tasks that the subject leader has to undertake, such as reviewing parts of the school science policy. The mentor then helps the teacher through the tasks. The teacher can gain a certificate on meeting the requirements to complete interim and final reports satisfactorily.

Other opportunities for tailored in-school support are offered by advisers and independent consultants, who can provide expertise in particular areas such as the development of thinking skills and the use of particular computer-based technology.

Opportunities for professional development out of school

Opportunities for staff development provided at other centres or institutions are widely available and often lead to a certificate or advanced degree. Out-of-school workshops and courses are generally well prepared and led by well-informed tutors, but they are not, by definition, tailor-made for the particular needs of individual schools or teachers. Moreover, some are available only at certain times at certain locations.

However, the increasing use of on-line courses releases personal study from these temporal limitations. For example, primary teachers anywhere in the world can study for a Master's degree at a University in the US wholly on-line (Harlen and Doubler, 2004).

Unique opportunities for teachers to experience science at firsthand were provided by the Primary Teachers as Scientists project. Teachers undertook an extended scientific investigation with support from academic and research institutions. The questions investigated were those that the teacher could talk to their children about and in some cases involve them. Positive outcomes were reported by Hobden and Reiss (1999), although they pointed out that not all teachers had completed their study because of competing demands on their time.

A key development of the 2000s is the establishment of a National Network of Science Learning Centres in the UK, which is extending the range and variety of courses available to teachers. Their purpose is

> to reconnect teachers with their subjects by keeping them up-to-date with the latest, frontier developments; give them time to reflect on their work in the company of fellow professionals; assist them in acquiring new skills, and above all, guide them towards being inspirational teachers.

> (Roberts, 2005, p. 9)

Although many of these provisions are inevitably directed at secondary science specialist teachers, there are opportunities for primary teachers to improve their knowledge and skills.

Finally, the achievement of Chartered Status by the ASE in October 2004 was followed by an agreement with the Science Council to award the status of Chartered Science Teacher (CSci Teach). Once the procedures for gaining this status have been clarified it will provide a further opportunity for the expertise of primary and secondary science practitioners to be acknowledged.

SUMMARY

In this final chapter we have been concerned with the structure and context that the whole school provides for science work in individual classrooms. The role of a member of staff given responsibility for science in the school – the subject leader – is a key one and was vastly extended in the 1990s. The aspects of this role that have been given attention in this chapter are those concerned with long- and medium-term planning, gathering and using information for evaluating the effectiveness of the school's provision for science and the provision of Continuing Professional Development.

Evaluation has been discussed as a formative process used at the school and class levels to improve provision for teaching and learning. At the school level, the science subject leader has the task of collecting evidence and judging how well what is being done matches the criteria of quality and effectiveness. It has been suggested that the process of evaluation, quite apart from the outcome, is itself of considerable benefit in identifying areas where improvements need to be made. Action taken is then evaluated as the cycle of school evaluation continues.

At the class level, teachers can also improve the effectiveness of their teaching through self-evaluation. Again this involves collecting evidence about how children go about and how they feel about their learning and then comparing what is found with the criteria that reflect intentions. Involvement of the science subject leader can help in deciding on any action needed to narrow the gap between intentions and practice.

Finally the provision of professional development opportunities has been considered. It has been suggested that greater use of ICT for this purpose can free teachers from time-bound and place-bound courses, and provide access at any time to information and to a community of teachers who are also learners. A dedicated Teachers' TV channel provides access to other teachers' classrooms and up-to-the-minute news and discussion of issues. Meanwhile the National Network of Science Learning Centres will provide diverse opportunities for teachers to develop expertise and innovative practices.

FURTHER READING

Bell, D. (2005) Keeping up to date: opportunities for enhancing professional expertise. In W. Harlen (ed.) *ASE Guide to Primary Science*, (third edition). Hatfield: Association for Science Education.

Bell, D. and Ritchie, R. (1999) *Towards Effective Subject Leadership in the Primary School*. Buckingham: Open University Press.

Ritchie, R. (1998) From science co-ordinator to science subject leader. In *Association for Science Education Guide to Primary Science Education*. Cheltenham: Stanley Thornes.

Wright, L. (2005) Within-school evaluation of provision for learning science. In W. Harlen (ed.) *ASE Guide to Primary Science*, (third edition). Hatfield: Association for Science Education.

References

AAAS (1993) *American Association for the Advancement of Science Benchmarks for Scientific Literacy.* New York: Oxford University Press.

Alexander, R. (2004) *Towards Dialogic Teaching: Rethinking Classroom Talk.* Cambridge: Dialogos.

Ames, C. (1992) Classrooms: goals, structures and student motivation. *Journal of Educational Psychology*, **84**, 261–71.

ARG (1999) *Assessment for Learning: Beyond the Black Box.* Available from the Institute of Education, University of London and the Assessment Reform Group website: www.assessment-reform-group.org

ARG (2002a) *Assessment for Learning: 10 Principles.* Available from the Institute of Education, University of London and the Assessment Reform Group website: www.assessment-reform-group.org

ARG (2002b) *Testing, Motivation and Learning.* Available from the Institute of Education, University of London and the Assessment Reform Group website: www.assessment-reform-group.org.uk

ASE (1998) *Primary Science*, No. 56. Hatfield: Association for Science Education.

ASE (2001) *Be Safe* (third edition). Hatfield: Association for Science Education.

ASE (2002) *ASE Science Year Primary CD-ROM.* Hatfield: Association for Science Education.

ASF (2004) Working paper 2: summative assessment by teachers: evidence from research and its implications for policy and practice. Available from the Assessment Reform Group website: www.assessment-reform-group.org

Askew, M., Bliss, J. and Macrae, S. (1995) Scaffolding in mathematics, science and technology. In P. Murphy, M. Selinger, J. Bourne and M. Briggs (eds) *Subject Learning in the Primary Curriculum: Issues in English, Science and Mathematics.* London: Routledge.

Atkinson, H. and Bannister, S. (1998) Concept maps and annotated drawings. *Primary Science Review*, **51**, 3–5.

Ausubel, D. R. (1968) *Educational Psychology: A Cognitive View.* New York: Holt, Rinehart and Winston.

Balkwill, R. and Rolph, M. (1990a) *Cell Wars.* London: Collins.

Balkwill, R. and Rolph, M. (1990b) *Cells Are Us.* London: Collins.

Barker, S. and Buckle, S. (2002) Bringing birds into the classroom. *Primary Science Review*, **75**, 8–10.

Barnes, D. (1976) *From Communication to Curriculum*. Harmondsworth: Penguin.

Baume, J. and Gill, D. (1995) IT puts the children in charge. *Primary Science Review*, **40**, 14–16.

Bell, B. and Barker, M. (1982) Towards a scientific concept of 'animal'. *Journal of Biological Education*, **16**(3), 197–200.

Bell, D. (2005) Keeping up to date: opportunities for enhancing professional expertise. In W. Harlen (ed.) *ASE Guide to Primary Science*, (third edition). Hatfield: Association for Science Education

Bell, D. and Ritchie, R. (1999) *Towards Effective Subject Leadership in the Primary School*. Buckingham: Open University Press.

Biddulph, F. and Osborne, R. (1984) Pupils' ideas about floating and sinking. *Research in Science Education*, **14**, 114–24.

Black, P. and Harrison, C. (2004) *Science Inside the Black Box*. London: NFER-Nelson.

Black, P. J. and Wiliam, D. (1998a) Assessment and classroom learning. *Assessment in Education*, **5**(1), 7–74.

Black, P. J. and Wiliam, D. (1998b) *Inside the Black Box*. London: NFER-Nelson.

Black, P., Harrison, C., Lee, C., Marshall, B. and Wiliam, D. (2003) *Assessment for Learning: Putting it into Practice*. Maidenhead: Open University Press.

Borrows, P. (2003) Managing health and safety in primary science. *Primary Science Review*, **79**, 18–20

Bransford, J. D., Brown, A. L. and Cocking, R. R. (eds) (1999) *How People Learn: Brain, Mind, Experience and School*. Washington, DC: National Academy Press.

Bruner, J. S. (1960) *The Process of Education*. New York: Vintage Books.

Bruner, J. S. (1964) The course of cognitive growth. *American Psychologist*, **19**, 1–15.

Bruner, J. S., Goodnow, J. J. and Austin, G. A. (1966) *A Study of Thinking*. New York: Wiley.

Budd Rowe, M. (1974) Relation of wait-time and rewards to the development of language, logic and fate control: Part II. *Journal of Research in Science Teaching*, **11**(4), 291–308.

Butler, R. (1987) Task-involving and ego-involving properties of evaluation: effects of different feedback conditions on motivational perceptions, interest and performance. *Journal of Educational Psychology*, **79**(4), 474–82.

Clarke, S. (1998) *Targeting Assessment in the Primary Classroom*. London: Hodder and Stoughton.

Clarke, S. (2001) *Unlocking Formative Assessment*. London: Hodder and Stoughton.

Claxton, G. (1999) *Wise-up: The Challenge of Lifelong Learning*. London: Bloomsbury.

Davies J. and Brember, I. (1998) National curriculum testing and self-esteem in year 2: the first five years: a cross-sectional study. *Educational Psychology*, **18**, 365–75.

Davies J. and Brember, I. (1999) Reading and mathematics attainments and self-esteem in years 2 and 6: an eight year cross-sectional study. *Educational Studies*, **25**, 145–57.

Deakin Crick, R., Broadfoot, P. and Claxton, G. (2002) *Developing The ELLI: The Effective Lifelong Learning Inventory in Practice*. Graduate School of Education, University of Bristol.

De Boo, M. (ed.) (2000) *Science 3–6: Laying the Foundations in the Early Years*. Hatfield: Association for Science Education.

DES (1989) *Aspects of Primary Education: The Teaching and Learning of Science.* London: HMSO.

DES (1991) *Your Child's Report – What it Means and How it Can Help.* London: HMSO.

DfEE (1998) *A Scheme of Work for Science at Key Stages 1 and 2.* London: Department for Education and Employment.

DfES (2003) *Excellence and Enjoyment: A Strategy for Primary Schools.* London: Department for Education and Skills. www.dfes.gov.uk/primarydocument

Dunne, M. and Lakin, L. (2005) Obtaining and managing resources. In W. Harlen (ed.) *ASE Guide to Primary Science,* (third edition). Hatfield: Association for Science Education.

Dweck, C. S. (1999) *Self-Theories: Their Role in Motivation, Personality and Development.* Philadelphia, PA: Psychology Press.

Earle, S. (2004) Using an interactive whiteboard to improve science-based skills. *Primary Science Review,* **85**, 24–6.

Einstein, A. (1933) Preface to M. Plank, *Where is Science Going?* London: Allen and Unwin.

Elliott, E. S. and Dweck, C. S. (1988) Goals: an approach to motivation and achievement. *Journal of Personality and Social Psychology,* **54**, 5–12.

Elstgeest, J. (2001) The right question at the right time. In W. Harlen (ed.) *Primary Science: Taking the Plunge.* (second edition). Portsmouth, NH: Heinemann.

Elstgeest, J. and Harlen, W. (1990) *Environmental Science in the Primary Curriculum.* London: Paul Chapman Publishing.

Evans, N. (2001) Thoughts on assessment and marking. *Primary Science Review,* **68**, 24–6.

Feasey, R. (1998a) *Primary Science Resources.* Hatfield: Association for Science Education.

Feasey, R. (1998b) Science and industry partnerships. In *Association for Science Education Guide to Primary Science Education.* Cheltenham: Stanley Thornes.

Feasey, R. (1999) *Primary Science and Literacy.* Hatfield: Association for Science Education.

Forster, M. and Masters, G. (1997) *Assessment Methods.* Camberwell, Victoria: Australian Council for Educational Research.

Frost, P. (1999) *IT in Primary Science: A Compendium of Ideas for Using Computers and Teaching Science.* Hatfield: Association for Science Education.

Goldsworthy, A. (2000) *Raising Attainment in Primary Science.* Oxford: GHPD.

Goldsworthy, A., Watson, R. and Wood-Robinson, V. (2000) *Investigations: Developing Understanding.* Hatfield: Association for Science Education.

Gordon, S. and Reese, M. (1997) High stakes testing: worth the price? *Journal of School Leadership,* **7**, 345–68.

Govier, H. (1995) Making sense of information handling. *Primary Science Review,* **40**, 16–18.

Gunstone, R. and Watts, M. (1985) Force and motion. In R. Driver, E. Guesne and A. Tiberghien (eds) *Children's Ideas in Science.* Milton Keynes: Open University Press.

Haigh, G. (2003) The ASE's Continuing professional development programme. *Primary Science Review.* **79**, 11–12.

Harland, J., Moor, H., Kinder, K. and Ashworth, M. (2002) *Is the Curriculum Working?* Slough: NFER.

Harlen, W. (1999) *Effective Teaching of Science: A Review of Research.* Edinburgh: Scottish Council for Research in Education.

Harlen, W. (2006) On the relationship between assessment for formative and summative purposes. In J. Gardner (ed.) *Assessment and Learning.* London: Paul Chapman Publishing.

Harlen, W. and Deakin Crick, R. (2003) Testing and motivation for learning. *Assessment in Education,* **10**(2) 169–208.

Harlen, W. and Doubler, S. (2004) Can teachers learn through enquiry on-line? Studying professional development in science delivered on-line and on-campus. *International Journal of Science Education,* 26(10), 1247–67.

Harlen, W. and Qualter, A. (2004) *The Teaching of Science in Primary Schools* (fourth edition). London: David Fulton Publishers.

Harlen, W., Macro, C., Reed, K. and Schilling, M. (2003) *Making Progress in Primary Science: A Handbook for Inservice and Preservice Course Leaders.* Second Edition: London: Routledge Falmer.

Hawking, S. W. (1988) *A Brief History of Time.* London: Bantam Press.

Hobden, J. and Reiss, M. (1999) The primary teacher as a scientist project. *Primary Science Review,* **56,** 1–2.

Hodson, D. (1998) *Teaching and Learning Science: Towards a Personalized Approach.* Buckingham: Open University Press.

Jelly, S. J. (2001) Helping children to raise questions – and answering them. In W. Harlen (ed.) *Primary Science: Taking the Plunge.* (second edition). Portsmouth, NH: Heinemann.

Johnson, C., Hill, B. and Tunstall, P. (1992) *Primary Records of Achievement: A Teacher's Guide to Recording and Reviewing.* London: Hodder and Stoughton.

Johnston, J. and McClune, W. (2000) Selection project sel 5.1: Pupil motivation and attitudes – self-esteem, locus of control, learning disposition and the impact of selection on teaching and learning. In *The Effects of the Selective System of Secondary Education in Northern Ireland,* Research Papers Volume II. Bangor, Co. Down: Department of Education, pp. 1–37 (ISBN 1 897 592 663).

Kellaghan, T., Madaus, G. F. and Raczek, A. (1996) *The Use of External Examinations to Improve Student Motivation.* Washington, DC: American Educational Research Association.

Keogh, B. and Naylor, S. (1998) Teaching and learning science using Concept Cartoons. *Primary Science Review,* **51,** 14–16.

Kluger, A. N. and DeNisi, A. (1996) The effects of feedback interventions on performance: a historical review, a meta-analysis, and a preliminary feedback intervention theory. *Psychological Bulletin,* **119**(2), 254–84.

Kohn, A. (1993) *Punished by Rewards.* Boston, MA: Houghton Mifflin.

Lave, J. and Wenger, E. (1991) *Situated Learning: Legitimate Peripheral Participation.* Cambridge: Cambridge University Press.

Layton, D. (1990) *Inarticulate Science?* Occasional Paper No. 17, University of Liverpool, Department of Education.

Lias, S. and Thomas, C. (2003) Using digital photographs to improve learning in science. *Primary Science Review,* **76,** 17–19.

Masters, G. and Forster, M. (1996) *Progress Maps.* Camberwell, Victoria: Australian Council for Research in Education.

Match and Mismatch (1977) Materials include three books: *Raising Questions, Teacher's Guide* and *Finding Answers.* Edinburgh: Oliver and Boyd.

Millar, R. and Osborne, J. (1998) *Beyond 2000: Science Education for the Future.* London: King's College London, School of Education.

Mitchell, R. (2005) Availability and use of ICT. In W. Harlen (ed.) *ASE Guide to Primary Science,* (third edition). Hatfield: Association for Science Education.

Nuffield Primary Science (1995) 11 Teacher's Guides and 22 Pupils' Books for Key Stage 2, *Teacher's Guide for Key Stage 1, Science Co-ordinator's Handbook* and INSET Pack. London: Collins Educational.

Nuffield Primary Science Project (1997) *Understanding Science Ideas.* London: Collins Educational.

Oakley, D. (1998) Inspection and the evaluation cycle. In *Association for Science Education Guide to Primary Science Education.* Cheltenham: Stanley Thornes.

OECD (1999) *Measuring Students' Knowledge and Skills: A New Framework for Assessment.* Paris: Organisation for Economic Co-operation and Development.

OECD (2003) *The PISA 2003 Assessment Framework.* Paris: Organisation for Economic Co-operation and Development.

OFSTED (Office for Standards in Education) (1994) *Science: A Review of Inspection Findings 1993/4.* London: HMSO.

Ollerenshaw, C. and Ritchie, R. (1988) *Primary Science: Making it Work.* London: David Fulton Publishers.

Osborn, M., McNess, E., Broadfoot, P., Pollard, A. and Triggs, P. (2000) *What Teachers Do: Changing Policy and Practice in Primary Education.* London: Continuum.

Osborne, J. and Simon, S. (1996) Primary science: past and future directions. *Studies in Science Education,* 27, 99–147.

Osborne, R.J., Biddulph, F., Freyberg, P., and Symington, D. (1982) Confronting the Problems of Primary School Science. Working Paper No 110, Science Education Research Unit, University of Waikato, Hamilton, New Zealand.

Osborne, R. J. and Freyberg, P. (1985) *Learning in Science: The Implications of 'Children's Science'.* Auckland: Heinemann.

Peacock, A. (2004) Choosing and using science books for children. *Primary Science Review,* **84**, 6–7

Peacock, A. and Dunne, M. (2005) Learning science outside the classroom. In W. Harlen (ed.) *ASE Guide to Primary Science* (third edition). Hatfield: Association for Science Education.

Piaget, J. (1929) *The Child's Conception of the World.* New York: Harcourt Brace.

Piaget, J. (1964) Cognitive development in children: Piaget papers. In R. E. Ripple and D. N. Rockcastle (eds) *Piaget Rediscovered: Report on the Conference on Cognitive Studies and Curriculum Development.* Ithaca, NY: School of Education, Cornell University.

Plowman, L., Leakey, A. and Harlen, W. (2000) *Using ICT to Support Teachers in Primary Science: An Evaluation of the Science On-Line Support Network (SOLSN).* Edinburgh: Scottish Council for Research in Education: www.scre.ac.uk/resreport/rr97

Pollard, A., Triggs, P., Broadfoot, P., Mcness, E., and Osborn, M. (2000) *What Pupils Say: Changing Policy and Practice in Primary Education* (Chapters 7 and 10). London: Continuum.

QCA (2003a) *Assessing Progress in Science*. Units for Key Stages 1, 2 and 3. London: Qualifications and Curriculum Authority.

QCA (2003b) Assessment practice and developments in England with particular reference to the role of teachers in assessment for summative purposes. Paper presented at the ASF Seminar, March 2004.

QCA/DfES (2003) *Teaching, Speaking and Listening in Key Stages 1 and 2*. London: QCA/DfES.

QCA/DfES (2004) *Teaching through Dialogue* (video with handbook). London: QCA/DfES.

Quail, B. (2001) Scientists in the classroom. *Primary Science Review*, **69**, 8.

Qualter, A. (1996) *Differentiated Primary Science*. Buckingham: Open University Press.

Richardson, J. (2000) Farm visits: health and safety issues. *Primary Science Review*, **62**, 20–2.

Ritchie, R. (1997) The subject co-ordinator's role and responsibilities in primary schools. *Proceedings of the 3rd Primary Science Conference*, Durham University.

Ritchie, R. (1998) From science co-ordinator to science subject leader. In *Association for Science Education Guide to Primary Science Education*. Cheltenham: Stanley Thornes.

Roberts, G. (2005) SET for success: a key role for Chartered Science Teachers. *Education in Science*, **211**, February, 8–9.

Sadler, R. (1989) Formative assessment and the design of instructional systems. *Instructional Science*, **18**, 119–44.

Schilling, M., Hargreaves, L., Harlen, W. with Russell, T. (1990) *Assessing Science in the Primary Classroom: Written Tasks*. London: Paul Chapman Publishing.

Schunk, D. (1996) Goal and self-evaluative influences during children's cognitive skill learning. *American Educational Research Journal*, **33**, 359–82.

Scott, P. (1998) Teacher talk and meaning making. *Studies in Science Education*, **32**, 45–80.

SCRE (1995) *Taking a Closer Look at Science*. Edinburgh: Scottish Council for Research in Education.

Shulman, L. S. (1987) Knowledge and teaching: foundations of the new reform. *Harvard Educational Review*, **7**(1), 1–22.

SPACE Research Report (1990a) *Evaporation and Condensation*. Liverpool: Liverpool University Press.

SPACE Research Report (1991a) *Electricity*. Liverpool: Liverpool University Press.

SPACE Research Report (1991b) *Materials*. Liverpool: Liverpool University Press.

SPACE Research Report (1993) *Rocks, Soil and Weather*. Liverpool: Liverpool University Press.

SPACE Research Report (1996) *Earth in Space*. Liverpool: Liverpool University Press.

SPACE Research Report (1998) *Forces*. Liverpool: Liverpool University Press.

Sutton, C. (1992) *Words, Science and Learning*. Buckingham: Open University Press.

Toynbee, P. and Walker, D. (2005) *Better or Worse? Has Labour Delivered?* London: Bloomsbury.

TTA (1998) *National Standards for Subject Leaders*. London: Teacher Training Agency.

Vosniadou, S. (1997) On the development of the understanding of abstract ideas. In K. Harnquist and A. Burgen (eds) *Growing up with Science*. London: Jessica Kingsley.

Vygotsky, L. S. (1962) *Thought and Language*. Cambridge, MA: MIT Press.

Watkins, C. (2003) *Learning: A Sense-Maker's Guide*. London: Association of Teachers and Lecturers (ATL) and Institute of Education, University of London.

Wenham, M. (2005) *Understanding Primary Science: Ideas, Concepts and Explanations*. (second edition). London: Paul Chapman Publishing.

White, R. and Gunstone, R. (1992) *Probing Understanding*. London: Falmer Press.

Willis, J. (1999) *National Curriculum Science: Walls*. Hatfield: Association for Science Education.

Woolnough, B. (1997) Motivating students or teaching pure science? *School Science Review*, **78**(283), 67–72.

Wright, L. (2003) Science under scrutiny. *Primary Science Review*, **79**, 8–10.

Wright, L. (2004) . . . and then we'll write about it. *Primary Science Review*, **84**, 4–5.

Wright, L. (2005) Within-school evaluation of provision for learning science. In W. Harlen (ed.) *ASE Guide to Primary Science* (third edition). Hatfield: Association for Science Education.

Index

Also available from SAGE Publications:

Teaching Science in the Primary Classroom
A Practical Guide

Hellen Ward, Judith Roden, Claire Hewlett
and **Julie Foreman,** *all at Canterbury Christ Church University College*

'Initial teacher education students, teachers and science leaders-ordinators will find the book accessible, yet challenging. The examples and case studies are current and designed to help teachers make science learning active and creative' –
Professor Hugh Lawlor, Director of AstraZeneca Science Teaching Trust and DfES Adviser

'An excellent book written with the class teacher in mind, it is practical and filled with loads of ideas. I found it an inspirational read' – *Carol Stringer, Class Teacher and Science Co-ordinator, Cartwright & Kelsey Church of England Primary School, Kent*

Based on courses run by the authors for trainee and practising teachers, this book will provide clear and practical guidance for teaching science in the primary classroom. It offers practical examples for use in the classroom and will explain how to turn theory into creative and lively science lessons.

Each chapter focuses on practical day-to-day issues and offers guidance on:

- questioning techniques;

- planning and assessing learning;

- the use of role-play in learning;

- classroom organization and management;

- safety.

Examples of children's work are included, case studies and different aspects of science are covered in each chapter. The emphasis is on providing the reader with ideas for interesting lessons and enjoyable classroom activities.

This book will appeal to class teachers and student teachers needing a practical guide to teaching primary science.

Paperback: 1-4129-0341-6   Hardback: 1-4129-0340-8
2005   176 pages

www.paulchapmanpublishing.co.uk

Also available from SAGE Publications:

Understanding Primary Science
Ideas, Concepts and Explanations
Second Edition

Martin Wenham, *University of Leicester*

'This is a useful and interesting resource book
for primary teachers and would help to
develop their knowledge and teaching of
science – I will certainly be using it to inform
my planning and teaching of the subject' –
*Juliette Green, Primary School Teacher,
Environmental Education*

'Every teacher, however well trained in science, will have areas of uncertain
understanding. This book is a prime resource for primary teachers of readable,
accurate and relevant explanations of scientific phenomena, supported by
impressively clear drawings. It has been revised to include recent scientific
developments such as DNA and environmental issues, and continues to give
sound advice about likely misconceptions whilst maintaining its focus on
explaining the science for teachers' – *Wynne Harlen, Professor in Education,
University of Bristol*

In a thoroughly revised and updated version, this book provides the background
knowledge teachers need in order to plan effective programmes of work and
answer children's questions with confidence. It is based on the belief that children
learn most effectively when they can interpret their own experiences and
investigation in scientific terms.

The content of this book has been guided, but not limited, by the National
Curriculum and the detailed requirements for teacher knowledge of the Teacher
Training Agency (TTA). It sets out the facts, develops the concepts and explains
the theories which pupils at primary level, including older and very able children,
are likely to need in order to understand the observations and investigations they
undertake. For this edition some new topics have been added, in response not
only to TTA requirements and ongoing developments in science and technology,
but also to the queries of children and teachers about observations they find
relevant and puzzling.

As a work of reference to answer specific questions and clarify ideas, or as a
resource for planning an effective primary science programme, this is an essential
book for teachers, student teachers and anyone interested in the roots and growth
of science education.

Paperback: 1-4129-0163-4   Hardback: 1-4129-0162-6
2005   320 pages

www.paulchapmanpublishing.co.uk